VETERINARY ADVICE FOR GUNDOG OWNERS

Gillian Averis
BVMS MRCVS

Ringpress Books

RINGPRESS

Published by Interpet Publishing,
Vincent Lane, Dorking, Surrey, RH4 3YX

First published 1997
© 1997 RINGPRESS BOOKS

This Edition Published 2003

ISBN 1–86054–028–7

Manufactured in Singapore

10 9 8 7 6 5 4 3 2

CONTENTS

1 *INTRODUCING GUNDOGS*

MY FIRST advice to anyone thinking of buying a gundog is to make sure you are in a position to give the lifestyle which the dog has been bred to need. Ask people who have the breeds you are interested in, ask about their bad points as well as the good ones, and if, at the end of your research, you feel sure you can give the dog a suitable home, then look for your puppy. Do not buy the first pup you see advertised in the local paper just because you feel sorry for the dog. Go to a reputable breeder whose stock is sound in body and mind, and whose dogs are producing working gundogs.

A reputable breeder will give you full post-purchase support, advice and help on rearing and training and, if the unpredictable happens, will always take the puppy back at any time. Such a breeder will have bred a well-planned litter, not just used the nearest and most convenient dog, and may have travelled to the other end of the country to use a suitable stud. Such breeders will probably know which families of dogs, when put together, will reproduce certain vital breed characteristics. They will also probably have put their breeding stock through programmes to eliminate any hereditary problems that a breed may have.

In some of the gundog breeds, the show side has concentrated on looks, to the detriment of working ability, and the workers do not adhere closely to the Breed Standard. This is detrimental to the breeds. Gundogs should look like the breed that they are registered as, and they should also be capable of doing the job for which they have been bred, over the years, to do. Ideally we should look for a breeder whose stock is shown and worked. This is easier in some breeds than others. The Hunt, Point and Retrieve (HPR) Group is still not divided, but to compete in field trials with a Cocker Spaniel, you would definitely have to forego bench wins in favour of a dog from a working kennel.

The Gundog Group is a wonderful group of dogs, bred to be biddable and loyal to their owners. They can make ideal family dogs and also great working companions. I feel sorry for the owners who cannot experience the thrill of taking your best friend out on a shoot and seeing the dog switch on, tremble with excitement, work for you and proudly bring back the bird to you. Even if you do not go on a formal shoot, to see these dogs hunting woods and hedgerows is a joy.

THE DEVELOPMENT OF GUNDOGS
The types of gundogs vary tremendously in

THE POINTS OF ANATOMY

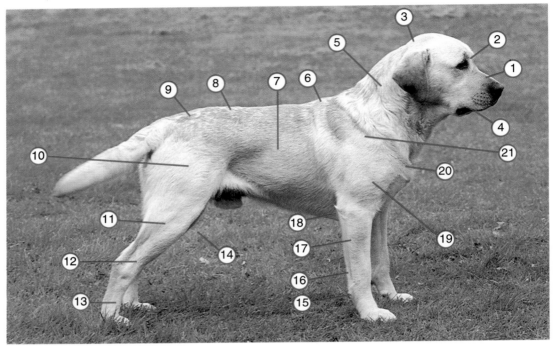

1. *Foreface* 2. *Stop* 3. *Occiput* 4. *Flew* 5. *Neck* 6. *Withers* 7. *Ribs* 8. *Loin* 9. *Croup*
10. *Upper Thigh* 11. *Second Thigh* 12. *Hock* 13. *Pastern* 14. *Stifle* 15. *Pastern*
16. *Wrist (carpus)* 17. *Forearm* 18. *Elbow* 19. *Upper arm* 20. *Shoulder Joint*
21. *Shoulder Blade.*

size, coat colour and, to a lesser degree, temperament, but we are blessed with a group of dogs who have been selectively bred to be biddable, and to hunt, flush and retrieve game for their owners. This is a long way from the behaviour of the wolf, from which all our dogs are descended. Wolves hunt as a pack and eat what they have killed for themselves; they do not bring it back, unmarked, to present it proudly to their owner.

Over the centuries huntsmen have selectively bred from dogs which showed the working qualities which were required. In Britain shoots were formal affairs for the landed gentry. Dogs were developed for specialised purposes. The Setters and Pointers were the game-finders on moors and open fields, where they had to be free-running hunters with tremendous stamina and endeavour. Their sense of smell had to be outstanding, and they carried their heads high in order to get the maximum chance of catching the slightest scent on the air. If they had their noses on the ground they would trip over the quarry and flush it too soon, out of the range of the guns.

The Spaniels, such a varied sub-group, were not as far-ranging but were expected to go into thick cover, so they were bred for

THE SKELETAL SYSTEM

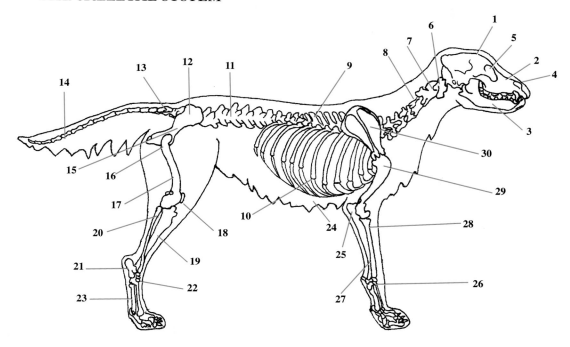

1. Cranium 2. Maxilla Bone 3. Mandible Bone 4. Nasal Bones 5. Orbit 6. Atlas. 7. Axis
8. Cervical Vertebrae 9. Thoracic Vertebrae 10. Ribs (13) 11. Lumbar Vertebrae
12. Wing of Ilium 13. Sacrum 14. Coccygeal Vertebrae 15. Pelvic Bones 16. Acetabulum
17. Femur 18. Patella 19. Tibia 20. Fibula 21. Hock 22. Tarsal Bones 23. Metatarsal Bones
24. Sternum 25. Olecranon 26. Carpal Bones 27. Ulna 28. Radius 29. Humerus 30. Scapula.

the local terrain – the short-legged Sussex for the undergrowth of the Sussex valleys, the lighter and slightly finer Welsh Springer for the hills of Wales. All the Spaniels have plenty of coat to protect their skin from the tough and sometimes ripping undergrowth which they will willingly dive into.

The Retrievers were developed to sit patiently with the guns, and enthusiastically retrieve any shot game, being equally happy on land and water. They tend to be medium-sized but heavier than the Setters, as they need the strength to carry game over great distances time after time after time.

On the Continent the requirements for the Gundog were different. Hunting started as the sport of noblemen, but in the 1800s the middle classes were able to buy and lease hunting land as more became available following various revolutions. More importantly, for both nobleman and countryman, because shoots tended to be walked up and not driven, the fashion was to have a dog who would hunt a variety of game over diverse terrain, and be steady to point, flush and retrieve. The type of game was varied and the dog was asked to hunt fur and feather, track wounded deer and bring it down, and track wild boar and hold it at bay until the hunters arrived. The dogs often lived within the family and had to be friendly and protective, and so the large group of Continental Hunt, Point and Retrieve dogs was developed. There was one Continental dog to do the job of six in Britain – sounds a familiar story! The HPR group is the ideal roughshooter's dog.

CONFORMATION

Every dog from a Cocker to a Chesapeake Bay Retriever has the same number of bones in the skeleton, but it is the size and shape of these bones which give each dog its different structures. The angulation and length of the bones in the front leg are important, enabling the dog to stride out and cover plenty of ground. All gundogs require a well-laid back shoulder blade and a long upper arm. This is essential to give the dog reach. A straight shoulder or short upper arm does not allow the leg to reach forward and cover plenty of ground. A dog with a short upper arm or upright shoulder will have to take more strides to cover the same amount of ground than a correctly-made dog would.

The hind legs give the propulsion to the dog. A straight hind leg will not have the power to push the dog forward. Low-set hocks give the best leverage and power to move the dog on. Lack of angulation at the stifle joint is undesirable, as it will not permit much reach and so would lead to a restricted stride.

To obtain the maximum benefit from the conformation and muscles, it is important that the forces of contraction are in a straight line. If the elbow sticks out or in, the pull of the triceps muscle will not be in a straight line and so will not be as effective. It will also increase the chance of damage to the elbow joint due to uneven pressure. Similarly in the hind legs: if the dog has cow hocks, or bandy legs, the pull of the muscles will be inefficient and energy-wasting.

The ribs enclose the lungs and heart. Oxygen is needed by the body to enable the dog to run and work. The harder the dog works, the more oxygen is required. If the rib cage is small, the volume of the lungs will also be small and this restricts the amount of oxygen which can be passed into the blood. Dogs with small rib cages tire quickly. A large rib cage encloses a greater mass of lung, so more oxygen can be transported to the blood and therefore exercise can be more prolonged.

The rib cage is increased in size by having a deep chest dropping to the elbow, and a long sweep of ribs reaching back to the loin. A slab-sided dog will have a restricted width to the chest and, consequently, reduced lung volume. If the ribs are barrel-chested, this will increase the volume of the lungs, but they will interfere with the free flow of the forearms and will result in more energy being used to do the same amount of work, so the increased lung volume will be cancelled out. An elliptical well-sprung rib is the best shape of chest to give maximum lung efficiency.

2 RETRIEVERS, SETTERS & POINTERS

THE LABRADOR RETRIEVER

The Labrador is the most popular gundog, with most working Labs being black, some yellow, but rarely chocolate. It is not clear whether their working ability varies with the coat colour or not. Not only are Labradors excellent gundogs, but they have also made their mark as Guide Dogs for the Blind and as Sniffer Dogs for the security forces. Labradors were brought to England from Newfoundland about 1760 but were not recorded as gundogs until 1810. In Newfoundland they were used to retrieve fish, nets and buoys from the water, and on land they were used for pulling loads. Once in England they soon became popular gundogs and the landed gentry and nobility started up kennels where precise records were kept about all breedings. In 1903 the Labrador was recognised by the Kennel Club.

Lord Knutsford, one of the early enthusiasts, believed that a Labrador should work and look good, and his dogs did well in the show ring and in the field. Since then the two disciplines have gone their own ways and it is very rare for a top show dog to be a top worker, and vice versa. The show dog tends to be heavier and taller, whereas the field trial Labrador has become very fine,

and light-boned to give the dog the speed and flashiness needed to win. In between there are some which can do both, but if you know what you want to do with your dog, you would be well advised to go to a breeder who specialises in that particular area.

TEMPERAMENT

The Labrador temperament should be intelligent, biddable and with a strong will to please. The dog should be good with children and have a kind, loving temperament. Unfortunately, due to lack of thought about temperament when breeding, some Labradors can have a very poor temperament and can be very vicious. This is a travesty of this wonderful breed, and now most reputable breeders can be relied on to have bred only from dogs with the truly wonderful Labrador temperament. Labradors are well-known for being destructive in the house, they seem to have an uncontrollable desire to have something in their mouth at all times – and if a pheasant is not handy, your chair will do!

CONFORMATION

The Labrador should give the appearance of a strongly built, short-coupled, active dog and have a keen love of water. The head is broad in skull, with no loose skin, a defined

The Labrador Retriever.
Photo: Carol Ann Johnson

stop and medium length of jaw. As the dog is bred to retrieve, the jaw needs to be long enough to carry game easily. In order to find game, the nostrils should be wide and well-developed so as to trap as much scent as possible. The neck should be powerful, to enable the dog to carry game with ease. Too short a neck would lead to difficulty in picking up the game and the dog would be likely to trip up over the retrieve. Too long a neck will lead to weakness and, again, a poor retrieving dog.

To enable the dog to move easily all day, the shoulder is long and sloping to give good forward reach and ground-covering gait. As the dog is strongly built, the leg bone should be good and strong to take the weight of the dog. To reduce potential damage to joints due to uneven strain, the legs should be straight when viewed from the front. Similarly, the hind legs should have a well-turned stifle and low-set hocks to give maximum propulsion to the dog.

To absorb concussion forces, the feet are well-padded with arched toes. The foot should be round and compact, which limits the chance of injury. The otter tail of the Labrador is a distinctive feature. It should be thick at the base and tapering to the end, be of medium length and covered thickly with short, thick, dense coat. Labradors will

thrash their tails all day when working, or when just enjoying themselves. If the tail is thin, long, or poorly covered by hair, it will be damaged by the ground, brambles etc. and will bleed. Once this has started, the scab is continuously knocked off and it is often necessary to have the tail amputated to a length of about eight inches to allow the dog to be injury-free. The coat of the Labrador is short and dense, hard to the feel and with a weather-resistant undercoat. This gives the dog an insulating layer essential for extensive winter water-work. Although the Labrador has a short top coat, the dog will drop mountains of hair when moulting, due to the water-resistant undercoat. I have heard many an owner bemoaning all the hair that their dog drops everywhere.

THE GOLDEN RETRIEVER

The Golden is the second most popular gundog registered at the Kennel Club but, as is the case with the Labrador, the show and the working Goldens are, usually, quite dissimilar. A few dedicated people do strive to produce quality, dual-purpose dogs, but this is uncommon. Most working Goldens are darker in colour and lighter in build than those bred for the ring. The origins of the breed are not clear. A romantic story has them coming from a Russian Circus, but a more plausible theory is that Lord Tweedmouth bought a yellow pup from a litter of Flatcoated Retrievers in Brighton and then took her back to Scotland. She was mated to a Tweed Water Spaniel and the four yellow pups were then selectively bred to an Irish Setter, Flatcoat, Bloodhound and a Labrador until the Yellow, or Golden Retriever, was recognised by the Kennel Club in 1913. The heavy coat of the Golden can need a good grooming after a day's shooting to remove burrs, mud etc. In their favour, they have tremendous scenting ability and, although not as fast as the Labrador, they will work thick cover as well as the

Spaniels and they have great stamina and thoroughness.

TEMPERAMENT
The temperament of the Golden should be biddable, kind and friendly. They can make excellent household pets and are good with children but, because it is expected that they will have this wonderful temperament, this aspect has been ignored on breeding programmes, and some Goldens can be extremely aggressive. As with the Labrador, a nasty Golden is really nasty and very untypical. Well-bred Goldens will have that wonderful affectionate, kind temperament and will make easily-trained, marvellous dogs. The dog should have a kind expression. You should smile when you look into the eye of a good Golden.

CONFORMATION
The head is broad without being coarse and the muzzle is of equal length to the skull from the top to the occiput to give the Golden Retriever a large enough mouth to carry large game. The neck must be of good length, and muscular, to allow the dog to carry game easily over long distances. As with the other gundogs, the shoulder is well-laid back and the upper arm of equal length to give maximum extension of the leg, and hence good ground-covering. The hind legs should have good muscle and well-bent stifles and low hocks to give a powerful hind propulsion. The body should have deep ribs, well-sprung to give good respiratory function. The loin is short but muscular, to prevent weakness and to give flexibility. The movement of the Golden should be powerful with good drive and a long stride to cover the ground effortlessly. To get this long stride, the Golden should have quite a long body, or else the long, striding hind legs would crash on to the front legs.

THE FLATCOATED RETRIEVER

The Flatcoat is a reliable shooting dog who

Golden Retrievers.   *Photo: Graham Cox.*

had great admirers in gamekeepers in the late 19th and early 20th centuries. They need firmness and consistent initial obedience training, as they are full of spirit, independence and natural ability. Due to their lack of popularity with the pet owner, they are still a sound, natural working dog. Their origins are not clear, but the first "Wavy-Coated Retriever" appeared in 1860. It was similar to a Labrador but larger and with a thicker coat. This breed was crossed with Gordons, Irish Setters and possibly with Collies. Dr Moore bred these dogs and culled any non-black pups to produce consistency of type. The Flatcoat was an extremely popular gundog at the beginning of the 20th century. A liver colour was introduced and, although they are still in a minority, they have proved their ability in the ring and field. Flatcoats were especially appreciated on the grouse moor, being tireless, excellent retrievers and their coat and feathering prevented damage to the skin.

TEMPERAMENT
They may be slower to mature than other Retrievers, but they are brave, persistent and have an excellent nose. They are confident, friendly and full of enthusiasm. The head is long and with only a slight stop, which gives Flatcoats their distinctive appearance. The nose is of good size to capture any scent, and

The Flat-Coated Retriever.

Photo: John Sellers.

the jaw long and strong, capable of carrying a hare or a pheasant.

CONFORMATION

The neck should be of a reasonable length and strong, to enable the carrying of game. The chest should be deep to give plenty of room for the lungs, but should not be so broad as to interfere with the movement of the foreleg. The loin is short to give strength to the back. The hind legs are muscular, with moderate bend of stifle, but with the important low hock to give propulsive power. The feet are anti-concussive with deep pads and well-arched toes. The tail should be short and not carried too high, to reduce the risk of injury during work. A long whippy tail is more prone to damage than a shorter, well-feathered, level tail. The Flatcoat should move freely and easily to cover plenty of ground in the most efficient way. The Flatcoat is a tireless worker, an excellent water dog, and a fearless swimmer, but with an exuberant temperament which does not suit a solitary kennel existence.

THE CURLY COATED RETRIEVER

Before the appearance of the Labrador and the Flatcoated Retriever, the Curly was the most common of Retrievers on a shoot. However, they are slower to mature and more demanding in training than the Labrador and so have lost some of their popularity. Their coats make them unique. They are covered in tight waterproof curls from the back of their heads to the tip of their tails. The coat cannot moult or grow very long, which means they do not require trimming. Their origins go back to the 16th century when an English Water Spaniel was crossed with a Retrieving Setter and, possibly, an Irish Water Spaniel.

TEMPERAMENT

They are bold in cover and are excellent water dogs. They are the largest of the Retrievers, being up to 27 inches high and 80 pounds in weight. They have a friendly, confident temperament and are intelligent and independent.

CONFORMATION

As with the other Retrievers, they have a strong jaw, a long but flat head with the hair short on it. The fore legs have typical gundog structure with muscular, well-laid back shoulders to give good free front movement. The hind legs are strong and muscular, with low hocks to give the dog the necessary drive to cover the ground. The chest is deep, with well-sprung ribs to give plenty of lung room. The loin is, again, short, to give strength to the back and prevent injury. The Curly Coat is an excellent retriever, with good scenting ability, excellent in water, strong and persistent, and the dog's slower rate of maturity and independence can present a rewarding challenge to the enthusiastic gundog trainer.

THE CHESAPEAKE BAY RETRIEVER

The Chesapeake is a well-respected dog in the USA but the breed is still in its infancy in the UK. Chesapeakes originate from Maryland, where two puppies from Newfoundland were shipwrecked. They were mated to yellow and tan coonhounds to produce the basis of the breed we see today.

TEMPERAMENT
Chesapeakes are alert and keen to work, intelligent but quite independent and can prove a challenge to their owners. They can withstand icy water, and their courage and endeavour make them an ideal duck dog.

CONFORMATION
The head is broad and possesses a medium stop, with a medium length of muzzle. As with all the scenting dogs, the nostrils are well developed to allow them to find the faintest of scents. The neck is not long but is muscular and strong, which makes them ideal swimmers. The shoulder blade is well-laid back with an equally long upper arm to give the dog excellent reach and front movement. The hindquarters are slightly higher than the shoulders but very muscular to supply the propulsion for swimming. The stifles are well-angulated and the metatarsals are longer than in the other gundogs. The feet are large, webbed and a bit hare-like, which makes them ideal swimmers but more prone to injury on hard, dry ground. The coat is very distinctive, of dead grass colour to brown, which camouflages the dog in the wetlands. It is thick, with a short and oily outer coat and a fine woolly undercoat. The coat is not curly but can have a tendency to wave. The texture of the coat is vital to enable the dog to work under all sorts of weather, even ice and snow. The coat is very water resistant. Because of their ability and

coat, Chesapeakes will soon be seen more frequently in the UK as a duck retrieving dog.

THE NOVA SCOTIA DUCK TOLLING RETRIEVER

When this breed was first mentioned in the UK most people though it was someone's idea of an April Fool's joke. But this is a popular Canadian dog with a unique game-finding technique. The dog has a foxy appearance and plays on the shore, enticing the inquisitive ducks to come and see what is happening. Once within the range of the guns, the ducks can be shot and the dog will then swim and retrieve them. This Retriever has been recognised by the Canadian Kennel Club since 1945 and is now becoming popular in the UK, being regularly shown at Kennel Club Championship shows.

This is a friendly, affectionate breed, 18 to 20 inches high to the shoulder, with a medium-length, fox-red coat. White markings are found on the chest and occasionally on the head, but always on the tip of the tail. They are good, persistent and enthusiastic retrievers and swimmers, and will make a useful contribution to the wildfowler's craft.

THE IRISH SETTER

The Irish is one of the most attractive and popular Setters, with a rich mahogany coat and elegant lines. Originally Irish Setters probably came from a mixture of Spaniel, Pointer and Setter, and were often seen with a large amount of white on them. This has now been selectively bred out, but frequently a few white hairs are seen on the chest. In the field they show tremendous agility and speed and have a keen nose. In recent years their popularity has been seen more in the show ring than in the field and, like many of the gundogs, the show Irish and working Irish are almost unrecognisable as being the same breed, the show dog being more refined, heavier in coat and taller than the smaller, plainer working Setter.

TEMPERAMENT

Training for both types can be difficult but, with perseverance, they can become responsive and loyal. They are dogs of very high spirits and natural friendliness, so lots of human attention and exercise are vital. The Irish must be racy in appearance. A heavy cloddy dog could not be untiringly ready to hunt and range; too light a dog would lack the stamina to be as active as required, so a medium, well-proportioned, refined dog is most desirable. Irish Setters are friendly, affectionate dogs and can make ideal family dogs as well as workers, but this really is a breed where the show dog and the worker are quite separate, and the dual-purpose dog is hard to find. Choose your worker carefully from a kennel where the dogs' working ability has been proven.

CONFORMATION

The head must be lean and long. Too coarse a head is extra weight to carry, which would slow the dog down. A good wide nostril and long foreface increase the scenting ability by allowing as much scent as possible to be drawn into the nostril and to flow over the turbinate bones in the nose where the scent receptors are found. The neck is moderately long and very muscular to keep the head held high when air scenting. Being an active, hard-running dog, the shoulder blade must be long and sloping with an equally long upper arm to allow the dog to reach far forward and cover the ground freely. If the shoulder and upper arm are upright or straight, this not only reduces the reach of the dog, and hence the amount of ground that the dog covers at each stride, but it would also increase the pressure on the shoulder joint and thus the chance of disease and injury to the joints. Similarly, the pastern needs to be fairly long and slightly sloping to

protect the carpal (wrist) joint.

As with other dogs in this group, there must be a deep chest to give the lung capacity to deliver oxygen to the tireless muscles. The chest is not too wide in front, as this would force the front legs out at the elbow and increase the risk of injury to the elbow joints, but the ribs are well-sprung and carried well back to the loin. The propelling force of the Irish is the hindquarters, and these must be powerful and wide to give that free-flowing driving motion. A long thigh and second thigh give maximum reach and the low hock is a most efficient lever to transmit the power to a forward motion.

The Irish needs a small, firm foot with well-arched toes. The dog's feet should not be forgotten. Any horseman will tell you to always look at the feet first. Big splayed feet are easily damaged and do not act as a cushion to absorb the weight of the dog as the feet hit the ground. Instead the joints are jarred, which will lead to early arthritis and joint damage. The tail of the Irish does not affect working ability except that it is an indication of what the dog's nose is finding; but an over-long tail, or one carried too high, is more liable to be damaged and, once the end of a tail has been cut, it can be extremely difficult to get it to heal. Many a room has been redecorated with red polka dots by dogs with damaged tail tips!

THE ENGLISH SETTER

The most important time for the English Setter's development was between 1819 and 1874. There were two outstanding breeders, Laverack in Scotland, and Llewellin. Laverack, with his gamekeeper Rattray, wanted a Setter of excellent appearance that would find birds. They would work eight dogs and expect a bag of 3,000 grouse in a single day. Llewellin wanted a dog who could win Field Trials. The appearance was not as important as the working ability and he used crosses with Gordons, Irish and English to achieve his goal. Between these two influential people the English Setter developed into the Laverack, or bench English Setter, and Llewellin, the field trialler. In reality the types mixed and each produced good dogs in both fields. The Llewellin type tended to have more white, with patches of body colour, heavier heads and shorter muzzles, and they excelled on speed and keen noses. The Laverack strain tends to be all-white, ticked with black, blue, red, orange or lemon. This colour is referred to as 'Belton'. Laveracks are taller dogs and heavier in build. Their heads are larger and narrower through the skull and the muzzle is longer and more square.

TEMPERAMENT
English Setters have a wonderful kind temperament, loyal, devoted and with a loveable disposition. The mild sweet disposition of the English, together with their beauty and aristocratic demeanour, make them well-loved by sportsmen, show-goers and pet lovers. Their disposition makes them ideal for a family with children. The typical English has a wonderful temperament, but some aggression towards other dogs has recently been seen, and this should be watched, so as not to spoil this wonderful dog. For English Setters, love and affection are more important than food. Their natural instinct of bird-finding has to be encouraged by exposing them to birds in the field. Contrary to many people's view, their hunting ability is improved by making the English part of the family.

CONFORMATION
The English Setter must range wide and for long periods on moors and fields and anywhere that game may be found. They carry their head high so as to find as much scent as possible. If they run with their head low they are likely to bump the game, as they will only pick up the scent when very close to the birds. Once a bird has been found, the dog should go on point and be steady to the flush. The head has a long muzzle to give plenty of length to the turbinate bones and hence to the scent receptors. It is held high on a long muscular but lean neck; no strength is needed to carry game but just to support the head. The conformation of the legs has to be such that the dog can range all day. Well-laid shoulders and muscular, well-angulated hindquarters give the dog the equipment to cover the ground tirelessly. The rib cage is well-sprung and deep to give the lungs plenty of capacity. The Setter tail is of medium length and should slash from side to side, at no higher than the level of the back. As the Setter tail is carried low and the dog works in open terrain, there is little chance of tail injury, so their tails are not docked. The action must be free, with power from the hocks to give speed and endurance. The English Setter is a wonderful dog, a great worker and a faithful family pet.

THE IRISH RED AND WHITE SETTER

These dogs are not just an Irish Setter with white on them, although probably their showier country mate did come from the Red and White originally. This is a heavier dog, with a broader skull, described as an athlete rather than racy, as is the Irish. They are good-natured and are increasing in popularity. Like their more glamorous cousin, they need powerful quarters, and they move with a long, free-striding gait. They probably can be traced back to the Red and White Spaniel and possibly the Brittany. Irish Red and White Setters first appeared in the English Kennel Club Stud book as recently as 1985.

TEMPERAMENT
They have a biddable, intelligent character and are good-natured and affectionate.

CONFORMATION

The head is broad with a good stop and a square, clean muzzle. The nostrils are well-developed to allow plenty of air to enter and allow the dog to pick up the slightest scent. The neck is moderately long and muscular to hold the head high while working. The forequarters have a well-laid shoulder, strong bone with good musculature to allow plenty of forward reach and the sloping pasterns absorb some of the concussive forces when running. The hindquarters are wide and powerful and the legs are well-angulated and long to give plenty of propulsion and speed. This construction allows the dog to have a long, free-striding, effortless gait. The body is strong and muscular, with a deep chest and well-sprung ribs to give the all-essential lung capacity. This structure enables the dog to cover ground with ease and perseverance and to find, hold and flush game. These dogs are not as popular as the Irish Setter, but their greater power can make them suitable for hard ground.

THE GORDON SETTER

The Gordon is the heaviest of the Setters. Developed over two hundred years ago by the fourth Duke of Gordon, these are hardy dogs with excellent stamina and recuperative powers. They are not the fastest Setters, but are very stable and dependable. Originally Gordons occurred in various colours, some black and tan, some black and white, and others tricoloured, but now they are only found in the wonderful rich mahogany tan and black.

In the fourth Duke's day these dogs were highly esteemed, and various dogs are thought to have been introduced to arrive at the standardised version. The Pointer Collie, Field Spaniel, Bloodhound and Irish Setter are all possible ancestors. They are a slow-maturing breed, sporting dog first and foremost, and will expect plenty of free running. Show and working type vary to a small degree – the worker tends to be lighter in bone and body, but there are some well-known kennels where beauty and working ability are equally treasured – and long may they pursue this joint approach so that the breed does not split completely into those that look good, and those that can work.

TEMPERAMENT

Although Gordons are one of the slower Setters, their intelligence and natural ability allow them to work steadily all day, rarely missing any game. They were probably first developed by selectively breeding from an old-fashioned Spaniel. At first they were somewhat clumsy and heavy in appearance but, with the introduction of the flashy Irish Setter, they became more elegant and fashionable. They are willing workers and have made a big impact on the shooting scene in America. They are loyal and make a good family dog, but will often attach themselves to one person.

CONFORMATION

The head is deep rather than broad, but has sufficient width to give plenty of brain room. The nose must be large and broad to give good scenting ability. The head is held high by a long, slightly arched neck. The shoulder blade is well-laid to give forward reach, and the hind legs are long and muscular, with low hocks to give the dog power and speed. They are heavy dogs and need plenty of muscle to propel them forward. Their pads are particularly well-cushioned to allow the concussive force to be dissipated and to reduce the chance of joint damage. The chest is not too wide, but the rib cage is deep and well-sprung to allow plenty of room for the lungs. The tail is carried below the level of the back and should not reach beyond the point of the hock. This type of tail is rarely damaged when working open land, but can be damaged in the house or kennel and it can be difficult to stop it from bleeding. This Setter is the heavyweight hunter but is noble, dignified and a glorious picture to see ranging on the open moors.

POINTERS

These aristocratic athletes originated from Spanish gundogs. They are thought to have been brought to Britain by soldiers returning from the war in Spain in the early 18th century. They were a little slow for the English sportsman and so, by selective breeding, a faster dog was produced. They are used to indicate the presence and position of game and are at their best when covering great areas of land – the grouse moor in particular. They carry their head high while hunting and need great speed and stamina. The show and working Pointers are not too dissimilar in appearance, but if you want to trial your dog it is probably sensible to go to a kennel where the dogs consistently win field awards. If you can secure good looks with working ability, then that is even better. Remember, you have got to look at your dog for 365 days each year, so your Pointer must be appealing to you.

TEMPERAMENT

Temperament is one of the most important considerations when choosing a puppy. A shy nervous dog is unlikely to make a good hunting dog, and can be unpredictable as a family pet. Pointers can be run together in groups quite happily, but you can have dominance problems and fights between males and between bitches. I have seen some nasty wounds resulting from rivalry in a pack. If you are the pack leader, this can help to prevent these fights – the pack leader can usually control situations with a stern voice and eye contact. Physical punishment is rarely acceptable or needed. The Pointer is a fine, aristocratic dog. The sight of a fit dog galloping across the ground and suddenly coming onto a staunch point is quite beautiful and breathtaking. Any potential owner must be able to give this dog plenty of running exercise if the breed's true sociable, even temperament is to be seen. Pointers are regal and graceful, and soundness is most essential in this athletic breed.

CONFORMATION

The movement of a Pointer should be smooth and ground-covering, allowing the dog to cover the yards with ease. Pointers should not waste energy by picking up their front legs in a hackney action, which is, wrongly, often thought to be the true Pointer movement. It is not. The movement should be easy, reaching out with the forelegs and driving with the hind legs. To achieve maximum ground coverage the Pointer must have a long sloping shoulder and a long upper arm to allow maximum reach. The hindquarters need plenty of muscle to propel the dog forward, and moderate angulation but a short hock, which aids in the driving action.

The height of the Pointer is important. If the dog is too small, then negotiating tall banks of heather will be an energy-sapping obstacle. If the dog is too tall, then the body weight will reduce the dog's endurance. The show standard ranges from 24 to 27 inches, which would be suitable to allow the worker to do the job for which the dog was bred. The Pointer has a tremendous sense of smell. This is facilitated by wide, open nostrils to suck in large quantities of air and scent and then a long foreface, where the sensory receptors sift out the scent. To allow the dog to carry its head high when quartering the ground, and hence pick up air scent, the neck is moderately long and slightly arched. A short stuffy neck would not enable the Pointer's head to be held in a position which gives the greatest chance of finding quarry.

A hard-running athletic dog requires an excellent set of lungs and a good heart. To achieve this, a Pointer must have a deep chest, down to the level of the elbows, well-sprung but not barrel-chested, which would force the forelegs out and lessen the foreleg efficiency. The Pointer has a short loin which must be muscular. This enables the dog to gallop easily. The short loin is a strong, flexible connection between the body and the propelling force of the hind limbs; a muscular, short, slightly arched loin can flex to allow the hind legs to get well under the dog and spring it forward.

The Pointer should have oval, well-knit feet with deep pads and arched toes. This type of foot will enable the dog to cope with uneven terrain, but more importantly from a veterinary point of view, the deep pads and arched toes help to cushion the concussive impact every time the dog gallops, and all the weight is taken on the front legs. Similarly, a slightly sloping pastern reduces the impact on the carpal or wrist joint. If the hard-running Pointer had an upright pastern, this would lead to more pressure in the wrist joint and increase the chance of osteoarthritis and lameness.

3 *SPANIELS*

Spaniels were used as gundogs long before the Retriever became part of the shooting scene. They were used to produce game for the falconer, and the hunter who used nets and arrows. With the advent of the gun, the Spaniel breeds were developed by big kennels to suit the requirements of the local nobility and landed gentry. Spaniels have to work close to the hunter, in thick cover, hedgerows and woodland. Their job is to find and flush game for the guns. Their colour is important and often white is included to allow the guns to see the dogs and avoid accidents. In the 14th century the Spaniels were split into two groups, the Water Spaniels and the Land Spaniels. The Water Spaniels existed as a separate breed until the 20th century, and were shown as small, curly-coated parti-colour dogs. The Land Spaniels became further divided, by their weight, into three groups, Toys, Cockers and Springers.

THE ENGLISH SPRINGER SPANIEL

This is the most common working Spaniel and bears little resemblance to its brother show type. The show Springer is taller, heavier and possesses more coat than the worker. They tend to be more relaxed and slower in nature than their working namesake. They have become a popular show dogs and pets. The working Springer is a smaller, lighter, livelier dog who is not so suitable as a family pet. Its working instincts are so strong that, in a pet home, they can develop behavioural problems if not given sufficient exercise and work. I am convinced that somewhere under the working Springer there is a key which is used to wind it up like a clockwork toy! If only you could remove that key when the dog is not needed for work, what an advantage that would be. The Springer works with speed and enthusiasm, will retrieve naturally and is good in cover and water.

At the beginning of the 19th century Spaniels were divided into three groups according to their weight. The lightest, under 14 lbs, were classified as lapdogs; 14 to 18 lbs were the Cockers, and finally came the heavy-weights, the Springer. Around 1800 the Boughey family of Aqualate in Shropshire began to develop a pure line of the Spaniels and they started a stud book, beginning with Mop 1 in 1812. At the end of that century a Springer Spaniel, similar to that which we are accustomed today, could regularly be seen, and was first called a Norfolk Spaniel because the Duke of Norfolk owned several of them at this time. This name was soon changed and the

English Springer Spaniel was officially recognised by the Kennel Club in 1902. The first recorded English Springer Spaniel Field Trial winner was the result of an English Springer Spaniel mated to a Cocker dog in 1901.

TEMPERAMENT

The Standard for the Springer requires a symmetrical build, a compact, merry, active dog, with a friendly, happy and biddable temperament.

CONFORMATION

The head should be fairly broad with enough strength to carry game. The nostrils are well developed to allow plenty of air to be inhaled and hence find the slightest amount of scent. The Springer's ears are lobular, with plenty of feathering to protect them from damage by brambles and cover, but the hair must not be too dense, as that can trap mud, thorns etc. and cause infection. A serious problem with too much hair in the inside of the ears is that there is an increased chance of the dog developing otitis externa, as the hair prevents the cooling and drainage of the ear canal.

The Springer must possess a strong and muscular neck to allow the dog both to carry game and to take scent. The shoulder is well-laid back, to give good reach with the fore limb. The elbows should fit closely to the body to increase efficiency of movement and reduce the chance of injury. A lot of working dogs have poor elbows which turn out, giving them a 'Queen Anne' front. This is more likely to be injured and it requires more energy from the dog in order to move, but most dogs cope with this handicap, though they would be faster, and have a longer working life, if their conformation was correct.

The ribs are deep, giving plenty of room for the lungs, and the back is muscular but not very long, to produce great flexibility and strength. The hind legs should be

The English Springer Spaniel .

Photo: Steve Nash.

muscular with good angulation to give the dog plenty of power. The pads are thick and the toes well arched, which absorbs some of the concussive force and prevents damage to the joints during exercise. Springers wag their tails non-stop while working and can damage the tip of the tail quite easily. The feathering on the tail will help to protect the skin from whipping injury. To minimise the risk of tail damage, most Springers' tails are docked within the first few days of life.

The Springer's movement is free and easy, the foreleg being swung forward from the shoulder to cover plenty of ground. The hocks drive from well under the body to give plenty of forward propulsion. The English Springer is one of the best gundogs for a family dog and as a worker. They hunt further and faster than any of the other Spaniels and are excellent retrievers and water dogs, their coat providing some protection in wet and cold conditions. They are tireless and have great enthusiasm and endurance.

THE COCKER SPANIEL

Cockers got that name because they were used to flush woodcock into nets strung across narrow rides in woodlands. Their popularity was high, especially in the south-west of England and in Wales. Many outcrosses were used – English Setters, Border Collies, Springers and Cavalier King Charles Spaniels, Fields and Sussex – to produce a variety of colour and markings. A black dog, Champion Obo, was a consistent winner in the 1880s and was used extensively at stud. The Cockers were classified separately in 1893, the year of the first stud book entry.

TEMPERAMENT

The Cocker is a willing worker but is better where there is scent. They are eager workers in woodland and natural cover, often preferring this to open root fields. Many enthusiasts think that the Cocker is more intelligent than the Springer, and is not responsive to hard training. Jim Wyke wrote: "You train a Springer and guide a Cocker." The Cocker became Britain's most popular gundog by the mid-thirties and held that position for many years. Their temperament makes them sensitive and affectionate and this makes them ideal house dogs. They are sturdy, merry dogs, compact and symmetrical.

CONFORMATION

Their overall body length is oblong, as the measurement from the withers to the ground equals that from the withers to the base of the tail. The head has a square muzzle, with a distinct stop midway on the head. A small, snipey muzzle would reduce the capacity of the dog to retrieve game. The nose is sufficiently wide to give the dog excellent scenting power.

The lobular low-set ears are covered with long, straight, silky hair to reduce the risk of traumatic injury and to prevent foreign objects entering the ear canal. As with most of the gundogs, the Cocker's neck is moderately long and muscular, leading into well-laid shoulders. The forelegs have good bone and should be of medium length to give plenty of leverage so that this bustling little dog has plenty of ground-covering

The Cocker Spaniel.
Photo: Carol Ann Johnson.

ability, but not too tall so as to restrict entry into thick cover. The body must be strong and compact. Deep ribs give the dogs plenty of respiratory capacity, allowing them to work tirelessly. If the chest is barrel-shaped it will interfere with the forcing movement of the forelegs. The ribs are elliptical to give plenty of volume at the top of the chest, reducing at the bottom where the front legs move across the chest. The back is short over the loin and well-muscled to give flexibility and power to the dog. The hind legs are well-angulated and very muscular to give these little dogs a power-packed action. The Cocker is the smallest of the Spaniels but has one of the biggest followings.

THE WELSH SPRINGER SPANIEL

The Welsh Springer was probably one of the oldest of the Spaniels – red and white hunting dogs were mentioned in the 12th century. There was considerable trade between Brittany and Wales and it is thought that part of the Welsh Springer's origins may have some link with Brittany. In Wales they are sometimes known as "Starters". They are midway between a Cocker and a Springer in size, but they are always rich red and white in colour. Their coat is silky and their ears vine-shaped. The WSS was recognised by the Kennel Club in 1908 and at this time they competed successfully in Field Trials. After the war the standard of work fell, and although a successful trial was run in 1985, most WSS are used for show or as pets.

TEMPERAMENT

Welsh Springers needs scent to encourage them to work and they are not as fast as the ESS, but they are steadier and more thorough in work. They are a sensitive breed and will not work for an unsympathetic handler. They have a natural ability to take a line, and this is useful when there is wounded game, but it is not helpful when hunting live game. Not all WSS are natural retrievers, as the trait was not encouraged in their evolution. They were used in teams, where Retrievers picked up the game at the end of the drive, not the Springer. They are agile and can cope with varied terrain, from gorse and mountain to bogs and rocky gorges.

CONFORMATION

They should be compact, merry dogs built for endurance and hard work. Their construction must give them the capability to cover ground effortlessly. The head has to be balanced, and in proportion to the rest of the dog. Too heavy a head would be weighty and would tire the dog quickly. The muzzle must be of medium length to give plenty of room for the air to circulate around the turbinate bones in the nose which support the scent-finding organs.

The ears are the smallest of the Spaniels

and do not need as much feathering to protect them from injury, because they do not flap around as much, and so are less prone to damage. The neck is long and muscular, leading into well-laid shoulders, thus giving the dog the reach needed to cover the ground smoothly. The rib cage is well-sprung to give the dog the capacity for endurance, and the loin muscles give flexibility and strength to the back. The hindquarters are muscular and wide to produce power, with well-developed second thighs. To produce a smooth powerful ground-covering stride, the hindquarters must be muscular.

THE CLUMBER SPANIEL

This Spaniel is quite distinctive within the Spaniel group and has changed very little over the years. There are several theories about the Clumber's origins. Possibly the first of them arrived in the UK when the Duc de Noailles presented some to the second Duke of Newcastle, from whose estate, Clumber Park, the breed was named. The Clumber's ancestors may have included the Basset, the Bloodhound or the Blenheim Spaniel which had red, lemon and white colouring. A portrait in 1788 depicted the 2nd Duke and Colonel Litchford with his head gamekeeper Marsell and three Spaniels. The abundance of game in the 18th and 19th centuries did not require a fast-moving Spaniel; a good nose and an efficient worker was more valued.

TEMPERAMENT

The Clumber has one of the best noses of the Spaniels and possesses a natural inclination to hunt with stamina and perseverance. The breed's large frame makes them slower than the other Spaniels, but they are agile and natural swimmers. No Clumbers have featured in trials in recent years and the continuation of the breed is mainly thanks to the show fraternity.

CONFORMATION Clumbers should weigh about 80 lbs, making them substantial, heavily-boned dogs. The head is square and massive with a well-developed stop and a medium length of muzzle. As a retrieving Spaniel, too short a muzzle would restrict the game-carrying ability. The neck is fairly long, thick and powerful. A weak neck would not be able to support the weight of the head. As the legs are short, the dog needs a well-laid shoulder to give some reach in movement. The legs must be well-boned to support the heavy frame. The body is long and low to the ground. The chest is deep with well-sprung ribs to provide the essential lung room. The hindquarters, being the powerhouse of the dog, must be powerful and well-developed. To carry this heavy-weight, the feet have to be large and round. Feathering offers protection from rough ground and cover. The Clumber has a rolling gait due to its long body and short legs, but the dog should still cover the ground with effortless drive.

THE FIELD SPANIEL

This is one of the oldest Spaniels. It is believed to have been produced by crossing Sussex with Cocker-type Spaniels, but a Cocker/Springer and Welsh/Sussex cross have also been suggested. In their early days, these dogs were divided into blacks and the coloured type. At first the Blacks were the most important colour and, at one time, the Field was known as the Black Spaniel, but later on the coloured dogs achieved the same status.

Fashion dictated that the Field should be low on the leg, heavy-boned and with a long body. Breeders strived to this end by using Basset Hound outcrosses, but the dog became useless in the field, and numbers declined to a point, in the sixties, when registrations were in single figures. Now the breed is on the increase, thanks to dedicated breeders and the use of Springer outcrosses

to get the well-proportioned dogs of today which resemble their ancestors.

TEMPERAMENT
They are well-balanced and handsome, with agility, speed and endurance, plus the benefit of intelligence and the ability to be easily trained. They are stronger and longer in the leg than the Cocker and work well in heavy going and roots. Their ability to spring from the ground and leap from tussock to tussock makes them a valuable dog. They have a good nose and will retrieve which, together with a friendly nature, makes them an ideal gundog or family pet.

CONFORMATION
The head should give the impression of nobility and has only a moderate stop. The muzzle is long but not coarse. The long muzzle helps with game carrying, and also provides excellent scenting ability. As with all the gundogs, the nostrils are wide and open, to allow plenty of air to enter the nose and carry scent to the scent organs. The ears are set low, are long and heavily feathered. This protects the ears from damage but the low set and heavy feathering can increase the risk of otitis externa occurring. The hair can also trap dirt and brambles and so should be groomed regularly.

The neck needs to be long and muscular to allow the dog to retrieve game without undue fatigue. The shoulder blade is long and sloping to give the forward reach necessary to cover the ground easily. The chest is deep and the ribs moderately well-sprung, giving good respiratory capacity without restricting movement. The back and loin are muscular to give spring and flexibility to the dog. The hindquarters are muscular and moderately angulated to provide power and spring. The feet are tight and round with strong pads to absorb the concussive force, but not too small, as this prevents the foot sinking too far into soft ground.

The tail is customarily docked to prevent tail damage while working in heavy cover. Because the Field is longer than the Springer and Cocker, the dog's movement has a long, unhurried stride, with great drive from the rear. The coat is long and silky, dense and weatherproof with plenty of feathering on the chest and under the body, but not from the hocks down. If the hair there was profuse it could become weighted down with mud and tire the dog. The Field is virtually free from hereditary defects. Considering its temperament, which is gentle and affectionate, and its soundness, it is surprising that it is not more popular as a working gundog.

THE SUSSEX SPANIEL

This breed is recognised by its golden liver colour. It is believed that this colour originated from a bitch belonging to Dr Watts which came from the famous Rosehill line of Mr Fuller. The breed could have died out following the death of Mr Fuller, but his head gamekeeper kept a dog and a bitch to maintain the strain. In the early part of the century, the numbers of Sussex were still small and this was said to be due to their difficulty in breeding. The bitches were not very fertile, and the pups often weak and delicate. This was put down to excessive inbreeding, which was difficult to avoid due to the lack of available breeding stock. At the end of the First World War only five pure-bred Sussex spaniels were registered and there were only eight after the Second World War, but dedicated enthusiasts have developed the breed and now its future looks safe.

TEMPERAMENT
The Sussex is unusual in Spaniels, in that it gives tongue when on game, which can be an asset if the dog has disappeared into thick cover! As beater's dogs they do excellent work, as they can face heavy thick cover and carry heavy game, due to their strong necks. They are comparatively slow workers, but conscientious and thorough.

CONFORMATION
They are strongly built with a wide skull and a pronounced stop, which gives protection to the eyes in thick cover. The neck is long and strong, allowing the dog to carry heavy game, although retrieving is not the breed's strong point. The shoulder is long and well-laid back to enable the short forelegs to reach forward to cover the ground. The rib-cage is well-developed to give the lung capacity, but the dog has no waist, just a wide, muscular loin. The hindquarters are strongly-boned to support this heavyweight, and they must be muscular. The dog has a distinctive roll when moving and the impression is given that the legs are not attached to the dog's body! This is a dog full of character and is not one who will allow others to dominate. It is wise to be firm with Sussex Spaniels when they are youngsters so they do not get too full of themselves. They have wonderful temperaments with people and their appealing movement makes them humorous and fulfilling pets. They often have poor-looking hips but rarely have any problems.

THE IRISH WATER SPANIEL

It is believed that the origin of this dog was the old European Water dog, which was also the ancestor of the Poodle. There were two distinct types of this breed originally – a Northern Water Spaniel and a Southern Water Spaniel. The Northern Spaniel was sometimes referred to as the "Old Brown Irish Retriever", but this confusing name has now gone and there is only one Irish Water Spaniel. From the middle of the 19th century Irish Water Spaniels were exhibited at dog shows and enjoyed some degree of popularity between 1880 and 1890. From then the breed started to decline and looked in danger of disappearing, but during this century the numbers have increased again.

TEMPERAMENT

These dogs have a very distinctive appearance, being covered with dense tight ringlets which cover virtually all the body except the face and tail. This waterproof coat makes them ideal water dogs, as they are extremely good at working in marsh and bogland. They hunt, flush and retrieve like the other Spaniels but are particularly good dogs for wild-fowlers. They are very intelligent and courageous and possess great stamina, which is needed to work strong tidal waters and estuaries.

CONFORMATION

The head is of medium size, with a good length of muzzle and width of skull. The muzzle is long, to ease the carriage of game. The neck is long and muscular with a slight arch to allow the dogs to carry their heads out of the water. The forelegs are constructed with a long sloping shoulder to allow a good forward reach when swimming and running. The chest is deep and extends well back in the body, and is somewhat barrel-shaped behind the shoulders to provide a large lung capacity and hence stamina and endurance.

The hindquarters are well-angulated and powerful, with particularly low-set hocks which give the dog powerful propulsion. The feet are large, round and spreading – ideal for swimming and running on soft ground. The tail is covered with curls for the first three to four inches and then, as it tapers to a point, it is only covered by short, straight hairs. As the tail is low-set and never carried above the back, it is less likely to be damaged and, as these dogs do not go through dense cover, the tail is not customarily docked. The coat has a natural oiliness which gives the dogs such an advantage while swimming and makes them such excellent companions for wild-fowlers.

4 THE HUNT POINT RETRIEVE GROUP

All the dogs in this group have been imported into the UK since the Second World War. During the 19th century Europe was covered by large estates, owned by noble families, which contained large numbers of game, both big and small. The European breeds were developed on these estates to accompany the huntsmen. They were needed to point partridge, quail, pheasants and fur, work the marshlands for waterfowl and hunt for wild boar and deer. They all needed to be able to hunt, point and retrieve the game. The different breeds were designed to cope with different types of terrain, and so there is some variation in their size, structure and movement. The breeds in the HPR group can be used as shooting dogs, and also by falconers to find the game and then hold it until the bird is released when the guns are in the correct position.

THE LARGE MUNSTERLANDER

At the beginning of the 19th century dog breeding to type rather than just for performance began to be taken seriously. One of the breeds which was being developed was a longhaired pointer and, over a period of time, the only puppies which were acceptable were brown and white dogs. Any black and white dogs were given away to farmers and 'keepers. In the area around Munster, the farmers began to breed these cast-offs and developed their own black and white, long-coated pointer. This dog became known as the Large Munsterlander. The first Large Munsterlander to be imported into Britain arrived in 1971, closely followed by three in-whelp bitches. These were of good-quality stock and have been a sound foundation for the breed in the UK. The Large Munsterlander Club was founded in 1972 to encourage good breeding of typical dogs in looks and working ability.

TEMPERAMENT
These are dogs with great stamina and they are good at working equally well on land and water. They are sensitive by nature and are easy to train, but they do need a firm but understanding hand. Their thick coats give them an advantage over the smooth coats of other HPR dogs. They will work on moorland, roots, stubble or grassland and also work thick cover, as their coat gives them protection from the thick undergrowth.

CONFORMATION The Large Munsterlander's head is built to allow for intelligence, with a sufficiently broad skull. It is also elongated to give plenty of length to the jaw for carrying game, and with wide, well-formed nostrils for good scenting ability. The broad close-hanging ears are moderately feathered to give protection from thick cover. The neck is strong and muscular, to enable the head to be carried high and for the dog to carry game. The shoulder is well laid back to give excellent forward reach. The hindquarters are broad and muscular with good angulation to give power and forward propulsion. The chest is wide at the front with good depth and well-sprung ribs to give plenty of lung room. The back is firm and well-muscled with a wide croup and loin to give strength and suppleness. The feet are well-knuckled and rounded to absorb concussive forces when working. The tail is carried level with the back and is well-feathered to give protection. The gait must be free, long-striding and springy, to give the dog the ability to cover the ground effortlessly all day.

THE HUNGARIAN VIZSLA

The very early ancestors of the Vizsla may have been the native Pannonian hound and a yellow-coloured bird dog from Asia, about one thousand years ago. The nobility of Austria-Hungaria developed this dog to be used as a pointer/retriever on the open grasslands. The dogs were used on birds and would also chase a large native hare, round it back towards the guns and drop to the ground, to allow the hare to be shot. Vizslas had to be quick, possess stamina and be able to cope with the extremes of temperature that are found in their place of origin. They had to point their game to allow the guns time to get in range before it was flushed. The retrieve could either be on land or in water. The Vizsla has continued to be owned by people strongly interested in their working ability and so the breed has not lost its natural instinct.

TEMPERAMENT

The Vizsla is an affectionate, very lively and busy dog which would give up most things for affection. The short coat, gentle manners and affectionate nature make this an ideal pet as well as gundog.

CONFORMATION

The Vizsla is a medium-sized, elegantly built dog, with an aristocratic air, and is an unusual yellow-gold to rich russet colour. This is an extremely attractive and distinguished dog. The Vizsla's head is lean and noble, moderately wide to give plenty of brain room, but not too big so as to cause the head to be heavy. The muzzle has a good length to help with game-carrying, and the nostrils are broad and wide. The neck is strong and muscular and moderately long to enable the dog to air scent and carry game. The construction of the limbs is such as to allow a ground-covering gallop, with well-laid shoulders and muscular, well-angulated hind legs. The bone of the Vizsla is robust but medium. Being medium-sized, very active and lively, these dogs could not do their job properly if their legs were heavily-boned, for they would then weigh more. If the bone was too fine, it would cause more damage to the joints when running. The rib cage is well-developed, a prominent breast bone showing the rib cage reaches well forward and, with well-spring ribs, the dog can obtain the oxygen needed to maintain work. The feet are rounded, cat-like, with tight arched toes which act as shock absorbers when moving.

THE HUNGARIAN WIREHAIRED VIZSLA

The Wirehaired Vizsla is recognised in many countries throughout the world but not in the USA. Wirehaired Vizslas in Hungary have to do various jobs, not just hunting the open plain, but also water work on the great lakes. The Wirehaired Vizsla is ideal for water work because the dog's thicker coat sheds water readily and is warmer. The origins of the Wirehaired were the same as the shorthaired, but the dog has been bred consistently to wirehaired dogs to create a separate breed. German Wirehaired Pointer blood was introduced to stamp the wiry coat into the breed.

These are a very new addition to the English dog scene and, being a distinguished looking breed, they are becoming popular. They have excellent working ability, they are fast and wide-ranging and will be a force to be reckoned with once in the field. The build of the Wirehaired is as the shorthaired, except for the coat and the heavier bone gained from the German Wirehaired Pointer.

THE BRITTANY

This has long been an established breed in France, and has proved to be very popular in America, but it is only since 1981 that the breed has been seen in the UK in any sort of numbers. In the 19th century, a Spaniel called the "le Pourgerès" (the High-Spirited one) was a popular dog in that he pointed both fur and feather. At this time English gentlemen used to go to Brittany with their dogs, Pointers and Setters, where they would shoot partridge and snipe. Often these dogs were left behind with local gamekeepers and farmers, and they mated with the native dog, which produced a dog with longer legs and with a tendency to "set" not point. They also had superior scenting ability and that was an advantage over the le Pourgerès. In 1907 the short-tailed Brittany Spaniel Club was founded. Careful breeding returned the dog to the original type, while maintaining the improved nose. When the Brittany came to Britain, it was first called the Brittany Spaniel as in France but, as the dog is a pointer and retriever, it was confusing to use the name Spaniel, so this was dropped and the dog is now known as the Brittany.

TEMPERAMENT

This is not the most handsome of dogs, but the working ability is well-proven and as the breed is affectionate, busy and eager to please, the dog's popularity is bound to increase.

CONFORMATION

The head is moderately broad to give brain room, but the muzzle is not as deep as the skull, though this does not stop the dog retrieving hare or pheasant. The nose is open and well-shaped to give good scenting ability. The neck is medium length and flows into sloping shoulders, giving forward reach. The hindquarters are strong and broad with well-bent stifles and low hocks to give the all-important forward movement. The ribs are deep and well-sprung but the body is short, with a strong loin giving strength but flexibility. The tail is naturally short, or is docked to prevent injury. The coat is dense, fine and slightly wavy, with light feathering on the legs and ears.

THE GERMAN SHORTHAIRED POINTER

This versatile gundog was developed by the Germans to locate game, point it until the guns arrived, and then retrieve any shot quarry. The dog must be sensitive, with a good nose to follow wounded large game, and also have the courage to face wild cats and foxes. The Germans in their efficient manner went about this task with great success and one of the dogs they produced was the GSP. This dog is medium-sized, of noble appearance, but sturdy, strong and with stamina, showing perseverance when hunting, and is equally good on land and water.

The GSP Club was founded in 1891 and under its umbrella many regional clubs existed. At this time the breed varied greatly in type. Some people bred purely for looks, but an important group, including Dr Paul

Kleeman, bred for performance and through that they got type. They believed that the performance went hand-in-hand with physique and temperament, enabling the dog to work. The breeding of the dogs in Germany is more controlled by their working ability than their looks. During the Second World War the breeding programme was disrupted and their development was stopped by the political split in Germany. However the breed is very popular all over the world, particularly in America and the UK and is very successful in field trials.

TEMPERAMENT
The GSP is designed as an all-purpose gundog and has to hunt wide sweeps of ground, air-scenting and pointing staunchly when game is found. The dog also has to work through heavy cover and flush the game for the guns. The breed's retrieving skills are excellent, and the dog is good on land and water and has a keen nose to help find wounded game. The GSP is a very popular, versatile gundog and is totally suitable for the roughshooter.

CONFORMATION
The GSP is a noble, alert and energetic dog of medium size, with a graceful outline and covering plenty of ground while standing. The head is sufficiently broad to give plenty of brain room, but not heavy. The jaw is powerful and sufficiently long to enable the dog to pick up and carry game. The neck must be moderately long and muscular to give strength and to aid movement. The shoulder must slope well to give forward reach, and the fore-limbs are straight, lean, muscular and strong without being coarse-boned. If the dog were coarse-boned, the extra weight would reduce speed and stamina. The hind legs are broad with plenty of muscle and well-angulated to drive the dog forward. This gives the dog a smooth gait, covering plenty of ground, and forceful propulsion.

The rib cage is deep, but not too wide, which would interfere with the swing of the shoulder blades. The ribs are well-sprung but not barrel-shaped. The back is firm and short to give a powerful coupling to the hindquarters. The tail is customarily docked to prevent injury. The short coat does not give much protection from cover. It is a disadvantage in that it gives little protection in general, and cuts and tears are a common occurrence after a day out in rough cover.

The Weimaraner.
Photo courtesy: Gillian Averis.

THE WEIMARANER

This breed is often known as the "Grey Ghost" due to the coat colour which takes on a ghostly hue at night. This aristocratic breed was recognised in its native Germany in 1896. At first there was opposition to the establishment of this dog as a separate breed because some people felt this was just a colour variant of the GSP, but it was argued that this unique colour made the dog a separate breed, and so the Weimaraner became accepted. There are numerous theories as to the breed's origins, but a type of Bloodhound known as a Schweisshund was one of the main ancestors. Pointers and Great Danes have also been involved.

Over a period of years the breed was perfected. The Germans were trying to produce the ultimate gundog, and the Duke of Weimar was an enthusiastic admirer of the breed. The early Weimaraners were referred to as Weimar Hounds and Weimar Pointers and were used to hunt big game, which was abundant in that area. Later on the huntsmen had to make do with birds and small game, which this breed still excels at. The estates of Weimar tended to be on the small side, so the dog was not bred for speed, but needed to be a thorough hunter which excelled in retrieving instinct. The dog had great tracking ability and, because not too much Pointer was introduced, this ability, gained from the Bloodhound ancestors, was retained. These dogs were jealously guarded by the nobility and up to the 1700s they were the only ones allowed to own them. German breeding was very secretive and it was not until the late 1920s that specimens were allowed into the USA. It was another 30 years before they appeared in the UK.

TEMPERAMENT
The Weimaraner is an excellent rough shooter's dog and works better in woodland than open fields. The dog is slower than the GSP at covering ground but is unlikely to miss anything. Because of the tracking instinct, Weimaraners tend to follow ground scent and not air scent, so the latter has to be encouraged. Their temperament is friendly, fearless, protective, obedient and alert. They are medium-sized, although bigger than the GSP, and present a picture of power and stamina. I am very biased towards Weimaraners as they are my first and favourite breed. They are intelligent, dominant and a mental challenge to most owners. They will learn good and bad behaviour easily and, like the elephant, do not forget. They are good in water if

introduced to it gradually, and they are strong swimmers. Because they have a short coat, they are not suitable as a wild fowler's dog, and they do feel the cold when inactive, but once sent off to hunt they will forget about the weather. As intelligent dogs they are not robotic hunters and will be unlikely to hunt if there is no scent, but once game is around they can be stylish hunters, steady pointers and obsessive retrievers.

CONFORMATION
The head is moderately long and aristocratic. The long nose and wide nostrils give the dog excellent scenting ability. The jaw is powerful to help in carrying game – a hare should be carried with ease. The ears are the longest of the HPR group, a legacy from the Bloodhound, and they are prone to trauma and cuts when going through cover, due to their long length and lack of thick hair. The neck must be moderately long to allow the dog to carry game and also to carry the head high and help with air scenting. The shoulder blade is well laid back, and the upper arm long to give the ground-covering reach needed for the dog to work. The hindquarters are moderately angulated, with low-set hocks and well-developed muscle to propel the dog forward.

The body of the Weimaraner should be quite long. This gives a long, deep, well-sprung rib cage which contains a large volume of lung and, hence, excellent respiratory function and stamina. When viewed from the side, this is an oblong dog, whereas most of the other dogs in this group are more compact in shape. The loin is short so that, although the body is long, it is not weak. The feet are often not good in this breed, but they should be well-arched and compact with thick pads to absorb the weight of the dog when running. The tail of the Weimaraner is carried with confidence and is extremely long if not docked. The whipping, long tail is quite prone to injury and so is customarily docked. The dog should cover the ground effortlessly, with a smooth, co-ordinated gait. The coat is normally short, smooth and sleek but there is a long-haired Weimaraner where the coat is of moderate length with feathering on the ears, legs and tail. Because the tail is covered in hair it is not docked.

THE ITALIAN SPINONE

Like many of the Continental gundog breeds, this dog's origins are not clear. The Coarsehaired Segugio is said to have been one of the ancestors, this dog being very common in Piedmont, but as the Spinone was found outside this region, this theory has its faults. Some experts believe that the Spinone is the result of a cross with a Griffon, but another more plausible history is that the Spinone was formed by crossing an imported coarsehaired Setter from the Western Adriatic Coast with a native White Mastiff. The Spinone was first imported into the UK in 1981 by Mrs Mary Moore (Odivane) and these dogs formed the foundation stock for the breed in the UK. The breed was granted Championship Show status in 1994 and is becoming very popular.

TEMPERAMENT
Spinones work at a characteristic fast trotting gait, giving them the ability methodically to cover a large area of land. They can work any terrain but their coarse coat and thick skin make them particularly good in water and marshes. Their coat and temperament will enable them to go through any cover and they are strong retrievers. They have a sweet, almost human, expression and thrive on companionship. They are country dogs, working untiringly all day, but are equally happy by the fireside. They need lots of socialising and sensitive training when young. They are solid, squarely built dogs, with strong bone and good musculature, and are faithful and intelligent.

CONFORMATION
The head is long and lean with a long muzzle to give good scenting and a strong jaw for game carrying. The nose is particularly large, open and spongy, so plenty of air can be inhaled and the faintest of scent detected. The neck must be strong and muscular but fairly short compared to other gundogs, which may be due to the fact that this dog works at a fast trot and not a gallop. The shoulders are strong and well laid back, giving free movement, but the shoulder blades are well apart. This has to be, because the chest is broad, and so the forelegs have to be set quite wide apart to keep the pull of the muscles in a straight line. The hindquarters have long thighs, low hocks with moderate angulation which drives the dog forward, with strong musculature. The pasterns are slightly sloping and the feet well-arched with a thick pad to help absorb any concussive forces and hence not damage the joints. The rib cage is broad, deep and well-sprung, giving the shorter ribcage plenty of volume, which this heavy dog requires. The top line in the Spinone is a little unusual as it has a slight rise to the hips, but it should be strong and muscular to give flexibility but no weakness.

These dogs have a most appealing character and expression, and their undoubted working ability will soon make them popular both as pets and as show dogs and, most importantly, as excellent workers.

THE GERMAN WIREHAIRED POINTER

Prior to the late 18th century only the nobility in Germany could hunt, and the dogs were specialised and highly guarded. In the 19th century with, as I have said, the changes in the political scene, hunting became more popular and a dog was needed who would hunt, point and retrieve all types of game including wild boar, and to do this from any terrain including water. The dog

The German Wirehaired Pointer.

needed to be able to trail wounded game and have a biddable and intelligent nature – no small feat for a breeder to achieve.

To develop the GWP, German Poodles, Pointers, Griffons and Stichelhaars were used. In 1902 the Verein fur Deutsch Drahthaar (German Wirehaired Club) was formed, with the aim of breeding a dog of great hunting ability, good build and, finally, beauty. Hunting ability was produced quite easily, but the coarse wiry coat was more difficult to achieve and, in order to produce dogs which only conformed with the breed type, the German Club opened a Stud book, into which only dogs over one year of age and conforming to the desired standard could be entered. A dog who was not in the stud book could not be used for breeding. This meant that only the best were used.

In 1928 the German Wirehaired Club was accepted by the German Kartell; it is now the leading sporting breed in Germany. The Wirehaired was exported to the USA in the 1920s and has proved to be a worthy all-round gundog. A few dogs came to England after the Second World War, but many of these were not registered and so have not become important to the present gene pool.

The breed made its official entry to the UK in 1972 when Major Wilkinson, who trained gundogs, imported a bitch, and, as she proved to be an excellent worker, so another dog and a bitch were imported to breed from. Several more dogs were then imported and these formed the basis of the GWP in the UK by the later 1970s. Other dogs were imported to improve the coat, temperament and hip status of the stock already in the UK. Some of these came from Holland and, although longer in coat, they were excellent physical specimens and had great working ability. Overall this dog is slightly longer in body compared to height, giving an oblong appearance.

TEMPERAMENT

The GWP is powerful, versatile, biddable and very loyal, as well as being an excellent worker and a good family dog who will prove to be an excellent gundog in most fields.

CONFORMATION

The head is medium-sized, broad enough to afford adequate brain room, but not coarse and heavy. The muzzle is long to allow game-carrying and to produce good scenting ability. The neck is strong and medium length to allow the head to be carried high for air scenting and easy game-carrying. The shoulder blades are sloping and muscular to give forward swing and reach of the foreleg to cover plenty of ground. The hind legs are broad, muscular, with good angulation to give the powerful forward movement. The chest is deep, long-ribbed and well-sprung to give the lung capacity to enable the dog to have endurance and stamina. The pasterns are just slightly sloping and these, coupled with the compact, well-padded, arched toes, act as the shock absorbers to protect the joints from damage. The coat is thick and harsh, with a dense undercoat in winter to give all-weather protection. The GWP is particularly suitable for water work.

5 STARTING RIGHT

In order to have a healthy and successful life your gundog must be looked after carefully and special attention paid to how the dog is reared, fed, housed and socialised. If the pup is not housed and reared correctly you are more likely to see illness and health problems develop. If you have an expensive car you would not fill it with cheap fuel or leave it out on the street to rust! So do take special care with your husbandry to produce an excellent adult dog.

Having decided on the type of gundog you want, and having found the breeder from whom you would like to purchase such a puppy, you must expect a grilling as to whether you are a suitable prospective owner. If you are not asked about your circumstances – what hours you work, where the dog will live, whether you have had a dog before, if you have any children and what their ages are, why you want a gundog, whether you intend to work the dog, do you want a dog or a bitch and why you have made your choice, etc. – then possibly find a different breeder! Do not take offence about being asked such questions; the breeder wants to make sure you are offering a suitable home for the dog.

You may strike lucky and find your breeder has a litter due very shortly, or even has one already born, but if not, it is worth putting your name on a waiting list. The puppy you are going to buy will, hopefully, be a close companion for the next 12 years, so a short wait is well worth enduring. I know a lot of people like to have a puppy in the spring, so you can do some basic training and have them ready for the next shooting season, but is that really so important, when the right dog is going to have many seasons with you, whereas the unsuitable dog will probably be lucky to see one!

The cost of the puppy should be asked at the outset. A well-bred and reared puppy may sound expensive, and the temptation may be to find a cheaper pup, but once the pup is yours, the feeding will cost the same, vaccinations the same, vet's fees the same – or they could be more expensive if the puppy has hereditary conformational faults or has been poorly reared. So do be patient for the right pup.

LOOKING AT THE LITTER
Ideally, when a litter is available, go and see the puppies as soon as the breeder allows, so that you can see the mother and the pups together and see where they are being reared. It is important to realise that the mother may be protective towards her puppies and keeping a wary eye on you. If she seems nervous, it may just be her maternal instinct. If the breeder has other

dogs, they will probably be related and so their temperaments can give you a good guide as to the probable way the pups will grow up. Also the bitch is unlikely to be looking her best. She will have lost muscle, her teats and mammary glands will be pendulous and her coat likely to be falling out and thinning. I often feel I would like a picture of the bitch in excellent condition prior to pregnancy to pin above the whelping box to show what she can look like!

Be cautious if the stud dog lives on the premises. Did they use him because it was convenient, or did his pedigree really tie in well with that of the bitch? It could well be the latter, in which case it is nice to see the father as well, but a good breeder would travel *any* distance to find the most suitable dog for their bitch, so it may not be possible to see him.

Now back to the puppies. Are they in a suitable environment? Very young pups, up to about three weeks, are not very conscious of their surroundings; so as long as they are warm, clean and mum arrives regularly, they will be fine. After three weeks they need to be exposed to people and noises which they may experience when older. I use a radio tuned to a pop station to provide varied noise, and encourage friends to visit and handle the pups. As they get a little older, they need toys to play with to develop their inquisitive natures and character. The toys do not have to come from an expensive shop – empty plastic bottles, cardboard boxes, or the centres from toilet rolls are ideal.

DOG OR BITCH?

Assuming that the pups live up to your expectations, and you are acceptable to the breeder, the next thing is to decide whether to have a bitch or a dog. You may have the choice made for you if only one sex is available but if you can choose, this has to be a personal decision. There are valid arguments on both sides. Dogs do not come on heat, whereas bitches are likely to have a season every six months, which will stop them working for three weeks, and some can be a bit moody afterwards. However, many bitch owners will say that at least bitches' hormones are only a problem for that time, whereas a dog has hormones all the year round! Some dogs are more interested in the opposite sex and in being dominant than others, but if a dog becomes too amorous or dominant he can always be castrated. Similarly if you are not going to breed from your bitch, spay her before her first season. As her hormones are dormant for three months of every cycle, by spaying you are extending that period permanently, so there are no grounds for saying that she will not work as well. In fact she should work more consistently without having her hormones to interrupt the serious business! Both dogs and bitches can be affectionate or aloof, but as a general rule dogs tend to be more dominant than bitches. If it is your first dog you may be better having a bitch, but I would recommend you take the advice of the breeder who will be able to assess you as well and help you make the choice.

It is normal procedure to leave a deposit so the breeder knows you are serious about buying the pup and you know that one will be reserved for you. This first visit is a good time to make arrangements for the collection of the puppy, and to ask what will be needed when the pup first comes home. What food the pup will be on is the most important question. A good breeder will give you a sample of food so the diet is not changed at a time when everything else will be.

IMPORTANT LITTER LEARNING TIME

The best time for puppies to leave their litter mates is at around eight weeks. The bitch will have stopped feeding them by about six weeks, but the following two weeks are important to enable the puppies to learn to play with their siblings. They learn the body language which says "I want to play", or "go away I have got a headache". They learn to understand the "play bow" – front legs on the ground, bottom up in the air, tail wagging, and the "aggressive dominant walk", head held high, legs straight, back slightly arched, tail upright and eyes staring. This means "back off". They learn how hard to play and that if they get too rough, then they will be chastised. It is a very important stage in their behaviour learning and should not be jeopardised by collecting the puppy too early. A puppy who does not have these learning play sessions will not understand the behaviour of other dogs and is likely to get into trouble, as an older dog, when moving into a working environment. A gundog who does not understand other dogs is a problem.

The bitch will often start to play with the puppies as they get older and teach them how to play and to understand just how far they can go before they are told off. When she tells them off, she will make a lot of growling noises and roughly hold the pup by the neck. But she is unlikely to hurt them physically. However, mentally she is dominating them. It is an important lesson to learn. Single puppies can miss out on this "nursery education" but often the mother will play with a single puppy, and she should be encouraged to do this so the pup can be properly socialised. So do not be put off by a single pup, but I would make extra efforts to introduce such a puppy to other dogs as soon as possible. I had a singleton puppy whose mother did not look after her, so she had never played with other dogs as a youngster and, as she got older, she was forever getting into trouble and causing friction because she did not understand when the other dogs had had enough of her game. She would push and push, not reading the body language, until eventually the other dog would bite her.

PREPARATIONS FOR THE HOMECOMING
Preparation for the pup's homecoming need not be elaborate. You will need to provide a draught-free bed, food and water bowls. Stainless steel bowls are probably the best as they can easily be kept clean and free from germs, and also they are harder to chew! If you are getting a Spaniel, I would recommend a Spaniel bowl. These are deep, with a narrow diameter which allows only the dog's nose into it, so the ears should stay out of the food and water and hence stay cleaner.

The pup's bed can be as simple as a cardboard box, which can be changed as the pup grows or as the bed is chewed. Alternatively you can buy a hard plastic bed which can be covered with a synthetic fleece or blanket. I would advise using the synthetic fleece type of bedding at all times as this allows moisture to seep underneath while the surface remains dry and warm. It washes extremely well and is difficult – but not impossible – to chew. Blankets are OK but they can be chewed and, if the strands are swallowed, they can cause very nasty foreign-body blockages in the intestine, which can be a potential disaster. Similarly carpet, especially nylon ones which unravel, are extremely unsuitable as bedding. The threads will not be softened by the body's digestive juices, and they can cut through the wall of the small intestines with fatal results.

INDOOR KENNELS
I would strongly recommend that you buy an indoor kennel if the pup is going to live in the house. Most gundogs are happier in the house with their owner so, if possible, let them be house dogs rather than kennelled ones. Indoor kennels are, basically, collapsible constructions made of wire, which come in a range of sizes. They are not cheap but they are far less expensive than a new chair leg or new floor covering! They are also the puppy's own domain in which the puppy will soon feel safe and secure. I put a cardboard box inside the kennel, with a

clean synthetic fleece, and a small bowl of water hooked onto the wire at the side. I then cover the top and sides with a blanket, which makes a very draught-proof snug area. The pup will cry at first, but will soon learn that this is bed, and will go into it when tired.

Another great advantage of the indoor kennel is that the pup becomes house-trained much more quickly than when sleeping in a large area. Pups are unlikely to soil their own bed and, if you take your pup out immediately after you return home, your training will be much faster. Indoor kennels are also portable, so they can be put in the car or taken with you on holiday. If I am staying in a hotel with my dogs, I take a kennel so I can leave them in my room, safe in the knowledge that they will not get into trouble while I am out.

OUTDOOR KENNELLING

As I have said, if your pup can live in the house with the family, that is the ideal situation. Some training can be done in the evening while watching the television and the dog feels part of the family. The Hunt, Point, Retrieve breeds in particular are happier with human contact and, if left alone in a kennel all day, would not be content. However, it may be more practical to have an outdoor kennel and run for use either during the day or night. With a little thought a very suitable kennel can be built. There are numerous ready-made kennels and runs on the market which can be bought "off the shelf". The "runs" with these are often small and only suitable to enable your dog to go to the toilet but are not big enough to allow play and exercise. These small runs are OK if only used for short periods, or overnight sleeping. A run which is going to be used for longer periods, especially if two or more dogs are going to be in it, needs to be much bigger.

I would look for one at least 12 ft long and preferably 8 to 12 ft wide. The best base

must be one which is easy to pick up from and keep clean – grass and soil will soon turn into a quagmire; pebbles are good for feet, but are difficult to pick up any mess from. Out of choice I would lay either concrete or paving slabs, making sure that there are no puddles and that it slopes down to a drain. A little planning at this stage will save a lot of hard work later. If you are using concrete, it is a good idea to seal the surface so that the dog's urine does not soak into it and cause a permanent doggy odour. The walls of the run can be made in several ways; half brick and half wire-mesh, or all wire. The frames are best made of galvanised metal as that is maintenance-free but if you want to use wood, make sure the mesh is flat on the inside and the wood is on the outside, or it will be chewed and destroyed. Any wooden structure must be preserved with a treatment which is not harmful to animals – read the labels. Wood is difficult to disinfect and is banned by most Local Authorities in boarding kennels, but it is warmer than brick and cheaper to buy in the first place.

Do not use horizontal bars, as the dogs will use them as a set of ladders and climb out. I once had a Weimaraner bitch who regularly scaled a 6 foot fence made out of horizontal slats of wood. I will not repeat that mistake! A six-foot high fence will normally keep in most dogs, but there is always the escapologist who will climb any height, so it can be advisable to put a roof on the run. Wire will suffice, but part can be clear polyurethane which gives some protection from the weather. Shelter from rain in winter is helpful, but also some shade in the summer is necessary. Trees are the best shade, if the kennel can be positioned for this. I would advise that you have a gate on the run, opening inwards, which can be locked. This will help deter the thief who, unfortunately, is becoming more frequent in modern society. When positioning the kennel and run, if possible plan it so you can see the dogs from the house and they can see you. Social contact is important to your dogs and they will be more content if they can see what is happening.

Always provide clear, fresh water in the run. Use a non-tip container and ideally one that is raised off the ground and held by a metal ring – this will help keep the floor dry by preventing the dog from tipping it over. A raised wooden platform will keep your dog off the wet floor and is a good sitting bench. A covered wooden pallet is fine. Make sure there are no protruding nails and check the kennel regularly for wear and tear.

Put some toys in the kennel for your dog to play with; plastic bottles are fine but must be removed once they start to be chewed. There are numerous healthy toys for your dog to play with. The type which help keep teeth clean are excellent, such as treated bones. Special knotted rope toys are also ideal. They help keep teeth clean and keep the dog amused. Do not give bones to your dog. They can cause great pain and, at worst, peritonitis and death. Nine out of ten dogs may manage them well, but the one that does not can suffer badly. I have seen some awful cases of dogs trying to pass rock-solid faeces composed of chewed up bone. Believe me, if you have seen how these dogs suffer you will not "give your dog a bone".

Now on to the kennel itself. This must be dry, cosy and draught-proof. A minimum size of six ft by four ft is needed for one dog. Wooden kennels are warm but can be chewed. Try and make the inside as smooth as possible, as any protruding edge will be chewed. It is a good idea to line the kennel with plywood and put a layer of insulating material between the two sides. Any edges can be covered with metal. Brick or concrete block kennels are maintenance-free, although they will need sealing and pointing. If using blocks, get the type which have a smooth surface and then they will be easier to keep clean. It is well worth sealing all the surfaces, walls and floor because urine will be absorbed into concrete and can start to

smell. The other problem with these kennels is that they cannot be moved if you want to move house.

A small cosy kennel will be warmer than a huge open space. The height of the kennel should be at least six foot to allow easy access to humans to clean out and to observe the dog. A shelf three foot wide and two foot six inches in height across the kennel can provide a cosy cubby-hole underneath for a bed and a handy sitting place for the dog during the day. The bed area needs to be raised and at least have a six-inch board in front to keep draughts out. A lot of people use straw as a bedding, out of which the dog can make a nest, but it must be changed regularly and it can contain insects and may cause skin allergies. I prefer the synthetic fleece bedding, as it is very warm, difficult to chew and allows moisture to soak through to the underside. Shredded paper is warm and hygienic and is very suitable as bedding, although I find it ends up everywhere and when soiled has to be thrown away, whereas the fleece bedding can be easily washed and dried.

You need a power supply to your kennel and this must be installed in such a way that the dog cannot get to any wires to chew them. It is important to be able to check the dogs at night and also to be able to provide heat when needed. A young pup in winter will require some heat if the dog is going to grow properly. Heat lamps are quite suitable, but make sure they cannot fall down on to the pup and the bedding. Always use a chain to support the light and keep the flex well out of the reach of the pup. If the flex is in the kennel, you can thread it through a metal pipe. A mesh cover over the bottom of the light is extra protection, as it will stop the pup catching the bulb and if the light did fall, the heat would not lie directly on the bedding. Test the area under the lamp for the correct heat. The heavy-coated Retriever and Spaniels can keep warm much better than the thin-coated Weimaraners or Vizslas.

You need a "bob hole" in the kennel so the dog can come and go at will. This can be just a simple small door, or can be as elaborate as a self-closing dog flap. To prevent draughts you can use a piece of material drawn across the opening or strips of thick plastic attached at the top, but loose at the bottom. You do not want the bob hole to be too close to the bedding area, in order to help prevent draughts if the door is to be left open at night.

COLLECTING YOUR PUPPY

The best time for you to collect your puppy is in the morning, because then the puppy will have the rest of the day in which to get used to the new home before being left for the night. The breeder should provide you with a diet sheet and information about worming. You should also get a full pedigree or family tree and also the Kennel Club registration document. Occasionally this might not have been returned from the KC but do make sure it is forwarded on to you as soon as possible. In the UK, apart from confirming that the puppy has been registered at the KC, the registration document will also carry on it details of any hereditary schemes that the parents have been put through. So if the breeder says the parents have been hip-scored for hip dysplasia, this should appear on the registration paper. American registrations will bear similar warranties.

Now, all the preparations are complete – you have collected your diet sheet, registration document, pedigree, food samples and, most importantly, your pup. Put your pup in the place in your car which you intend the dog, when older, should use. A puppy who is carried home on a passenger's lap will get used to sitting in the front and seeing your eyes and responses. Then that puppy gets older and is too big to sit on laps and is banished to the rear of the car behind a dog gate, or in a crate – and will consequently feel rejected and cry and bark.

A dog who has always travelled in the back will soon acknowledge that this is the proper place and you will all arrive at your journey's end refreshed and happy. The puppy may be car sick on initial journeys, so have some paper towel or newspaper ready. Try to make any car journeys short to start with and, as soon as the puppy is vaccinated, go in the car and then for a short walk, so car journeys become associated with something enjoyable. Most pups will grow out of car sickness but if not, your vet can give you some tablets to alleviate the problem.

Your pup has been used to feeding with litter mates, so do not expect the newcomer to tuck into the first meal with gusto. The pup may not eat to start with. Ignore this. Put the food down for ten minutes and if it is not eaten, take it away. Make sure there is fresh water down at all times. Do not be tempted to alter the diet to induce the pup to eat. If you do, you are likely to cause diarrhoea. The pup has enough changes to cope with and will eat when ready. Most pups will eat on the second day. If the puppy is still not keen, you can try feeding the food warm, or adding a small amount of gravy on top of the original food. But be patient. Healthy dogs will not starve themselves!

Finally the puppy should sleep in the permanently allocated place. If this is outside, then put the puppy in the kennel with some food early in the day to become acclimatised to the new home. Similarly, if you have an indoor kennel, the pup should be put into this reasonably soon after you all arrive home. The pup will cry. You can go back once to give reassurance, but after that, ignore it. A puppy who knows that crying will bring you back – will cry! The puppy will soon realise that the bed is safe and secure and will probably start going there immediately when tired. When this happens you can all get some sleep.

FEEDING YOUR PUPPY

People will give you conflicting advice on

diet, but you should stick to the one that your breeder recommends to start with, unless your vet advises against it. If you change the diet too quickly you are asking for digestive upsets and diarrhoea. Generally speaking you should feed four meals a day until 12 weeks of age, and then, as the size of the stomach increases, you reduce to three meals daily, but increase the amount at each feed. It is very difficult to overfeed a gundog puppy because they are growing so rapidly that they need a huge input of nutrients. The exception to this would be the Labrador Retriever, who seems capable of putting on weight on lettuce leaves, so just be a little watchful, and if you can no longer feel the ribs, then it would be wise to cut down a little bit. If in doubt, ask your vet.

I would recommend that you feed a good-quality complete food suitable for puppies. There are several excellent foods on the market. The premium type of dry complete food is excellent. This gives puppies the best start at this vital period of their lives. The complete foods are balanced for protein, carbohydrate, vitamins and minerals, so it is extremely important not to add any extra vitamins, cod liver oil or minerals to the diet, as you will upset the delicate balance, which can lead to abnormal bone growth. It is possible to rear your puppy successfully on a meat and biscuit diet and many of the old breeders prefer this, but making up your own diet is a very skilled job, one which can only be learned with experience, and even then it can go wrong, so I would not recommend it.

Leave the balance of your pup's diet to the experts. The major dog food manufacturers spend massive amounts of money on research into diets, employing highly qualified staff to perfect a food which is ideal for every stage in your dog's life. I have tried the cereal and milk, scrambled egg, rice pudding and mixed meat approach and produced puppies which looked like forced rhubarb – tall and thin. I now stick faithfully

to a premium puppy food and am very pleased with the bone, condition and happiness of the pups.

UNDERSTANDING VACCINATIONS
As soon as possible after bringing your pup home, make an appointment to see your vet to have the puppy checked over. If a problem is found, it is much easier to return a puppy who has not yet had a chance to become part of the family. Just as important, your vet can advise about vaccinations, worming and diet. If you do not have a vet before getting your pup, telephone around your local practices to see if you can find one that suits you. Ask friends with dogs who they use and if you can find a vet who is particularly interested in gundogs, then they will have a little more understanding about your needs. Inquire at training clubs, or ideally at your local shooting meets.

Vaccinations are usually started at eight weeks, and consist of two injections, the second given at 12 weeks The vaccinations can protect your dog against the major infectious diseases. Most brands of vaccine are compatible with each other, so if your breeder has had the first vaccination done, then, as long as you have a certificate giving the details of it, your vet will be able to complete the course with one more injection.

Why do we vaccinate dogs at 8 and 12 weeks and why do they need annual boosters? Vaccination causes the dog to produce antibodies against the disease. Antibodies are the body's soldiers who seek out the enemy and kill it. They are specific to a certain disease. Antibodies are passed on to the pups from a vaccinated bitch via the colostrum, the first milk. Antibodies have a short life. In the vaccinated animal, once the "scout" cells find an invading infection, they send messages to the body to produce masses of antibodies to surround and neutralise the invader.

In the young puppy the antibodies have

been passively obtained and the pup cannot make any new ones so, as the passive antibodies are lost, there will come a time when an invading infection could get past this passive immunity. If the bitch has a high level of immunity following booster vaccinations, she will pass on eighty per cent of this to the pup. As the loss is exponential, about forty-four per cent per week, it can be seen that the pup from a well-protected bitch will have protection for longer than a pup whose mother had a low level of immunity and, hence, the pup started off with a correspondingly low level.

Without blood-sampling every pup, we do not know if the pup has still got some maternal antibody or not. Maternal antibody will stop the vaccine working, because it recognises the vaccine as alien and neutralises it. If we left vaccination until 12 weeks of age, you could virtually guarantee that one hundred per cent of pups will have no maternal antibody and the vaccine would "take" and cause the puppy to produce the cells which then produce their own antibodies. However, from 8 weeks, some fifty-five per cent of pups have lost their maternal antibodies and would be vulnerable to infection. So, as a compromise, the first vaccine is often given at 8 weeks and the second at 12 weeks.

Booster vaccinations are necessary as a reminder to the body's immune system not to let its guard down as there are nasty things about – a bit like doing a revision course. The streetwise town dog, who wanders the streets sniffing every available scent, is likely to be challenged fairly regularly with field virus which act like a continuous booster so, as long as the dog is initially vaccinated, these challenges will probably be survived. However, the dog who is more isolated from sources of infection and not allowed to wander – which should be the case with every dog – will not get this natural boosting and so it is vital to have annual boosters – particularly for the

country dog. Vaccinations are not expensive compared to the cost of your gundog, should the dog catch one of these totally preventable diseases.

I was taught (many moons ago) to tell owners that their puppy should not mix with any dog or go anywhere public until 10 days after the second injection which meant that they could not socialise until they were nearly 14 weeks old. However the Guide Dogs for the Blind Association did some research which showed that behavioural problems were far more common in poorly socialised dogs, and the critical time for socialisation was from six to 16 weeks. We are now left with a dilemma. Do you allow your dog to mix at an early age and risk disease, or do you risk behavioural problems by keeping to strict isolation? A sensible approach has to be taken. Once the first vaccination has been given, then your puppy can mix with fully vaccinated healthy dogs. Visit friends, invite them to you, find out if your vet holds puppy parties where pups can play together. Take your pup out in the car to see the buses, watch the people and hear all the noise of modern life. If possible, carry the puppy around some shopping streets – but this can soon become difficult as your gundog gets heavier and heavier and heavier! I would avoid like the plague any area where stray or latch-key dogs roam. They are likely to be the main source of infection.

DISEASES PREVENTED BY VACCINATION

Distemper. Fortunately this is seen less frequently than in the past. It is a particularly nasty disease because it has two phases. The first is when the pup can have diarrhoea, pneumonia and a nasty muco-purulent discharge from the eyes and nose. The pup is usually very depressed, having a moist cough and raised temperature. If treated, it is possible to get through this stage, but the virus affects the central nervous system

(CNS) and at some future date can cause fits and/or chorea, which is a regular constriction of a group of muscles causing a twitch. These CNS signs are not curable, although the fits may be controlled by drugs. Vaccination is very effective and no dog need suffer from distemper. It used to be called hard pad in the past because it can cause hyperkeratinization of the pads and nose leading to a thick, cracked pad or nose.

Infectious Hepatitis is caused by a virus, canine adenovirus type I (CAV). This virus causes sickness, diarrhoea, intense thirst, abdominal pain, increased temperature and it can cause inflammation in the eye. Interestingly, as the dog produces antibodies which fight off the virus, this can lead to the front of the eye taking on a milky appearance which is called "blue eye". This is transitory and is a good sign that recovery is occurring. Again, this disease is now very rare due to regular vaccination.

Canine Parvovirus is still a problem in certain areas but regular vaccination of the mother should remove any risk. Parvovirus attacks growing cells. If the puppies are born with no protection, the virus can damage the growing hearts, which can lead to the sudden death of young dogs. Nowadays this is unusual and, more commonly, the pup is very depressed and initially vomits, but quickly progresses to passing bloody diarrhoea. The smell is awful and the puppies have abdominal pain. The diarrhoea is the colour of strawberries and custard and has one of the most depressing smells I can imagine. If treated quickly it is sometimes possible to bring the puppy through this awful stage and they can make a full recovery, but unfortunately a lot do not respond and do die. Treatment is with intravenous fluids and antibiotics. Regular vaccination can virtually eliminate the risk of parvovirus and once someone has seen a dog with parvo, they would never allow their dog's vaccinations to get out of date.

Para influenza is not a fatal disease but it can cause a nasty cough, plus eye and nasal discharge, so it is well worth including in a vaccination programme.

Leptospirosis covers two types of disease. The first, leptospirosis icterohaemorrhagiae, is caught by contact with rat's urine which has contaminated food or water. Affected animals are very depressed, often vomit, and have pale gums, often with small bruises on them. The disease affects the liver and kidney, with surviving animals becoming jaundiced and, at a later stage, possibly developing chronic kidney and liver failure. Leptospirosis icterohaemorrhagiae is passed in the urine of ill animals and it can be passed on to man.

Leptospirosis canicola is another serious disease which causes acute kidney disease and can lead on to chronic kidney failure. The clinical signs are dullness, raised temperature, vomiting and thirst. If the kidneys are severely damaged the dog may die at this acute stage but if they do survive they are likely to go on and develop chronic kidney failure which cannot be cured, only managed. The vaccine against leptospiros is very effective and the disease is rarely seen now due to regular vaccination.

Rabies Vaccination. Rabies is a fatal viral disease which can affect many species of wild-life including dogs, cats, foxes and man. At present the disease is not present in the UK but it is common throughout Europe, America and Africa. The virus, a species of rhabdovirus, enters the body usually via a bite from an infected animal, and then replicates in the central nervous system and salivary glands. The incubation period depends on the amount of virus inoculated, and the severity of the bite, but it can be between 10 days and 4 months.

First signs of infection usually are a change in temperament and increased temperature. The saliva of infected dogs can contain large amounts of virus up to three days before clinical signs are first seen, which means that any dog-bite in an infected country should be taken seriously, even if the dog appears normal. About a quarter of infected dogs become hyper-excitable, restless and irritable and can have depraved appetite and chew wood, carpets, stones etc. They slip into a period of weakness and have difficulty in swallowing, and will soon die either during a fit or in a coma. A dumb form of rabies is more commonly seen in dogs and can be difficult to diagnose. The eyes are congested, the lower jaw drops and saliva drools from the mouth. The dog will have difficulty swallowing, there is generalised weakness and death occurs within 15 days.

In many countries control is via vaccination. Rabies vaccination is now quite effective and a dose will provide protection for one year. Annual boosters are then required. As there is no rabies in the UK, the Government feels that quarantine is the best method of preventing rabies from entering the country and infecting dogs, cats and wildlife. Any dog or cat entering Great Britain and Ireland has to undergo 6 months of strict isolation from other animals. The theory behind this is that if the dog is incubating rabies, signs will develop within six months. Vaccination in the UK is only allowed under a licence from the Ministry of Agriculture, Fisheries and Food, when a dog is to be exported or is already in quarantine. However modern vaccines are quite effective and there are now strong arguments for allowing dogs to be vaccinated, blood-tested to confirm the vaccine has taken, permanently identified with an identi-chip or tattoo and then allowed in. This is already possible under the Bali directive but there are strict criteria as to where the dog has been before coming into the UK. The argument about quarantine and vaccination is coming more to the fore and changes look possible.

WORMING

Roundworms, toxocara canis, are almost always found in young puppies. They are long, round-bodied worms found in the small intestine and may be passed in the faeces or vomited up, and appear like pieces of shiny, long, whitish-cream pieces of string. Infection of the puppy is via several routes. The main one is by the migration, during pregnancy, of the larvae which have been encysted in the bitch's tissue and these cross the placenta and infect the puppies. Routine worming has no effect on these encysted larva, which is why most puppies are born with worms. The second route is via the bitch's milk; the third is by eating an intermediate host, mice and sheep for example; the fourth is by direct ingestion of eggs.

The larvae do not develop into adult worms straightaway, but migrate through the intestinal wall, to the liver and lungs, and then back to the intestine via the trachea, as mature adults. The life-cycle happens in pups up to three months of age, but after this age the migration via the trachea stops and the larva encysts. Because of this unusual cycle, and the encysted larva, all puppies should be wormed at 3, 6, 9 and 12 weeks and then monthly, until they are six months old. After this all dogs should be treated against roundworm every six months.

If the mother has been wormed regularly the pups will not be heavily burdened with worms, but they will still have some, so regular worming is essential. Worming preparations, like every type of drug, have improved greatly over the years and modern ones are now very safe and effective. Get your wormer from your vet, who will recommend the best type for your gundog puppy. Some of the older worming preparations were quite aggressive and could damage the stomach and small intestine, causing abdominal pain, and make the pup more susceptible to bowel infections. These old wormers did not kill the worms but just caused them to be passed. Modern wormers kill the worms and are very effective, and they do not cause the damage to the intestines which can be so detrimental to the pups.

Roundworms are at the heart of the anti-dog lobby's case in the UK. The worm eggs are passed in faeces and, if a child gets toxocara eggs on their hands from playing with soil contaminated with infected dog faeces, and then ingests these eggs, the larvae can migrate from the small intestine into the body, and become dormant – a state called Visceral Larval Migrant (VLM). Very rarely a larva will migrate to the eye and form a cyst, causing loss of sight. Dog owners must be responsible, worming their dogs regularly and picking up any faeces which their dogs produce in public places. Special plastic bags can be bought at supermarkets which can be easily carried in your pocket and then put in a rubbish bin after use.

Tapeworms are not passed to the pups from the mother. Go to your vet to get a treatment which will remove the head of the worm as well as the body.

Heartworm is a parasite, dirofilaria immitis, and is transmitted in larval form by mosquitoes. It can be seen in dogs in Africa, Central America, the eastern seaboard of the USA, Asia and Australia, or in dogs imported from these areas. The larvae develop in the dog's tissue and then migrate into the dog's circulatiory system and finally rest in the right side of the heart and pulmonary vessels. It takes two to three months for the worms to develop. They can cause inflammation in the arteries and the clinical signs produced are coughing, difficulty in breathing and, on X-ray, the right side of the heart may be enlarged. The disease is diagnosed by examining a blood smear where the larvae can be seen.

Treatment is necessary to remove the worms and treat any cardiac failure. Dogs in areas where the disease may occur should be treated regularly with an effective drug.

Dogs imported from areas where heartworm can be found should also be treated.

IDENTIFICATION FOR GUNDOGS

All dogs must wear a collar and identification disc when outside, according to the law. For working gundogs this would be a potential hazard, as the collar can be caught on undergrowth and, at worst, could cause the dog to hang itself. This is why gundogs on a shoot do not wear a collar. Your pup should, however, get used to a collar so that if you ever need to use one it is not such a traumatic shock to the dog.

Permanent identification for your dog is a sensible idea. This can be achieved by tattooing or by inserting a microchip. Tattoos can be put on the inside of the ear, or inside the thigh, but personally I would not use tattoos. They can be very difficult to read but, more importantly to me, they can be painful when applied. I would favour the microchip, if this system is available in your area. This is a painless procedure whereby a microchip about the size of a grain of rice is injected under the skin between the shoulder blades. It cannot be seen from the outside and would be impossible for a thief to remove. The microchip contains a unique bar code which identifies the dog with the owner. This information is kept on a national computer. If a lost dog is taken to a police station, vet or rescue kennel and scanned, the information on the microchip enables dog and owner to be reunited. This prevents any dog being put to sleep because the owner could not be found. All strays are now scanned before they can be destroyed so no mistake should be made. Not one of us who cares for our dogs would let them stray, but there is always the chance that a strong scent will lead a dog in the wrong direction, or the horrible thought that, if you were involved in a car accident, your dog might escape and, in fear, take off. At least when the dog is finally found, identification can be made.

6 FEEDING YOUR GUNDOG

After spending considerable time, effort and money on buying a puppy who will work well with you, your next consideration should be how to achieve your dog's full potential through correct feeding. If you asked ten different experienced dog folk which was the best food to give their dog, you would get ten different and strongly held views! All of these methods will probably work for these experienced people if they understand their dogs and have perfected their nutrition over the years by trial and error. You need not make these errors.

Decades ago many dogs suffered from a condition known as "Black Tongue" because they were fed a diet of only flaked maize and skimmed milk. This condition was caused by a deficiency of nicotinic acid. When this was discovered, meat was added to the diet, which solved the problem because it contained the necessary nicotinic acid.

A diet of household scraps, which not so long ago most dogs were fed, could also lead to an unbalanced diet and so vitamin and mineral supplements became the norm. As the petfood industry began to expand it started to produce balanced, cheap, complete foods and so the need for supplements vanished. Unfortunately the health problems which could occur by giving too many vitamins and minerals were not understood, and so these supplements continued to be advised in the 60s and 70s, even when a dog was on a complete feed. In an already balanced food, adding extra vitamins and minerals makes the diet unbalanced, and can produce skeletal abnormalities, e.g. hip dysplasia (HD) and osteochondritis dissecans (OCD). These conditions are usually seen in the fast-growing, heavier breeds where a slight imbalance in the diet can be magnified when eaten in quantities. An "epidemic" of bone and joint abnormalities was seen in the 70s and 80s in these big breeds, caused mainly by over-supplementation of the diet, for example in Goldens and Labradors.

So let us look a bit more closely at dog food and what goes into it. Food consists of:
1. Protein
2. Fats
3. Carbohydrate
4. Vitamins
5. Minerals
6. Water
7. Fibre/Ash

PROTEINS
Proteins are basically the body's building blocks. They are essential for the growth and daily maintenance of the body. For

nutritional purposes, all protein sources are measured against chicken for metabolic use. In general, white sources of protein i.e. poultry, rabbit, tripe and fish, are higher in value than red protein. I never feed pork to my dogs as it will often cause diarrhoea. The protein in cereal is of a lower metabolic value than white meat protein.

FATS

Fats are essential for proper development, providing essential fatty acids and transporting the fat-soluble vitamins A, D and E into the body. They are an excellent source of masses of calories and are the most efficient way to provide energy in a food. A diet high in fat is an easy way to provide high levels of energy for the working dog. Ounce for ounce, fats contain the highest number of calories of all the foods.

Feeds high in fats also tend to be more palatable and because of this some dry foods have fat sprayed onto the outside of the feed to make them taste better to the dog. Fats can go rancid if not kept properly, so it is important that food is stored in dry containers, out of sunlight and used before the "date" runs out. Fats also contain the fat-soluble vitamins, and a diet low in fats may be low in the essential vitamins.

CARBOHYDRATES

Carbohydrates are either simple (sugar, lactose etc.), or complex – these are ones which have to be broken down by the body and provide a slower release of energy. Good sources of carbohydrate are cereals, potatoes and rice.

VITAMINS

Vitamins are organic compounds essential to life and required in very small quantities for normal metabolism. They are natural components of food and are generally present in sufficient amounts in a varied diet. Deficiencies can cause serious health problems. There are two groups of vitamins:

the fat-soluble vitamins A, D, E and K, and water-soluble B complex, including thiamin, niacin, riboflavin, biotin, folic acid and B12. Vitamin C may be required in certain conditions but it is manufactured by the dog in the liver and so is not essential in the diet. Fat-soluble vitamins can be stored by the body in body fat, whereas the water-soluble vitamins cannot be stored. Because of this, water-soluble vitamin deficiencies can occur much faster in an inadequate diet, rather than fat-soluble vitamin deficiencies.

Vitamin requirements are increased during growth, pregnancy and heavy work, because of increased tissue formation, limited reserves (especially in the young, thin animal) and increased activity. Vitamin A, if given in excess, can lead to skin thickening but, more importantly, faulty bone formation and remodelling in young dogs, especially in the spine, which can cause pressure on the nerves and degeneration, leading to limb weakness. Vitamin A can be found in cod-liver oil and carotene. It is found in high concentration in liver and because of this, liver should only be fed in moderation.

Vitamin D is involved in the delicate balance of calcium and phosphorus in the body. For our gundogs, Ca/P ratio is important in bone development. Vitamin D is quite resistant to damage by heat and it is also produced in the body, so routine dietary supplementation should be avoided. Too much Vitamin D in the body leads to an increase of calcium in the blood and a decrease in the bones, which can lead to joint abnormalities and "greenstick fractures" of the long bones. Too little Vitamin D, if found in conjunction with an imbalance of calcium and phosphorus, can lead to rickets.

Vitamin E is another of the fat-soluble vitamins and, if not found in sufficient quantities in the diet, can cause poor muscle formation and decreased production of sperm and hence reproductive failure.

The water-soluble vitamins cannot be stored in the body and so a regular supply is essential. A deficiency of this B group leads to vague signs of loss of appetite, weight loss and poor growth. Many of the vitamins are manufactured by the normal bacteria which live in the small and large intestine. Their production can be decreased if the dog takes oral antibiotics, so it is often advisable to supplement with B vitamins following antibiotic treatment. Thiamin, one of this group, can be destroyed by a chemical found in raw fish, so this should never be fed to dogs; the compound, Thiaminase, is destroyed by cooking, so cooked fish is not a problem.

MINERALS
The main minerals which we have to worry about in our gundog are calcium and phosphorus. They have a close metabolic association and so must be considered jointly. The ratio of calcium (Ca) to phosphorus (P), 1.2:1 to 1.4:1 by weight, is generally considered to be the optimal combination to have maximum utilisation. It will also minimise the need for Vitamin D. Ca and P are needed in the blood and also in bones. The bones are a reservoir of Ca and P which give the bones their strength. If the diet is low in Ca or P, the level in the circulatory blood is low, so the body, with the help of Vitamin D, releases Ca/P from the bony reservoir to top up the blood levels. If this goes on for too long, the bones will become weak and lead to joint abnormalities and greenstick fractures. If the diet is very high in Ca or P, the levels in the blood will be very high and so the body deposits the extra in the bones. If this is to an excess, the bones become deformed and lameness results.

If the diet has too much phosphorus, as in a cereals-only diet (with a Ca:P ratio of 1:8), the body will take calcium from the bones to restore the blood circulatory ratio to 1.2:1 to 1.4:1. This leads to a Ca deficiency in the bones. Similarly, a diet too high in calcium or too low in Phosphorus will cause a decrease in bone phosphorus. Imbalance of Ca/P in the diet in the growing dog can lead to deformities of the joints, abnormalities in the growth plates of the bones, lameness and poor tooth development. A diet containing 1.6g Ca and 1.2g P per 12,000 kcal metabolizable energy will meet the minimal requirements of a normal dog.

WATER
The adult dog's body is 60 per cent water. This level is higher in young pups. Water is vital for life and a dog can survive for a longer period if deprived of food than if deprived of water. Water can be obtained in liquids and from food. A dry dog food will still contain 10 to 20 per cent water, whereas a canned food is 74 to 78 per cent water. Water is lost from the body through the lungs, intestines, urine, and skin and from milk in the lactating bitch. Fresh clean water should always be freely available.

FIBRE
Fibre is not absorbed by the body but it is needed to provide faecal bulk, to absorb water and to slow intestinal transit to allow proper absorption from the large intestine. It can help in cases of diarrhoea because of these functions, and also in constipation, by encouraging faecal bulk and motility of the colon.

ACHIEVING A BALANCED DIET
As you can see from the preceding paragraphs, to create a balanced diet for your dog is a very scientific and skilled job, so I would strongly recommend that you use a commercially prepared food from a recognised manufacturer. The leading pet food producers spend enormous amounts of money on research and development to create the ideal food, so let them do the work. Your dog's health and working

performance are not worth a gamble. The quality of dog foods varies tremendously and the type of food your dog needs will also vary according to the different stages of growth, and also the amount of work you are expecting the dog to do.

A diet low in protein and energy can be fine for a couch potato but is not adequate for a hard-working dog. We have all seen the carefully monitored diets that the top athletes are given by their coaches and, with improved nutrition, their performances have increased tremendously. Roger Bannister's four-minute mile, such a massive achievement forty-odd years ago, is now regularly broken by many present-day athletes. No fast-food burger and chips for our record breakers, so just think about what you are putting into your dog's body if you want to get the best results and keep the dog healthy.

Commercially prepared foods can be split into three main groups:
1. Dry.
2. Semi-moist.
3. Canned.

Within these groups the quality of the foods varies tremendously. The quality of the ingredients and their value to the dog is important. If you were to analyse shoe leather, breaking it down into the percentage of protein, fat and carbohydrate, it would appear to be an ideal dog food. But we all know that that is not the case. This is because the dog's digestive system cannot break down the shoe leather and digest it, so the nutrients have no biological value. They would be passed out of the intestines virtually unaltered! As a general rule the more expensive the food, the higher the proportions of easily digested food will be found, and the better the diet is for your dog.

Manufacturers use many ingredients to put the protein into the diet including poultry, beef, tripe, lamb, fish, eggs, soya, wheat, maize, oats and barley. Animal protein is easier to digest than cereal protein for the dog. Poultry is the easiest protein for the dog to digest as the body needs to do less work to be able to utilise its stored nutrition and a higher proportion can be absorbed into the body.

Diets which obtain the majority of their protein and energy from cereals tend to be lower in protein than the premium or meat-based foods. They can be quite adequate for a sedentary, middle-aged dog who has little pressure on him, or her, but they are not suitable for a rapidly growing dog, or pregnant bitch or working dog. Eating a cereal-based food is, for a dog, a bit like us eating sausage, beans and chips every day – you can survive on it but it is not the healthiest diet and your health may suffer.

The protein level of foods varies from as low as 10 per cent (cereal-based) up to 35 per cent (premium chicken or lamb and rice). The growing dog, the pregnant or nursing bitch, and the working dog need larger amounts of protein and energy than a sedentary pet. If a diet has only 12 per cent protein, the dog would have to eat twice as much of it as compared to a diet containing 24 per cent protein, to obtain the same level of nutrients. When a dog has high nutritional demands, the volume of food which needs to be consumed on a low protein diet is vast, and can be physically impossible to consume. For this reason it is clear that our high-need group of gundogs should be fed on a high-protein premium diet. Similarly, the same group of dogs will have a high energy requirement, so, as fat is the best source of calories, a high fat diet is to be recommended.

The high cereal foods have a low metabolic value. The dog cannot digest all the cereal properly and quite a lot of the food passes through the digestive tract unaltered and is not available as nutrition for the dog. As a result, dogs fed on a low protein cereal diet pass larger amounts of faeces than a dog fed on a premium food.

They are often more prone to flatulence on the cereal foods, as bacteria in the gut feed off the indigestible food and produce gas which the dog then passes, usually when you have guests!

When looking for a food for your dog you should study the bag, look at protein and fat levels, and then study the list of ingredients. The best food for your working gundog will have a higher proportion of meat than cereals. Manufacturers of dog food list the ingredients with the food found in the greatest amount first, and the least last. So a food which starts its list of ingredients with poultry or meat is likely to be a better quality food than one which starts with cereal. However, beware – the manufacturers know that you want to feed meat to your dog, not cereal, so they will sometimes try to subdivide the cereal classification so that it appears lower down the list – for example, wheat can be split into wheat and wheat husks, thus lowering wheat's position on the ingredient list!

PUPPY FOODS

Your young pup requires twice as much energy per pound of bodyweight as an adult dog. The puppy's stomach is small in relation to the volume of food required so, even when fed on a premium food which is a low-residue food, you need to split the food into multiple small feeds. From three to twelve weeks the puppy should be fed four times daily. The ideal food will have a protein level of about 30 per cent protein and 20 per cent fat. Initially it should be fed well-soaked and gradually the soaking time is reduced until by eight weeks the food can be completely dry. Fresh water should always be available. The growing puppy is consuming energy so quickly that it is virtually impossible to overfeed a puppy. The only exceptions would be Labradors and Golden Retrievers, and I would watch their weight carefully. We want our puppies to have a bit of spare flesh, but not to be walking Michelin men!

As you will have gathered by now, I prefer the dry premium complete foods, but if you want to feed canned meat and biscuit, make sure you give the same volume of meat to biscuit to keep the balance. *Do not give extra vitamins or minerals.* Milk is not necessary for your puppy. Cows' milk will often cause diarrhoea because, as puppies age, they lose the enzymes which can digest the lactose which is in cows' milk and this will cause the loose faeces. Goats' milk can be used as an alternative if your pup is a poor doer, but should not be needed if the pup eats well.

When feeding, leave the food with your pup for ten minutes, then take it away. If you leave it down all the time the puppy may become a "grazer", or slow eater, which is no good for a dog who is out all day working. Do not be tempted to add to the balanced diet. Dogs will not starve themselves if presented with good-quality food, but they can soon decide whether you are a soft touch who will add tasty extras to their food if they do not eat it straightaway. However, if after three to four days of following this routine your pup is still not eating well, but is otherwise full of health, you can add a small amount of meat made into a gravy. But stop as soon as the pup is eating with more enthusiasm.

At twelve weeks reduce the meals to three a day but increase the volume of each feed so the dog is eating the same, or more, than before. With the bigger breeds it is sometimes a good idea to change the youngster from the puppy food at about eight weeks, to a food designed for active dogs. Check that the manufacturer says that it is suitable for puppies first, but the bigger kibble size is often preferred, as the pup grows, to the smaller puppy food. The nutrient level of these activity foods is usually ideal for your pup, but do a double check to make sure that it is suitable for growing dogs.

ADOLESCENTS AND JUNIORS

At six months you can start feeding twice daily. I continue with this regime throughout my dogs' lives, particularly for the bigger gundog breeds when two smaller meals are less likely to cause digestive upset than one large one. You are also spreading the dogs' energy intake over a longer period. Puppies need sleep to allow their bodies to grow properly. When I first started in dogs I heard the old breeders talking about the difference between pet-reared and breeder-reared puppies. At the time I though it was one of those "good old mother" stories, but over the years I have seen what was meant. At eight weeks my carefully reared puppies go to their new homes, and it is amazing the number of times they return for visits at nine months of age looking tall, thin and rangy, whereas the litter mate I have kept is well-covered, with plenty of bone and with more substance, despite the puppies having been very similar at eight weeks. My puppies play out all day, can sleep when they are tired, and are put to bed in the kennel when darkness falls. At meal times they can eat as much as they want until they are six months old and then the regime is altered according to body condition.

Puppies reared in the home do not get the opportunity to sleep as much. They are disturbed by the daily routine of the house. Someone is with them during the day, the vacuum cleaner has to be attacked, the washing basket emptied and, just when it's nap time, the boss puts on the coat and off we all go for a walk. Evenings, the rest of the family is around and so sleep is disturbed again. The bag of dog food says that the pup should eat "x" amount per day, and this is adhered to without looking at the condition of the dog. Invariably, with all this extra activity and less rest, the pup becomes thinner. Do give your pup a rest – indoor kennels are ideal. Just like putting a baby in its cot for a nap, put the pup in the kennel for regular periods during the day to allow the body to grow.

Dogs do most of their rapid growing up to the age of nine months. The smaller breeds reach the adult height earlier than the larger ones. The rate of growth then begins to slow down so that maximum height is achieved at 14 months. This is completed when the long bones stop growing, that is, when their growth plates close. The growth plates are found in the long bones, for example, the femur, tibia, humerus etc. The bones lengthen at these growth plates and when they have closed, no more lengthening can take place.

Age of Growth Plate Closure	Months
Wrist (carpus)	$5^{1/2}$
Toes (Phalanges)	6
Scapula (shoulder blade)	$6^{1/2}$
Hock (tarsus)	$6^{1/2}$
Front pasterns (metacarpals)	7
Rear pasterns (metatarsals)	9
Forearm (radius/ulna)	11
Second thigh (tibia and fibula)	13
Thigh (femur)	14
Upper arm (humerus)	15

These times are approximate and can vary by a month. The bones of the body, spine and skull continue to grow for up to two years.

As you can see from the chart, the bones lower down the leg tend to stop growing first. That is why, on a young pup, the feet and lower leg always look too big. It is because they reach the adult proportions earlier in life than the rest of the dog. Similarly, the legs have finished growing before the spine has reached its full length, so the junior dog, 12 to 15 months, can look long on the leg compared to the length of back. The flat bones of the skull can change shape up to two years of age, which is why you will often hear people say that a dog's head has "broken" at last – it means that the bones have reached their adult shape and size.

The calculated metabolic protein and energy requirements of dogs at different stages of life are as follows:

	Protein g Metabolization Protein Kcal per Wkg 0.67 per day	ME Requirements Kcal per Wkg 0.67 per day
Weaning 3 weeks	8.1	400
Weaning 6 weeks	6.5	374
Early growth	6.0	353
Half Growth	3.8	225
Adult	1.5	132-159
Pregnancy (late)	5.7	205
Lactation	12.4	560

WORKING GUNDOGS

The range of work gundogs are expected to do must be taken into account when deciding on the correct diet. The premium dog food range usually has a variety of food for active or working dogs. These dogs have high protein energy requirements with low residue. 25 to 30 per cent protein should be sought. In very cold weather energy requirements are much higher than in warmer weather as energy is used by dogs to keep warm. A layer of body fat will keep them warm but will also slow down their ability to work, so you should aim to keep a dog in fit condition with just the last two ribs showing. A dog out on a full day's shoot can need two to four times the normal energy requirements of a non-working dog. This is a large volume of food and so it is vital that a low-residue, concentrated food is fed, and this is split into two meals. On a working day, take some food with you for lunch time for the dog as well as for yourself. It is often an idea to feed an energy-rich food such as Mars bars, as this can give the dog's waning energy reserves an excellent boost to keep going until the end of the day.

Many gundog people will have seen a hard-working dog 'switch off' in the afternoon or, worse still, have a fit while out working. This is usually caused by hypoglycaemia (low blood glucose) caused by the extra demand put on the dog by all the exercise. In the worst scenario it can cause the dog to go into a coma, and death will result if sugar is not given. Honey is the best source of glucose but is not easily carried – so Mars bars should always be in your emergency box in case of need.

Usually dogs which become hypoglycaemic decrease their activity, pottering around rather than hunting obsessively, which therefore lowers their energy requirements and they can recover on their own, but you will have had a poorer afternoon's work from your dog than if you had topped up its reserves at lunch time.

During a hard season most dogs will lose weight so it is a good idea to start the season with a *little* body fat to provide a stored source of energy. Dogs who have no body fat and cannot eat all the calories necessary in order to work all the days required of them, will start to break down their muscle to provide the energy needed, and so their ability to do the work will be inhibited as they will have reduced muscle mass. Bones become weaker, joints are more liable to injury as tendons are weaker, and the immune system becomes less effective so that infections are more common. Reproductive function will also suffer.

If you are expecting your dog to do three days' work a week, in cold weather, it might be advisable to add extra fat (and hence calories) to the diet by pouring some olive oil over the food. On the way home from a day out, a bag of chips is a good idea to feed your dog until you get home. They have a high fat content to help replace the energy burned up during the day, and the warmth will help maintain the dog's body heat after a particularly cold day. A second bag for yourself is also an excellent idea!

NON-WORKING DOGS

Dogs which are not hard at work do not have the same high nutritional demands that the worker has, and if fed on a high activity diet will be prone to putting on weight. Also the high-activity foods are more expensive than those for a dog with a more sedate pace of life, so you can feed a food with a lower protein and energy content. I would still recommend a premium food, but drop down to a 15 to 20 per cent protein. You will still get the quality of ingredients and keep the dog in excellent condition. Just because a dog is not working, this does not mean that dog can be fed a poor-quality diet. The dog deserves better. Staying on a meat/poultry based diet and not cereal, will still result in excellent digestibility, so fewer faeces and less flatulence, but still a good coat and a fit dog. I have heard people say that these premium foods can make dogs hyperactive. I disagree. What you are doing is bringing out the true character of the dog. On a poorer quality diet the dog may be quieter because the diet is not sufficient to keep the dog in tip-top condition.

GERIATRIC DOGS

Dogs, like people, have changing nutritional demands at different stages of their lives As they get older they will benefit from a white meat diet rather than red meat. This is because their liver and kidneys may not be as active as when they were young, and the protein from white meat or fish requires less alteration by the liver and kidneys and, like a car and its various component parts, the fewer demands you put on these organs, the longer they will last!

In old age the dog is not building up muscle or using up the amount of calories of the younger dog, so the diet has a lower protein content, lower fat, but more carbohydrates where energy can come from. Oily fish is an excellent occasional addition to the diet as the essential fatty acids found in it are used by the body to form natural pain killers and have anti-inflammatory features to help with arthritis. There are special diets for geriatric dogs which have the lower protein, fat and calorific value but also have reduced phosphate levels which is beneficial if the animal's kidneys are working

less efficiently than normal. If the phosphate level rises in the blood, a mechanism comes into play which removes calcium from the bones and can lead to them becoming soft and weakened

Other nutrient levels are also changed in the geriatric diet to compensate for changes in the metabolism of the older dog. Although your old age pensioner is not working for you, it is worth providing the best possible diet so that the dog's last years will be as long and healthy as possible.

INJURY AND CONVALESCENCE

During illness or injury the nutritional requirements of your dog will change. Energy needs can quadruple, and protein is required in massively increased quantities to remove and repair damaged body tissue and to enable the body's immune system to work flat out. Food should be easy to digest and highly palatable to tempt the dog to eat. Small aromatic warm meals are more likely to be tempting to eat than an enormous cold bland meal. By this I do not mean a highly spiced curry!

Commercial pet food designed for 'puppies' or 'growth' are suitable, as a high proportion of their calories are from protein and fat and are usually highly palatable. Canned foods are usually more tempting to the convalescent dog than dry foods. Baby foods can be used for a short time as they are palatable, but the meat-based foods are deficient in Ca, Vit A and thiamine, so should not be relied on as a prolonged sole source of nutrients.

Sometimes it is worth offering fresh food in order to tempt the true anorexic. Chicken and fish with boiled rice are often acceptable. canned sardines in tomato sauce are tempting to most dogs, especially if they are warmed up a little. Water should always be available and should be changed regularly. Sometimes a dog which is reluctant to drink will lick an ice cube. Dogs who have had sickness and diarrhoea will have lost electrolytes from their bodies. These are vital to their circulation and should be replaced if the loss lasts for more than 24 hours. Electrolyte replacement sachets can be bought from your vet and offered to the affected dog, but if the dog will not drink this salty-tasting liquid, do provide fresh clear water as well.

PREGNANCY AND LACTATION
For the first six weeks of gestation you should continue to feed your bitch her regular food in normal quantities. As long as her diet is of good quality, she will not have any changed needs. The foetus is very small at this point, and most of the abdominal swelling is fluid. At this stage any increase in body size should be due to the pregnancy and not due to fat. After six weeks you should start increasing the amount of food that you give and, as the abdomen enlarges, you will need to give more frequent feeds, as there is not room in the abdomen for the stomach to be filled with a large meal. The type of food should be of high quality. With little room for the stomach, due to the increased size of the uterus, you do not want to be feeding a diet of large bulk. High-protein, high-fat diets suitable for working dogs are ideal. On such a diet you do not need to give any supplements and, in fact, they are to be avoided, or you are asking to produce metabolic imbalances and potential disasters. Milk is not needed at any time during pregnancy – just clear, fresh water.

Your aim is to keep some condition on your bitch so that you can just feel her backbone and last two ribs. If your bitch is too fat when she whelps, she is likely to have a more difficult labour than if she is in fit condition. If she is too thin, she will have started to break down her own muscle to provide her energy requirements and this will decrease her ability to have strong abdominal contractions. During labour itself most bitches will not eat, but it is useful to provide some milk to keep her energy levels up.

Post-whelping you must feed your bitch so that she can maintain her body weight and produce enough milk for her litter. The amount of food will obviously be dependent on the number of puppies which she has to feed and on her initial condition. Continue to feed your complete, top-quality meat-based food, but increase the quantity over the next few weeks to up to four times the normal amount. I always leave a bowl of dry food at the side of the whelping box, alongside the water bowl, so that she can eat what she needs. Some bitches may need to have their intake restricted a bit – Labradors in particular – but assess the amount of food in relation to the bitch's body condition. If you can see her backbone and more than the last two ribs, feed more. If her back looks like a boardroom table top, restrict her! There is no hard and fast rule, and each bitch must be fed according to her needs.

When she has first whelped, it is often difficult to get her to start to eat. She is too busy cleaning up after the pups, fussing over them, and the last thing on her mind is food. The first time I whelped a bitch, as soon as she had finished I was panicking because she would not each much, and she had all those puppies to feed. I brought her fresh beef, cooked scrambled eggs and was paranoid because she only picked at them. How could she feed her puppies? Would they all die through lack of milk? No, of course not. I eventually realised that at a few days old a puppy only takes a small amount of milk from the bitch, and so it is not necessary to force-feed mountains of food to her in the first few days of lactation. So long as she is drinking, offer small, tasty meals in the whelping box. She may take an offering hand-fed, but do not worry as long as she is drinking. Her need for food and her appetite will soon return, once the pups start increasing their intake of milk.

At three weeks the litter will really be

pulling your bitch down, so make sure she has plenty of top-quality complete ration at this stage, as well as lots of water. If you feed her a top quality complete food there is no need to give her any supplements – no extra calcium or milk. You will be providing her with the best balance of nutrients you can and this will enable her to rear her litter well and quickly return to her normal fitness and shape.

7 *KEEPING YOUR GUNDOG HEALTHY*

There are many things which you should do to keep your gundog in good health. A healthy dog should have a bright, clean eye, correct coat for the breed, good muscle tone and vitality. The "cold, wet nose" is a legacy from days when distemper was a common problem and dry crusting would be found on the nose of a sick dog. The most healthy of dogs will have a dry, warm nose after sitting in front of the fire, and an off-colour dog's nose will be cold and wet if it is rainy outside! It is an old wives' tale, and is not a good indicator of health.

EXERCISE

Exercise plays an extremely important part in the health and care of your gundog. It is not just a way of keeping the dog quiet; regular exercise is important in keeping the dog in good health. You know yourself that if you spend all week sitting at a desk and then decide to walk all day on Saturday, should you survive the shock then on Sunday your muscles, tendons and joints are stiff and aching. If, however, you take regular exercise, you suffer no effects after slightly longer or harder sessions.

The same theory applies to your dog. A dog who is given regular exercise will develop good muscles; the tendons and ligaments will be taut, the heart fit and ready for anything. The muscles and tendons, when well-developed, help to stabilise joints and reduce the chance of damage and so, apart from reducing the immediate day-after stiffness, regular exercise also reduces the incidence of arthritis in the older joints. Arthritis is most often caused by instability of a joint, resulting in damage or abnormal wear.

Young dogs have particular requirements when it comes to exercise. Twelve-week pups play for one hour then sleep for two. They are not capable of going for a three-hour walk at this age. Exercising a young pup must be a matter of common sense. Ideally puppies should have access to a large exercise area in which they can sleep and play as they wish. When tired they will sleep, when refreshed they will exercise. Play is a form of exercise and will begin to build up the muscles needed for work.

When you first start taking your pup out, just go out for 30 minutes to start with and gradually increase the length of time until the pup can go out for one hour of exercise at six months. That is exercise at the puppy's own pace. If you are running a dog in training and that dog is going flat out, then no more than 15 minutes should be attempted at this age.

The smaller breeds, Spaniels and Brittanys, reach their adult height sooner than the heavier Retrievers. Because they stop growing at a younger age, they can be exercised a little more than the heavier, slower maturing breeds – Weimaraners, Labradors, Curlycoats and Chesapeakes.

Exercise must be a gradual build-up. You must slowly develop the muscles and tendons to protect the bones and joints from abnormal movement. Labradors and Golden Retrievers are two breeds which commonly suffer from Osteochondritis Dissecans (OCD) which is a bruising of the cartilage in joints. Too much pressure put on young joints can predispose them to this condition, so these breeds must be exercised with care. That does not mean you lock them in a kennel until they are one year old, but you should give regular short, frequent periods of exercise. Lead exercise on roads is good for developing muscles and tightening tendons without allowing abnormal movement of the joints through twisting and turning.

Just as an athlete trains for a specific event, so you should plan your dog's exercise ready for the shooting season. Frequent short spells of exercise are better than one long session. Road walking is excellent for tightening up the ligaments of the feet and keeping the toes resilient with good, shock-absorbing bounce. Lead exercise is OK for developing muscle but you must also allow free running to develop the flexibility of the spine and joints. An unfit dog is much more prone to injury than a fit dog.

The body weight of your dog should be checked regularly. As the season progresses, dogs tend to lose weight and then recover over the summer. You do not want your dog to start the season too fat – or too thin – because too much extra weight will slow your dog down and put too much extra strain on the joints, which can damage them. An injury at the beginning of the season is a disaster!

It is a good idea to weigh your dog regularly. Often you will not notice the gradual increase or decrease in weight until someone who has not seen the dog for a while makes a comment. You can use your own bathroom scales, weigh yourself, then pick up the dog and deduct the first from the second reading. However, it is not always easy to do this with bigger dogs and you may need an extra pair of eyes to read the scales – that is, if you can pick the dog up!

Most vets now have dog weighing scales and a monthly check is ideal. You can then decide if you need to change the amount of food you are giving. Dogs do not all need the same amount of food. Some dogs, like people, need a higher calorie intake than other dogs of the same breed and size. This can be due to a higher activity level, better utilisation of food, or a less stressful life, and so on. Feed each dog according to its needs – body condition is an excellent guide.

VACCINATION

I have dealt with this subject in the previous chapter, but the importance of proper vaccinations for gundogs cannot be stressed enough. Once a year you must take your dog to your vet for the booster vaccinations. This is important, because immunity cannot be guaranteed if the boosters are not given. Of particular concern to gundog owners is Leptospirosis. Because one of the main sources of infection is via rats' urine, or ingestion of infected material, the gundog is particularly vulnerable because the organism enters the body through various routes including damaged skin, causing disease of the liver and kidneys, resulting, usually, in the death of the dog. Because gundogs are working on land where rats may be found, it is extremely important to keep up to date with this vaccination.

The annual booster also protects the dog against Distemper, Parvovirus, and Hepatitis, which can all be disastrous if the dog is not protected and comes in contact with the infection. When the dogs all meet at the beginning and end of a shooting day, the chance of infection being spread from one dog to the next is high, as they all investigate each others' ears, bottoms, faeces and urine!

While at your vet to receive the annual boosters, your dog will receive a health check. Teeth, eyes, ears, skin, heart, lungs, nails and weight will be checked. If any problems arise they can be dealt with in a preventative manner. It is worthwhile considering having annual blood samples taken to test that all is working normally. Any changes or abnormalities can be treated at an early stage, thus keeping your dog in excellent health.

NOSES

The nose should be clear of any discharge or scabbiness. Nasal discharges can be mucoid, purulent and bloody. If any of these are seen you should seek veterinary advice. These discharges can be signs of infection; a tumour in the nasal cavity, sinusitis or foreign bodies. It is amazing what foreign bodies can be found up the noses of dogs. The most common are grass or grass seeds. Occasionally the end of a blade of grass can be seen at the point of the nose but more often it works its way slowly up the nasal cavities and can cause a lot of sneezing and irritation and needs removing under general anaesthetic. Fungal infections can cause a unilateral discharge. They are very difficult to diagnose and to treat.

Tumours in the nose and nasal cavities can cause a bloody mucoid discharge, usually just down one nostril. Diagnosis can normally be made by X-ray examination. Their treatment is very difficult and often disappointing, but progress is always being made at specialist centres. However, early treatment will stand more chance of success so, if in doubt, find out – go to your vet as soon as possible.

Scabs around the nose can be the result of trauma, but are more commonly a form of

eczema and should be treated early to reduce any permanent damage to the skin, which will then be more susceptible to injury. Always check the nose for injury after a day's shooting. Most small cuts will heal nicely, but bathe them in clean water to remove any dirt or debris. A runny nose, where the discharge is just clear fluid, can be due to an allergy or the early stages of kennel cough. The dog will sneeze and may have red, swollen eyes in the case of allergy, but otherwise be quite well.

If the discharge is mucoid and pussy it could be due to a respiratory virus, distemper or Parainfluenza. Parainfluenza only affects the respiratory system and is often a complication of kennel cough in young dogs. The dog can be very depressed and poorly but will usually recover if treated with antibiotics to prevent infection.

EYES

Your gundog only has one set of eyes, so do not take any chances with their health. If in doubt seek early veterinary attention. The eyes are a delicate structure but are well-protected by the eyelids, which will close by a reflex action if anything approaches them. Dogs have a third eyelid, called the nictitating membrane, which moves across from the inside to the outside of the eye beneath the eyelids. This system, along with the normal eyelids, gives dual protection against physical trauma. However, sometimes, as with all good systems, it can go wrong and you can get an ulcer caused by trauma on the front of the eye, or a foreign body actually stuck into the cornea. Both these will cause pain and should be treated as soon as possible.

As a first aid procedure, you can wash the eye with clean fresh water to flush out any debris, but ulcers will need veterinary treatment. They usually heal very well, leaving no scars, but some can be quite resistant to repair and may need surgery to cauterise the ulcer and to sew the eyelids

EXAMINING EYES

Photos: Keith Allison.

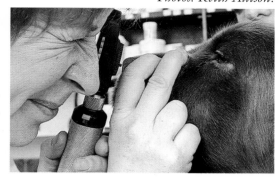

If your dog is experiencing eye discomfort, it is advisable to see a vet.

An ophthalmoscope may be needed for a more detailed examination.

ADMINISTERING EYE OINTMENT

Photos: Keith Allison.

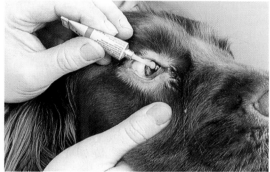

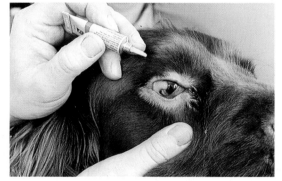

together for a few weeks to allow the ulcer to heal below them. Contact lenses are now being used to protect the ulcer and enable healing.

A serious complication which can occur is if the trauma penetrates right through the cornea. This is most likely to lead to permanent damage and loss of sight in that eye. Sometimes, particularly with gundogs working thick cover, a thorn or splinter can penetrate the clear cornea and become embedded in it. Initially it is very sore and will cause the eye to water and the dog will hold the eye closed, or half shut and blink repeatedly. If the penetrating foreign object is large, it can sometimes be seen with the naked eye, but often your vet will have to

look at the cornea with an ophthalmoscope, which magnifies and illuminates the eye and will make it easier to see abnormalities.

Any foreign object should be left for the professionals to remove if it is stuck in the cornea. If you try to remove it, you could cause more damage, if the dog moved at a vital moment. Foreign bodies sitting loose on the surface of the eye can be washed out with water, but take extra care if the foreign object is a thorn, as it could damage the surface of the eye if removed too forcefully.

CONJUNCTIVITIS

Conjunctivitis is an inflammation of the membrane surrounding the eye. It can be caused by an allergy (pollen, grass), irritants or infection. An allergy tends to produce red eyes, puffiness and a watery discharge. In humans it is seen in hay fever. It can be treated with antihistamines or steroids, but a correct diagnosis must be made before treatment because, if an ulcer is present, the use of steroids would make the ulcer worse. This is one of the reasons why your vet will not prescribe eye drops without having examined the dog first. The eye will weep, possibly with a purulent yellowy-green discharge, the normally white part of the eye (sclera) will be red and the eyelids may look swollen. The dog is likely not to open the eyes fully and bright light may be avoided.

Conjunctivitis caused by infection is most common in the summer when flies can pass on infection, and there is more dust in the air and hence more chance of bacteria. An uncomplicated case will respond well to antibiotics obtained from your vet, but bathing the eye in cold tea will aid in this, as it reduces the inflammation and soothes the eye.

If the dog's eyes are obviously uncomfortable and veterinary treatment cannot be obtained immediately, you can give your dog either an aspirin or a paracetamol as a one-off treatment. For Springers use half a tablet, and for the Retriever, HPR and Setter, one tablet. Aspirin and paracetamol are excellent anti-inflammatory drugs but can cause gastric bleeding in some cases, so they should be used with discretion.

Traumas to the eyelids themselves may need careful suturing to maintain their normal shape and function. If a lid is cut and it heals badly, this can lead to deformity of the lid which may prevent the eye from closing properly, leading to a greater chance of future injury. If in doubt, consult with your vet.

TEAR DUCTS

The surface of the eye should look moist and it is kept washed by the continuous production of tears from the tear (lacrimal) glands surrounding the eye. They act like your car windscreen wash, flushing debris off the surface of the eye and also providing the nutrition to the cells that form the cornea.

ADMINISTERING EYE DROPS

Photos: Keith Allison.

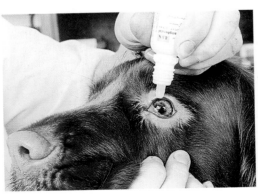 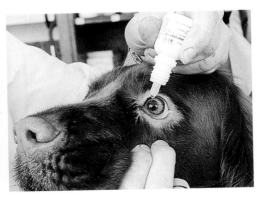

The eyelids are the windscreen wipers that brush the tears away. The tears drain from the corner of the eye down the tear duct, which ends in the back of the nasal cavity. This is why if you cry and produce extra tears, you need to blow your nose, because the increased flow of tears is cleared from your eyes, down the tear duct and into your nose.

Occasionally the tear duct becomes blocked or it may not be present. This means that the tears spill over the corner of the eye and drain down the face. This will cause staining of the hair on a light-coloured dog, which is unsightly but, more importantly, the underlying skin can be damaged and become infected because of the continual wetting. Your vet can check to see if the tear duct is open by putting a drop of sterile fluorescent dye into the eye. This bright green dye will then drain down the duct and appear on the opening of the nose. If the dye is not evident after one minute, the duct is not working properly. Sometimes the dye fails completely to make an appearance, which means the duct is totally closed.

If the overflowing of tears (epiphora) is of sudden onset in an older dog, it could be due to a swollen or blocked tear duct, or the overproduction of tears. In a young dog it might signify that the duct is not present at all, and if this is the case, there would always be a potential problem. If the duct is closed due to infection, this can be treated with eyedrops (antibiotics and anti-inflammatory) which will normally restore the normal patency of the duct. With over-production of tears, the ducts cannot cope and the extra tears will stream over the eyelids. Over-production will occur with conjunctivitis, irritation of the surface of the eye (foreign bodies, entropion, ectropion), allergies or inflammation of the lacrimal glands. Treatment of the initiating cause will solve the unsightly weeping. If your dog is prone to epiphora and the condition cannot be cured, you can help protect the skin by putting a small amount of Vaseline on the skin below the inside corner of the eye – do not let it go into the eye, however.

TEETH
In the wild, dogs' teeth were designed to tear raw meat, hide and bones, and this kept their teeth clean and the gums healthy. Dogs today do not use their teeth as nature intended and they commonly suffer from dental disease. The main problem is that tartar builds up on the teeth, mainly on the gum margin. Tartar is a deposit from saliva which, when it forms on the teeth, sets rock hard, like cement. It causes damage to the gums, allowing inflammation and infection, which undermine the gums, exposing the root, and eventually the teeth become loose as infection gets to the roots and causes abscesses.

True dental caries, as found in humans, is less common. The infection around the teeth (gingivitis) can cause pain but also bad breath. You can reduce the build-up of tartar by encouraging dogs to chew and use their teeth, and by brushing the teeth. Yes, you can brush your dog's teeth! Bones are excellent for dogs to chew to keep their teeth clean but they can cause horrendous intestinal problems, pain and distress, so I would *never give a dog a bone!* You can buy treated bones which only crumble in small pieces and will not cause colonic impaction and they are quite suitable. There are also numerous chews and specially-designed nylon bones which help dislodge debris from between the teeth. The dry dog foods will help remove some tartar and debris better than soft food, but do not be complacent, because the teeth still need some extra work done on them to keep them white and strong.

If you start when your dog is young, ideally you should clean the teeth daily, with a soft brush and special toothpaste. Do not be tempted to use the cheaper human paste as it is not as effective for dogs and can cause

Right:
If teeth are
neglected,
tartar will
accumulate,
leading to
tooth decay
and gum
infection.

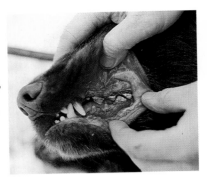

stomach upsets. There are lots of special dog tooth brushes, but an old, soft, human one is OK, although I like the small finger stalls which have a brush on the end, which are easier to use. It is important to brush the teeth on the gum margin; only the outer side is necessary as you will not get much tartar on the inside of the teeth. Daily brushing is the best, but it must be done at least twice weekly to be effective.

Traumatic damage can happen to dogs' teeth. Small chips can come away without causing much trouble to the dog, but if the chip is deep and reaches the pulp cavity, i.e. the centre of the tooth, it can lead to infection, death of the tooth, pain, and the need for removal. A common tooth abscess is caused by cracking the carnassial tooth, the large molar on the upper jaw below the eye. The infection causes a swelling below the eye and, if left untreated, the poison will seep through the skin and form a fistula, or open wound. The tooth needs to be removed under general anaesthetic and antibiotics given to kill the infection. When you go to your vet with such a swelling on your dog's face, do not be surprised to see your vet's face drop. The carnassial tooth has three very, very deep roots and it can be quite a tussle to get the tooth and roots out!

The large canine teeth can be damaged by trauma to the front teeth – running into a wall, kicks by cows and horses, or even biting on a stone. Often the tooth is only bruised, with bleeding into the pulp cavity

Above and Top: If a dog is accustomed to teeth-cleaning from an early age, he will be quite happy to accept the procedure.
Photos: Keith Allison.

but no damage to the outside of the tooth. These teeth will take on a purply-pink appearance, but usually will remain sound and pain free. If the tooth is chipped it is now possible to have orthodontic work done to fill the root canal and cap the tooth. This work is specialised and must be initiated soon after the damage has been done. If it is important for your dog to retain a full set of teeth, for showing for example, it can be worthwhile, but for most working gundogs I feel it is unnecessary. Most of the teeth will remain viable with a short course of antibiotics to stop infection. The teeth seal themselves off and no more treatment is necessary. If, however, the tooth becomes loose and painful, it can be removed without affecting the dog's working ability.

60

EARS

The ear is split into three parts. The inner ear, which contains the hearing organ and balance mechanism, the middle ear, consisting of the horizontal and vertical canals, and the pinna, or ear flap. The inner ear is completely out of sight, but can be affected by infection which can cause circling, head tilt and pain. This is a veterinary problem and professional advice should be sought. Treatment is usually successful.

The middle ear is divided into horizontal and vertical canals. The horizontal is out of sight and leads to the ear drum and then to the inner ear. The top of the vertical canal can be seen by the naked eye, but a special lens and light (auroscope) is needed to see to the bottom of it. These canals are lined by a modified skin which produces wax, which is used to transport any deposits found in the ear to the outside.

If the ear is inflamed by trauma or infection, the skin swells, becomes red and produces excess wax and secretions which fill the ear canal. The swollen skin decreases the lumen of the canal and prevents easy drainage of the ear. If the ear has lots of hairs in the vertical canal, which help to stop debris falling in, these also restrict the outflow of wax and add to the inflammation. This starts a vicious circle, with the inflammation encouraging infection, which causes pain and scratching, leading to more trauma, inflammation and infection.

It is important to treat otitis externa as soon as possible because permanent damage will be caused and the longer the otitis is present before treatment, the greater is the permanent damage and the more prone the dog will be to further attacks. This is because, although the inflammation and infection can be removed, the lining of the ears will be left more thickened than before the attack, which reduces the lumen of the ear canal, thus offering more chance of a

Otitis externa, seen in a Golden Retriever. Photo courtesy: Dick Lane.

In the Spaniel breeds, it is advisable to pluck the hairs from the vertical canal, as these can prevent the outflow of wax. Photo: Keith Allison

build-up of wax, and hence more chance of infection and another episode of otitis.

You can reduce the possibility of otitis occurring by cleaning the ears regularly with a good cleaner and gently plucking some of the hair from the vertical canal in the longhaired breeds. When cleaning the ear, be sure to use a good cleaner, as some are not the same pH as the ear and can cause irritation or inflammation and may increase the chance of infection. Ask your vet for a suitable preparation. It should be used weekly as a preventative measure. Flood the canal with solution and gently massage the base of the ear. *Do not poke cotton wool buds,*

ADMINISTERING EAR DROPS

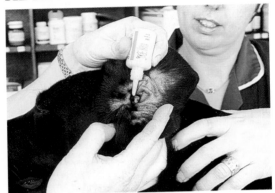

Ear drops can be administered to aid cleaning the ear.

Massage the base of the ear once the drops have been administered.

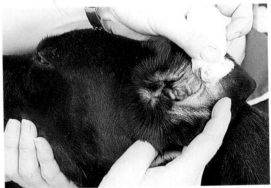

Use cotton-wool to clean dirt from the ear. Do not use cotton-wool buds to probe the ear canal.

Photos: Keith Allison.

or cotton, down the ear. You can cause irritation and trauma by fiddling down the ear. Only clean away any fluid or debris which you can see. The cleaner will make the wax flow out more easily and it does not need your help! If the middle ear becomes red, sore or smelly you will need antibiotics, so go straight to your vet. Remember, while you try your own remedies, you may be causing more permanent damage.

Otitis externa can be caused by many agents – fungal, bacterial, viral, parasitic or traumatic. Trauma can be due to the dog scratching or doing a lot of head-shaking which leads to inflammation and swelling, and infection will jump into this warm, moist environment. The infection, viral or bacterial, can be primary in origin, which leads to inflammation, and increased secretions, and then the dog will scratch and head-shake and perpetuate the cycle.

Ear mites can cause a very dry, scaly deposit in the ears and are a great irritant. The mite is a parasite which is often picked up from cats but can be cured by ear drops. *All* affected cats and dogs should be treated for seven days; if not, the cycle will not be broken and it will be passed from one around to another.

Another cause of head shaking and irritation in the ears can be foreign bodies. The most common culprit is the grass seed. The hairs on the seed make it very difficult for the seed to go backwards, so once the seed starts moving down towards the eardrum it only has one way to go, and that is into the ear canal. This is usually a problem in the Setters and Spaniels which have pinnae (ear flaps) which are more likely to trap the seeds, but it can happen to any dog. The signs are very acute and intense. The ear is hypersensitive, which makes the dog shake its head almost continuously. The only way to retrieve these awkward foreign bodies is to give a general anaesthetic and hope they will be easy to find. But if it has travelled down to the vertical canal, this can be quite tricky to retrieve. It is very painful to the dog, so veterinary attention must be sought at once.

CONDITIONS OF THE EAR FLAP (PINNA)

One consequence of head-shaking is an aural haematoma, commonly seen in Labradors and Golden Retrievers. This is seen as a painless soft swelling on the inside of the ear flap, which can range in size from about one inch to involvement of the whole ear flap. It is caused by the dog shaking its head and this can cause a blood vessel to break as it travels through the cartilage to the inside of the ear. Blood leaks from that tear and forms a haematoma – a blood clot between the skin and the cartilage. If no treatment is given the ear will become distorted as the blood clot is re-absorbed and leaves a fibrous knot of tissue. The end result can be a cauliflower ear. This can then pre-dispose the dog to more ear disease. The best solution is to have the haematoma drained and the cause of the head-shaking treated. There are two main techniques to resolve this. The first is to have an opening cut on the inside of the ear. The haematoma is then removed and the two sides of the skin are sutured together. Sometimes buttons are used to stop the sutures cutting into the skin. This allows the ear flap to return to its normal shape but the dog can look comical with half-a-dozen buttons in an ear! After the sutures and buttons have been removed, the ear will return to its normal shape.

Another method is to drain the blood from the ear and to inject an anti-inflammatory drug into the wound. It is necessary to do this several times and it can take longer to heal, but it has the advantage that usually no general anaesthetic is needed.

TRAUMA

The gundogs with feathering on their ears are protected from brambles and barbed wire, but the short-coated dogs,

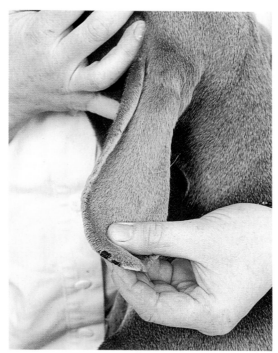

The short-coated breeds, such as the Weimaraner, are prone to damaging their ears by catching them on thorns or brambles.
Photo: Keith Allison.

Weimaraners, German Shorthaired Pointers and Vizslas, are prone to catching their ears, which can then bleed profusely. The irritation of the cut will cause them to shake their heads which, apart from causing everyone to be covered in blood spots, stops the scab forming and so they continue to bleed. A small nick can stop quite quickly, but a bigger tear can be quite a problem. As the dog shakes its head it will leave blood on the opposite side of the neck – which will leave you checking the wrong ear if you are not careful!

If the bleeding continues for more than a few minutes, or is profuse, you should make an attempt to bandage the ear to the head so that it cannot be shaken, and this will allow time for the blood to clot. A length of nylons, or old socks with the foot cut out, can be used to slide over the dog's head, but you will need some surgical adhesive to stick the front of it to the hair on the dog's head, or it will slip straight down the neck. If the cut is small, a piece of adhesive can be applied directly, and can allow healing to take place successfully.

Make sure you do not apply any dressing too tightly – test the tension with your fingers. Only leave the dressing on for four hours and then remove. If the wound is still bleeding you will probably need your vet's help. Short tears are best left alone, but cuts exposing the cartilage, or more than half-an-inch long, are better sutured.

When dealing with the gundog breeds with profuse hair on their ears it is important to groom the hair regularly to prevent knots forming. If a knot has formed, it will trap grass seeds which may cause a reaction if they are allowed to migrate into the skin. More commonly, the skin under the matt can become infected. If the knot is too advanced to comb out it may be necessary to cut it away, but be *very careful*: it is so easy to cut the skin by accident. Always put your fingers between the matt and the skin and cut between them. It can be a long job if the matter has been neglected – but it will encourage you not to let it happen again. This is seen in English Springers in particular.

NAILS

Dogs' nails grow continuously from the nail bed at the base of the toe. The outer part is hard and protects the inner sensitive quick, which contains blood vessels and nerves. The hard keratinized part of the nail wears away through contact with hard and rough surfaces. If the dog has particularly hard nails, or does not have enough exercise on hard surfaces, the nail will grow long and be prone to injury. If the long nail is not trimmed, it will have a tendency to split at the end and this can cause it to tear, eventually, up to the sensitive part of the

NAIL CUTTING

Photos: Keith Allison.

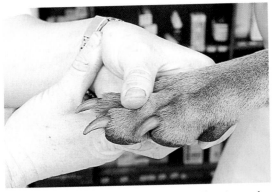

It is important to keep a gundog's nails trimmed.

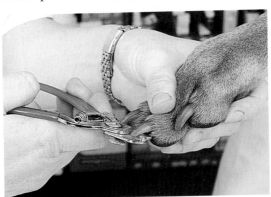

Be careful not to cut into the quick as this will result in bleeding.

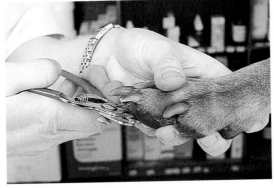

The lever double-blade cutter, with the safety back-stop, prevents you from cutting too much nail.

nail. Sometimes, if the tear is short, it can be trimmed and will not progress any further. But if the tear tracks up and exposes the sensitive part of the nail, it will be necessary to give a general anaesthetic and cut the nail right back, above the damage. The general anaesthetic is necessary because you are cutting into the sensitive part of the nail and this is too painful to be done when the dog is conscious. The centre of the nail is cauterised and the nail will grow again.

If your gundog has plenty of hair around the nails, be particularly careful to check the nails regularly. In some breeds the nails grow in a very tight curve and, if not trimmed, can grow round and dig into the pad. This obviously causes pain and the pad will become infected if the impinging nail is not removed quickly.

You can keep the nails trimmed. Start with the dog as a puppy, and only trim the tip of the nail. Dogs with light-coloured nails are easier to trim because you can see where the sensitive blood and nerve part of the nail is. Dogs with dark nails must be treated with a lot of care. If you cut the nail too short and it bleeds, the dog will always resent having the nails cut, and this can then be a battle. If in doubt, just keep nibbling a little bit of nail at a time, and stop when the pup starts to resent the trimming. If you begin when the dog is young, it will be much easier to keep the nails short and in good condition. Once the nail has grown too long, the quick will also grow long and you will always have a long nail.

A human nail clipper is ideal for puppies but, as the dog gets older, you will need something a bit bigger. The guillotine type of clipper can be good, as long as the blade is sharp but, from choice, I think the lever double-blade cutter with a safety back-stop is the best. With the back-stop in position, you are prevented from cutting too much nail off at any one time.

DEWCLAWS
Dewclaws are the fifth or, more correctly, the first toe (thumb) on the inside of the leg. They are always present at birth on the front leg, and sometimes on the hind leg. Dewclaws on the hind leg should always be removed as they invariably dangle and, particularly with a working gundog, they can be caught or torn on just about anything. If this happens you can guarantee it will be on a public holiday, it will bleed profusely and you will have to call the vet out! Hind dewclaws can range from being ugly double affairs to small single nodules. Always check your puppies at birth, as removal within the first few days is simple, but once their eyes are open, the puppies will have to have a general anaesthetic. Italian Spinones require the dewclaws to be present, but I would prefer to remove the hind ones and will only leave the front claws at the owner's specific request.

Front dewclaws are removed on some breeds and not others. Generally, if they fit closely to the leg they probably will not cause a problem but, as they are of very little benefit to the dog, if any at all, I would always recommend that they are removed as soon after birth as possible. Legally anyone can remove the dewclaws from a puppy whose eyes have not yet opened, but I would recommend you go to a vet who is experienced at removing dewclaws, or go to an experienced breeder. I like to remove them before the pup is four days old, and preferably earlier. I use a clean, old pair of curved scissors, cut the dewclaws off and then stop any bleeding with either potassium permanganate or a silver nitrate pencil. The latter is easier to use, but both, when dabbed on for a few seconds, will stop any bleeding which may occur.

Please do not do this with the bitch present, as it may upset her. The pups may give a little cry, but are quite settled once they are returned to their litter mates. I would much rather snip the dewclaws off at one day old than let them become torn and damaged in an older dog, which would be

REMOVING DEWCLAWS

Photos: Keith Allison.

Curved scissors are used to remove the dewclaws.

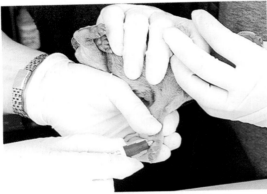

A silver nitrate pencil will stop any bleeding.

The puppy suffers no trauma if the procedure is carried out within a few days of birth.

extremely painful. If dewclaws are left on a dog, please make sure they are checked regularly, because the nail can grow round and get bedded into the pad, causing pain and infection – and this should not happen to a well-cared for dog.

FEET

After any walk, but particularly in the summer and autumn, you should check that there are no twigs, grass seeds, stones or other foreign objects caught in the hair between the toes. If the foreign object is not removed, it may burrow mechanically into the skin and migrate, moving up the leg. When the foreign object penetrates the skin there will be a small, infected hole, but this can heal over and the object will then continue to move up the leg. You might find a series of sores on the leg where the foreign object has moved near the surface of the skin, causing the dog to lick it, and a small fistula may form. Usually such a foreign object causes enough discomfort and pain to be noticed, and it can be removed when still around the pad area, but I have found a grass seed near the elbow on a Spaniel, and it had obviously started its journey at the pad!

It is a good idea to keep the hair on the pad, and up to the stopper pad of the Spaniel and Setters, trimmed so that the area can be kept clean and checked easily. Some hair should be left, as this will provide some protection from cuts and the cold, but you do not want to have so much hair left on the foot that it can trap dirt and debris – and, aside from the health implications, too much hair on the feet can make the dogs act like walking mops.

In the early spring the short new shoots of nettles can be a major irritant to some dogs' feet, causing the dogs to pick their feet up very sharply, and they can chew their feet to try and stop the stinging. If your dog does have a bad reaction, try getting the dog to walk on wet grass, as this seems to have a cooling effect. Some dogs seem to be much

In the Spaniel breeds, it is advisable to trim the hair that grows betweeen the pads.
Photo: Carol Ann Johnson.

more sensitive to nettles than others, so do be a little careful where you walk if your dog has a particularly painful reaction. As the nettles grow the problem disappears, probably because the dog is not standing on the leaves but walking between them. Dock leaves are said to soothe affected feet, and this remedy might be worth trying if the feet are so sore that your dog refuses to put them down.

GROOMING

I have already mentioned about trimming the hairs from between the toes but it is sometimes an idea to do a bit of generalised trimming if you dog has a profuse coat. There must be a balance between providing some protection from the cold weather and keeping the coat in an easily manageable condition.

With Spaniels and Setters trim some of the feathering at the back of the front legs from the foot to the stopper pad, and also on the hind legs from the foot to the hock. This will stop too much mud, and potential foreign objects, from collecting on the legs and causing damage. Some hair can also be trimmed from under the base of the tail to reduce the chance of faecal soiling. The hair on the ears can be thinned if the coat is profuse, particularly on the inside, which will

help reduce the chance of otitis, but do leave some, particularly on the outer edges, to act as protection against thorns and brambles. The coat should be groomed regularly in all breeds to keep it waterproof, knot-free and healthy. There are numerous brushes and combs on the market. For the short-coated breeds I like the rubber mittens which pull out any dead coat and remove mud without damaging the underlying skin.

Dogs with more coat need a more substantial brush. Make sure you are not damaging the skin with a brush with sharp bristles or pins. You can get a brush in which the pins are bedded on a flexible rubber pad, so that the pins can move up and down with the contours of the body. Pay particular attention to the hair behind the ears and between the legs. It is all too easy for a tangled mass of hair to develop in these sites. It is very easy to give the coat a brush over and not brush the underlying hair properly. Gently brush the coat the wrong way to make sure you are grooming the whole coat and not just the top layer. It may be necessary to use a steel comb to tease out any knots. Be careful. Hold the dog's skin above the knot so that you are not pulling the skin when you are pulling the knot out. Think how you would feel!

BATHING

You should not have to bath your dog at any time, unless for medical reasons, but if the dog has rolled or fallen into some foul-smelling substance, use a very mild soap or get a hypo-allergenic shampoo from the vet. The gundog's skin is very susceptible to bacterial skin infection and anything which upsets the natural balance of the skin, e.g. washing, can allow a skin infection to take hold. The dog's skin is unique in domestic animals in that the hair follicle does not have a lipid seal, which in other species acts as a barrier, preventing bacteria from getting into the hair follicle. The depth of the outer skin layer is also thin in the dog, which means it

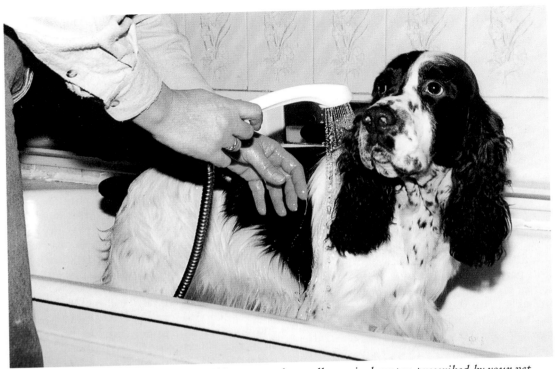

If you need to bath your dog, use a mild soap or a hypo-allergenic shampoo prescribed by your vet.
Photo: Carol Ann Johnson.

has two weak points which contribute to the reasons why skin infections in dogs are very common.

On the surface of the normal dog's skin various bacteria live in harmony and do not cause any problems. However, if the skin is damaged, for example by allergic reaction, trauma, or wetting, it can alter the normal skin balance and allow one strain of bacteria to multiply, invade the skin and cause a dermatitis. If you use a shampoo which irritates the dog's skin, by causing an allergic reaction, altering the pH or reducing the oil in the oat, you may initiate a skin infection. So bath your dog only when it is unavoidable and use a correct shampoo.

If your dog does develop a skin infection, the sooner you have it treated the quicker it is likely to heal. Skin infections can vary, from a small patch to one involving the whole body. It can be just on the surface of the skin, or deep in the hair follicles or right down to the tissue below the skin. Then it is called cellulitis and can be life-threatening. The causes of skin infections can be bacterial, parasitic, allergic, fungal or due to an underlying condition.

EXTERNAL PARASITES
FLEAS. Bacterial skin infections often are secondary to an allergic reaction. The most common allergy is caused by the flea. The flea is not always easy to find and it will spend most of its life off the dog. Most commonly you can see the flea dirt on the coat – it looks like coal dust. If you put a bit of this on your finger and wet it lightly, after a short time a ring of orange-red blood will appear around the dirt, confirming that it is flea dirt. Nowadays, when we live in warm,

dry, clean houses, the flea is in its element and can breed and live in ideal conditions. Fleas are dark brown wingless insects about 3mm long, the body is laterally compressed and looks a bit like a tea leaf on its edge. Fleas move rapidly through the coat, feed from the host by sucking blood, and can live away from the host for several months after feeding.

Fleas can be controlled by many methods. By choice I use a spray which has a residual action and stays on the coat for up to two weeks. This is vitally important, because the flea does not stay on the dog all the time, but jumps off and lives in the surroundings. If you use a spray from the supermarkets, it is unlikely to have any residual activity and so you will only kill any fleas on the dog at the time you are spraying and, as soon as you go outside again, a flea can jump onto your dog and cause a reaction or, worse still, visibly run across the dog's head when you have an important visitor!

I find flea powders a waste of time, as more seems to blow away than stays on the coat! Good-quality flea collars can work well if the flea challenge is not too high, but the chemical which kills the flea is concentrated at the neck, whereas the fleas are often around the tail and hind legs, a long way from the insecticidal chemical, so they are not always killed. Another problem with the collar is that it can sometimes cause a nasty skin reaction, with loss of hair, redness, pain and irritation. The collars must be changed according to the manufacturer's instructions if they are to have any chance of working.

Another form of flea control is to apply a solution to the skin on the back of the neck. This is then absorbed into the body and distributed to the skin. When the flea bites the skin it will ingest the poison and be killed. It is an effective way of controlling fleas and only has to be applied monthly, but it must be applied carefully and you must use gloves, as the drug can be absorbed through your skin if you get some on your hands.

As well as treating your dog, you should consider using a spray to kill fleas in the house and dog bed. Most of the sprays for the house will last for over four months and it is not necessary to spray the whole house, just the areas where the dog sits and under radiators, skirting boards, etc. It is well worthwhile protecting your home and dog from fleas before you have a problem, because fleas can reproduce so rapidly that, before you know what has happened, you can have an epidemic.

The fleas which your dog might have could not live on you, but they can bite you and some people can react and have red, itchy spots on their ankles and legs. An effective but more expensive way to control fleas in the environment is by use of a chemical, given monthly by mouth to your dog, which is then distributed in the blood. When a flea bites your dog, the chemical will, in effect, sterilise the flea and prevent it from reproducing. The chemical, by stopping the flea from reproducing, will prevent the enormous build-up of fleas in the house, but it does not kill the fleas, so it is usually necessary, initially, also to use a spray on the dog.

TICKS are occasionally found on the skin of dogs. They can vary in size from about only a couple of millimetres when they are light-coloured, up to about 1 centimetre when they are bluish coloured and bean-shaped. The tick is seasonally active, the two peak periods being Spring and Autumn. At these times the tick can be found on the tips of vegetation, from which it will attach itself to a passing animal, burying its mouth into the skin of the animal and feeding from between four to fourteen days, depending on the age of the tick. It then drops off into the undergrowth and continues its life-cycle, which takes three years. The adult female feeds for 14 days, then drops off and lays thousands of eggs in the undergrowth. The larvae from these eggs hatch the following year, feed for six days on the host before dropping off, and moulting to a nymphal stage. These, in turn, feed the next year for about six days, before dropping off and becoming an adult. Most ticks feed on sheep, but they will jump on, and feed off, any passing animal given the chance.

Ticks are a temporary parasite. They are usually found behind the ears, and on the upper neck and head, where the dog cannot remove them. They look like a lentil, or up to the size of a baked bean, standing on its end. At the base you can usually see the brown legs close to the skin. It is very important, if you try to remove the tick yourself, that you make sure you pull the head away and not just the body. If you leave the head in the skin your dog can get a very nasty reaction and infection. To remove the tick, grasp it right down at the skin and pull away firmly. You should be able to see the moving legs at the base of the body if you have done it properly. For the more squeamish, you can dab the tick with a small amount of alcohol or flea spray, which will kill the tick and it will drop off after a few days. If in doubt, go to your vet and let him or her show you how to remove the tick carefully.

MITES The other main parasitic group found on dogs' skin is the mite – Sarcoptic, Demodex, Cheyletiella and Otodectes.

Sarcoptic has a rapid life cycle of only three weeks, so you can soon have a large population on the untreated dog. Sarcoptic Mange (Scabies) is extremely itchy and the dog will scratch almost continuously in very bad cases. The skin becomes red and scaly and the coat is thin. In very bad cases the dog will be almost bald, and the skin can have secondary bacterial infection following damage to it by scratching. Infection is by direct contact with another dog.

Treatment in the form of special baths is effective, but must be carried on for at least four weeks, to kill all the larvae. You must go to your vet for a shampoo, which is effective, and you must dispose of it in the proper manner and not into the drain, as the chemical is very toxic to fish. Sarcoptic mange mites can infect people, and is usually seen as small red pimples around the waistband, ankles and wrists. If you have any of these signs you should see your doctor. All contact animals should be treated to stop the cycle of infection.

Demodex is seen in two forms, a dry, scaly type and a pustular weeping type with secondary bacterial involvement. Demodex can be difficult to diagnose and, again, needs prolonged, specialised baths. The mite can live in the skin of a dog without any clinical signs but, when the dog's immune system is weakened by stress, pregnancy or illness, the mite can thrive and produce clinical signs. Demodectic mange is not as itchy as sarcoptic mange.

Cheyletiella is a larger mite, and causes a scaly dermatitis, commonly called 'walking dandruff'. It is not always very itchy and the dandruff can be seen to move a little, hence its common name. Again, veterinary shampoos are very effective.

Otodectes causes ear mange in dogs and cats. Dogs will shake and scratch their ears, and a dry, dark brown debris fills the ear canal. Get some suitable ear drops from your vet and, again, treat contact cats and dogs, because it will spread from one to the other and, if you only treat one animal, the others will re-infect the original animal once treatment is stopped.

LICE are permanent parasites and can be found on the coats of all domesticated animals, including dogs. They are wingless insects with flattened bodies and up to 0.3 cm long, and cause damage to the host by either sucking blood or by biting and living on skin debris. The egg is about the size of semolina and is stuck to the hair, so if you find white, dusty particles attached to the hair, be suspicious, there may be lice present.

The adults prefer the longer hair areas of the ears, tail and neck, and cause irritation. The adult louse is easily killed with most insecticide sprays or shampoos, but the egg is resistant, so the treatment should be repeated two weeks later to kill the newly-hatched generation.

It is unusual to find lice on short-coated dogs but they are more common on the feathering of Spaniels. The adult louse can be seen on the skin close to the base of the hair. It will move, but not as fast as the flea; if you look long enough you may see a bit of movement, but do not expect much action. An important consideration, if you dog does have lice, is that the lice can act as the intermediate host of the tapeworm diplydium caninum and so it would be sensible to treat your dog for tapeworm, as well as for the lice infection.

FUNGAL INFECTIONS

Dogs can suffer from ringworm, which is the most common fungal infection seen on the skin. It can be quite difficult to diagnose as it can take many forms, from just a dry scaly patch of skin, to large areas of hair loss, redness and scabs. The classical ringworm lesion is rare. The fungus gets its name from the red, raised dry skin gradually spreading out to form the characteristic "ring", but all too often this is not seen, and confirmation of the infection has to be done in the laboratory, which can take up to six weeks if the fungus has to be grown. Treatment of the dog is with a course of tablets, which is usually very effective, but spores from the fungus can survive in the environment for extremely long periods, so all bedding should be either burned or treated. Ringworm can pass to people easily, so check for any dry, red patches of skin on yourself and, if in doubt, get advice from your doctor. Ringworm is not a dirty infection, or all that serious, but because it is a zoonosis (i.e. can pass to humans) and because the spores can last a long time, it is a nuisance if

your dog contracts it.

An unusual case of a fungal infection was found on the muzzle of an English Springer Spaniel. The skin was thick and scabby with loss of hair. It was confirmed by a laboratory that the dog had a fungal infection caught from a hedgehog! Treatment was successful, but we did advise the owner to stop him retrieving hedgehogs.

Malezzia is a yeast which is found on the skin of many dogs, but it can be involved in the development of itchy, moist, smelly skins. The infection tends to be on moist areas, in folds of the skin initially, but then it can be all over the body. Treatment is with anti-fungal baths and sprays, but it can take several months to control. It is likely to recur unless the underlying cause of the upset of the normal balance of the skin is treated, e.g. fleas, allergy or trauma.

If you are unlucky enough to have any of the parasitic or fungal skin infections on your dog, do keep the animal away from other dogs until the condition is cleared – or you will become very unpopular with your friends.

WORMS

Worm your adult gundog at least twice yearly. As I have said in the previous chapter when discussing the incidence of roundworm, toxocara canis, in young puppies, all puppies should be wormed at 3, 6, 9 and 12 weeks and then monthly, until they are six months old. After this all dogs should be treated against roundworm every six months. The adult dog is capable of ingesting roundworms by eating an intermediate host – mice and sheep's meat for example – and by direct ingestion of eggs. It is vital, both for the health of your gundog, and for the health of small children, that you dog is wormed properly, and that you do not leave your dog's faeces in a public place.

The main tapeworm found in dogs is diplydium caninum. It feeds in the small intestine but rarely causes more than a loss in body condition. The dog acquires the infection by eating infected fleas and lice. The mature tapeworm releases segments containing the eggs which are motile and pass out of the rectum. They can be seen either on the faeces or on the hair around the anus. They are flat, creamy-white and motile when first passed, but soon dry and look like grains of rice. They can cause anal irritation, so if you see your dog rubbing its bottom across the floor, examine the area around the anus for any tell-tale segments. The dog cannot be re-infected by ingesting these egg packets, only by eating the intermediate host i.e. fleas and lice.

Control is by worming every two months with a specific tapeworm tablet and by controlling any fleas or lice. Do get a wormer from your vet, or you are unlikely to remove the tapeworm's head and the cycle will soon return.

Another family of tapeworm which can become a problem is Taenia. The dog picks this up by eating cysts in an infected host – rabbits, mice, or in the meat of sheep and cows. The cysts can be found anywhere in the infected animal, but a major concern is the infection in sheep, where the cysts can lodge in the brain and then cause the sheep to circle and have nervous signs. The sheep will have caught the infection by eating tapeworm segments left by a dog, so it is very important that we worm our gundogs thoroughly so there is no chance that your dog can be infecting the farmer's sheep and causing a financial loss. Feeding cooked food at all times will prevent infection but, a dog who has eaten a rabbit carcass or mouse can become infected so – worm at least twice a year!

8 FIRST AID FOR GUNDOGS

There are times when it is necessary for an unqualified person to act in order to help an animal in an emergency. For the gundog owner a basic knowledge of first aid is vital, as our dogs are particularly at risk There are three principles of first aid:

1. To preserve life.
2. To prevent suffering.
3. To prevent the worsening of a specific condition.

When dealing with emergencies it is important that you keep calm and keep the dog as comfortable as possible and, if necessary, contact a vet as soon as possible. It is better to be over-cautious and see a vet, than to hope all is well, only to find that the condition was worse than you first thought and that the dog has deteriorated. It is an excellent idea to make a note of the telephone number of the vet who covers the area where your shoot is. This can save valuable time, as most people will shoot outside the area covered by their own vet and the last thing you want to do, when a genuine emergency occurs, is to have to hunt for the local vet's telephone number.

FIRST AID KIT
It is a sensible precaution to carry a basic First Aid Kit in your car at all times. This should contain:

1. A sterile gauze dressing to apply directly on to the skin.
2. Cotton wool (or cotton) – a sheet at least 12ins x 12ins minimum.
3. Conforming bandages. These are easy to apply and can induce pressure onto a bleeding wound to reduce haemorrhage. Used in conjunction with cotton wool, they will restrict the movement of joints or broken bones.
4. Adhesive tape.
5. Small strips of Elastoplast to apply to

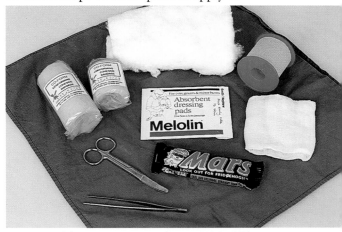

A first aid kit.   *Photo: Keith Allison.*

73

nicks on ears.
6. Mars bars – for hypoglycaemia.
7. Paracetamol – painkillers
8. Pair of scissors.
9. Pair of tweezers.

It is not necessary to carry disinfectants or anything to clean the wound – leave that to your vet.

PRINCIPLES OF FIRST AID

A routine examination should be made to assess the dog's general condition:
1. Is the dog conscious?
2. Is there a pulse?
3. Is the dog breathing? Are the chest movements normal, deep, shallow, rapid, or slow?
4. Is the dog withdrawn, staring blankly into space? This is a bad sign and can indicate serious trouble.
5. Is the dog conscious of its surroundings, following movements with his or her eyes and responding to voices? This is a good sign.
6. Is the dog bleeding? How much and from where? Is it pumping out?
7. What colour are the dog's gums – pink, blue or white? If you press your finger on the surface of the gum and then lift it off, the mark left by your finger should disappear in around one second. If not, the circulation is restricted and the dog may be in shock.
8. Do the dog's legs feel cold?

MOUTH TO NOSE RESUSCITATION

If the dog is not conscious, make sure that the airway is open. Pull out the tongue and stretch the neck out. If there is any danger of neck injury, do not move the head unless the breathing is restricted. If the dog is not breathing, make sure the airway is open, pull the tongue out, check there is no obstruction in the mouth – blood, vomit or foreign bodies – and pull the head up to stretch the neck and hence open the windpipe (trachea). If the dog is not breathing you can initiate mouth to nose

resuscitation. Close the dog's mouth. Place your mouth over the dog's nose and mouth and blow sharp, firm breaths about every 5 to 10 seconds. Watch the rib cage rise with each breath.

HEART MASSAGE

Check the pulse by feeling the inside of the thigh or, if you are not confident of finding this, place your hand on the left chest just behind the elbow. If you cannot feel the heart beating or find a pulse, you should start heart massage. Lie the dog on the right side, and press rhythmically with your palm, one hand on top of the other. Pressure should be applied behind the elbow and should be done every two seconds; then have a feel to see if you can find a pulse. It is worth continuing heart massage and artificial resuscitation for up to ten minutes, but after this time there is likely to be irreversible brain damage and so no more attempts should be made to revive the dog.

FURTHER EXAMINATION

Once you are satisfied that the dog is breathing and has a pulse, you can examine more closely.
1. Look for any blood from the nose and mouth. If possible, carefully open the mouth. If there is blood present, but no sign of injury, it might have been coughed up from the lungs.
2. Look at the dog's eyes. Is there any swelling or bruising around the eyes? What size are the pupils? Are they both the same? This can give information about possible brain damage. Are the eyes looking forward or do they flick from side to side (nystagmus)? This is often a sign of a stroke. Do the pupils change size with differing light?
3. What colour is the inside of the lower lid? Abnormal colour can indicate blood loss or shock.
4. Are there any swellings over the head?
5. Is there any sign of blood from the ears,

PUTTING ON A MUZZLE

A: A rope lead can be used as an emergency muzzle. First tie the lead in a loose knot.

B: Slip the loop over the dog's muzzle and tighten the knot.

C: Bring the two sides of the lead down underneath the muzzle and cross them over.

D: Tie the two ends of the lead behind the ears, at the top of the dog's neck.

which could occur with brain damage?

6. Can the dog stand?

7. Can the dog feel all four legs?

8. Is there any damage to the limbs – swelling, cuts, abnormal carriage of the limb? Fractured limbs often hang loosely. Do not feel any suspected broken leg too much as you will cause the dog pain and could make the fracture worse.

9. Feel over the ribs – if air is leaking from a damaged lung it will feel like crackly paper under the skin.

10. Can the dog's tail wag? A flaccid unresponsive tail can mean there is spinal damage.

11. Check the body surface for cuts and

Photos: Keith Allison

grazes. Most animals will suffer some degree of shock following any accident. Shock can be life-threatening and so measures should be taken to minimise its effects. You should keep the animal warm. Cover with a blanket and, if possible, lie the dog on a piece of bedding or a dry warm surface. Do not apply external heat as this can cause the blood vessels of the skin to dilate and increase the blood flow, diverting it from the essential organs – heart, lungs and brain – and can make the dog's condition worse. Just wrap the dog up in dry, warm bedding.

If possible the dog should be moved and placed in a vehicle for transportation to the vet. Beware that you do not get bitten. Talk quietly and calmly to the dog and move very slowly. If necessary apply a muzzle to the dog. A bandage or lead can be slipped around the mouth and tied behind the ears. This does not then give you "carte blanche" to pick up the dog without thought to the pain you might inflict. With dogs who can walk, it is often best to allow them to move themselves to the vehicle and only assist if they cannot jump up into the car.

If the dog cannot stand, the best way to pick up a Spaniel or a Brittany is by the scruff, using the other hand to support the hind quarters. Medium-sized dogs – Springers and small Labradors – can be picked up with one arm at the front of the sternum (breast bone) and with the other arm around the back of the hind legs. Large dogs need two people to move them, one holding the neck and chest and the other holding the abdomen and hind quarters.

If you suspect a spinal injury do not use these methods. Dogs with spinal injuries should be moved by using a stretcher. This can be made from a piece of board, or a coat suspended on wooden poles. Several people can roll the dog onto its chest, all acting together to stop any twisting of the spine, and then push the stretcher underneath the dog. Then roll the dog back and pull the stretcher underneath. It is possible just to drag the dog onto the stretcher by holding the skin across the scapula, back and pelvis. This can be useful if the dog has suspected broken limbs as there is no rotation of the limbs and so less chance of further damage increasing the injury.

SHOCK

Shock is a serious condition which can lead to death. It is the interruption to the normal blood flow to the body which can lead to cell death. When a dog suffers from shock, the body diverts blood from the skin and intestines and concentrates it in the vital organs – heart, lungs and brain. Shock can follow road accidents, burns, heat stroke, poisoning, fluid loss (e.g. diarrhoea), allergic reactions and insect stings. The signs of shock are: weakness or collapse; pale gums; slow capillary refill (press your finger on the gum and time the interval until blood returns to the finger mark); cold limbs; weak rapid pulse; shallow rapid breathing. Veterinary treatment should be sought immediately. In the meantime, keep the dog warm, try not to move the dog too much and, if there is no injury to the head, offer small, warm, sweet drinks. Your vet will treat the shock with intravenous fluids and will then try to treat the cause of the shock. Dogs which die after a road traffic accident usually die from shock and not from trauma.

AIRWAY OBSTRUCTION

Airway obstruction, if total, can be a real emergency and can soon lead to collapse and death. A common cause is when a ball becomes lodged at the back of the throat just in front of the larynx. The dog is very distressed, paws at the mouth and will quickly become blue and collapse. Sometimes it is possible to push the ball to one side to allow breathing and then hook the ball out but, if not, you can try the "Heimlich Manoeuvre". For this you should hold the dog up by the hind legs and then punch the dog sharply just above the xiphisternum, on the abdominal wall. The angle of the punch is down onto the diaphragm and this should stimulate a cough and hopefully the ball will be dislodged. This can be tried several times if at first you are not successful.

Partial obstruction will be seen as noisy, laboured breathing and although not as much of an emergency, you should see a vet immediately and keep the dog as quiet as possible in the meantime to reduce the oxygen needed by the dog. Blood and vomit can cause obstruction in a collapsed dog, so pull the tongue forward and hook out any matter from the back of the throat with your fingers. Be careful that you do not get bitten if the dog is conscious! If the dog has stopped breathing, once the airway is clear it is possible to give artificial respiration.

COLLAPSE

This is a term which encompasses many conditions. Collapse can quickly get worse, the patient becomes unconscious and can even die, or it can resolve and the dog makes a full recovery. It depends on the cause. Potential causes of collapse are:

Unconscious collapse
1. Fits – the dog is rigid, may have limb movements, drools at the mouth, defecates and urinates.
2. Metabolic dysfunction.
3. Poisoning.
4. Asphyxia – flaccid.
5. Metabolic disturbance – e.g. diabetes.
6. Physical cause – e.g. heat stroke, head injury.

Conscious collapse – the dog is unable to rise and is wobbly.
1. Respiratory distress – oxygen starvation.
2. Circulatory – loss of blood, anaemia, shock post-RTA, stroke.
3. Central Nervous System – e.g. slipped disc.
4. Locomotor System – arthritis.

5. Drugs – owner's sedative etc.

In the event of collapse, check first to see if the dog is conscious or not. If unconscious, is the dog breathing and is there a heart beat? If not, start heart massage and breath for the dog. What do the eyes look like? What colour are the gums and tongue? Make sure the airway is open. Stretch out the dog's head to straighten the windpipe. Keep the dog warm and if possible get to the vet immediately. Do not offer fluids to an unconscious dog unless you are sure there is a problem about low blood sugar and then you can wash the mouth with sugar and water. Be careful it is not inhaled.

If the dog is conscious, check the pulse, watch the breathing – is it fast, slow, deep, shallow? What colour are the gums? What are the eyes doing? Can the dog feel his or her legs? All these observations will help your vet to make a diagnosis as to what caused the collapse. In the field keep the dog warm and, when the situation has been assessed and it has been decided how to move the dog, then go straight to the vet for examination.

BLOAT

Bloat is an extremely serious emergency condition which all gundog owners should know about. If not treated promptly, within hours, your dog will be dead. It is seen in many deep-chested breeds but particularly in Irish Setters, Weimaraners, Flatcoated Retrievers, Italian Spinones and Gordon Setters.

For some reason the motility of the stomach and small intestines stops. The dog tries to be sick but cannot achieve this and only brings up small amounts of white froth. It is believed that the stomach swells with gas produced by fermentation, but tests show this gas to be swallowed air. The dog's abdomen becomes swollen and tight like a drum. The dog is extremely uncomfortable and restless, pacing up and down. The

LIFTING A SMALL DOG

Hold the dog by the scruff of the neck.

Use the other hand to support the hindquarters.

Now the dog can be picked up safely.

LIFTING A MEDIUM-SIZED DOG

Place one arm at the front of the dog, and the other around the back of the hindlegs.

The dog can now be lifted.

Photos: Keith Allison

pressure of the stomach restricts blood flow back to the heart and the dog quickly goes into shock.

The swollen stomach is unstable and can twist (torsion) cutting off the entrance to and exit from the stomach. Once this happens surgery is the only option open to the vet. If the stomach has not twisted, it can be possible to pass a stomach tube to release the gas and flush out any contents. Your vet will give the dog drugs to increase gastric motility, and antibiotics and large amounts of fluid to try and counteract the life-threatening shock. After giving drugs to increase motility it is a waiting game to see if this does the trick or if surgery is needed. It is a wonderful feeling if the room becomes filled with flatulent gas, showing that things have started working again!

If the gas continues to form despite stomach tubes and no wind is passed, or if torsion has already occurred, your vet will

LIFTING A LARGE DOG

Two people will be needed to lift a large dog such as a Weimaraner. One person should support the neck and chest while the second person takes the abdomen and hindquarters.   Photos: Keith Allison

have to operate to clear the problem. Surgery in these patients is extremely serious and there is a high mortality rate due to shock, release of toxins and interruption of the blood supply to the intestines, stomach, heart and lungs. Post-operative serious complications can occur, including peritonitis, enterotoxaemia and heart arrhythmias.

The cause of bloat or gastric Dilatation Volvulus Syndrome is not known for sure but there are several factors which can play their part in its occurrence. It tends to occur after the age of six years but I have seen it in a nine month old Weimaraner puppy which sadly died despite prompt treatment.

It is more likely to occur if you feed one large meal of a high fibre, bulky food, then take the dog for a walk and then allow the dog to drink a large amount of water. Stress is an important aetiological factor. I make sure that I feed my dogs twice daily on a low residue food and, if I have been out all day at a show, or on a shoot day, I feed them a little and often at the show but not at night when I return home. They get extra the next morning when I can keep an eye on them. Do not feed your dogs late and then put them straight into a kennel for the night. Bloat usually occurs after feeding.

I have heard of, and seen, several bitches who have blown after whelping and at weaning time. Whether this is due to stress, or due to the slackening of ligaments under hormonal control I do not know but this is another time when you should be vigilant.

There are several drugs which can be given to dogs who have had an episode of bloat, to maintain gastric motility and prevent a reoccurrence. Metaclopramide, Cisapride and Erythromycin are all drugs which can increase gastric motility and hence decrease the chance of bloat. It can be worthwhile fixing the stomach to the abdominal wall and so prevent a further torsion, although bloat is still a possibility. The stomach is sutured to the abdominal wall on the right-hand side under general anaesthetic.

Bloat is a genuine emergency and if you suspect your dog is suffering from it, phone your vet immediately.

VOMITING

One-off vomiting is not abnormal in the dog if it only occurs no more often than once a month. If it is more frequent it should be investigated. Persistent vomiting is a potentially serious condition, as the body soon becomes dehydrated and loses salt and

MAKING A STRETCHER

Photos: Keith Allison.

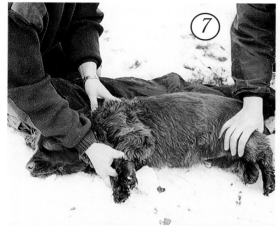

MAKING A STRETCHER –
Key to photographs

1. In an emergency situation, a stretcher can be made out of a coat and two strong branches.
2 & 3. Lay the coat flat and pull both sleeves inside the coat.
4. Zip up the coat.
5 & 6. The two branches are inserted into the sleeves of the coat.
7 & 8. The injured dog is rolled on to the stretcher.
9. The dog is now ready to be moved.

ions essential for normal body function. If a dog is vomiting you should withhold all fluid and food for 24 hours. If the vomiting continues despite no oral fluid, see your vet immediately. If the vomiting ceases you can try small amounts of boiled water the next day, but if the vomiting recurs you must seek veterinary help. It is often necessary to give intravenous fluids if vomiting persists despite drugs to stop it (anti-emetics). If your dog can keep fluid down for one hour, give a little more and then the next day start a bland diet of chicken, rice, fish etc. If at any time the vomiting returns, you should go back to your vet for more treatment.

Vomiting is potentially serious and must be monitored closely.

DIARRHOEA
There can be many factors which trigger diarrhoea, but if the dog seems bright and healthy otherwise, you can try your own treatment for 48 hours. If the diarrhoea contains blood or is profuse or if your dog is unwell, you should see your vet immediately.

If you are going to try to give treatment yourself, starve the dog for 24 hours, offering only boiled water which has cooled, and you can give Kaolin, bismuth or charcoal. If the diarrhoea has eased the next day, you can feed small frequent meals of boiled rice and either fish or chicken. If the diarrhoea is still present after 48 hours of this, take your dog to the vet for further investigation.

Do not give your dog milk, as this is likely to make matters worse. Gluten found in wheat is a common cause of diarrhoea as it can be an allergen to the dog and so I would not feed any biscuits, bread, etc. if the dog's stools tend to be loose. Diarrhoea can be caused by many agents but often it is due to ingested materials. If your own husbandry has not improved matters, take a faecal sample with you to your vet for laboratory examination.

COLITIS

Colitis is usually seen as loose stools with mucus and sometimes blood mixed in with them. Dogs with mild cases often pass fairly normal stools but they appear to have a skin on them like sausages – this is mucus and is an indication that all is not well. Blood in the stools shows that there may well be ulcers in the colon.

Colitis can be caused by stress, infection, food intolerance and/or inflammation of the colon. Often the initiatory cause is food intolerance, the most common culprits being wheat gluten and soya. Treatment involves antibiotics, anti-inflammatory drugs such as sulphasalizine, sometimes over a period of months, and a change of diet to gluten and soya-free, or a hypo-allergic diet. Sometimes extra bran in the diet can help but I find this unusual.

POISONING

There are many substances which can cause poisoning if ingested and if you are ever suspicious that your dog has eaten something which is poisonous, take a sample, and the label from the bottle if possible, to your vet. The signs of poisoning depend on the type of poison. If you think your dog has eaten something poisonous

you can put a crystal of washing soda onto the back of the tongue to cause vomiting. There is no point in making a dog vomit later than four hours after ingestion of the poison as it will have moved out of the stomach. To reduce absorption of a poison you can feed charcoal to bind with the poison. Symptoms of poisoning can vary from hyper-excitability to depression, vomiting and diarrhoea, collapse, respiratory distress etc.

Ethylene Glycol (antifreeze). This has a sweet taste and will attract dogs. Water containing this substance after draining out of car radiators is a common source of the poisoning. Initially the dog is dull and will then pass blood in the urine. Death can occur. Treatment within four hours can be successful but must be given by a vet.

Lead. This poison is found in putty, paint, linoleum and metallic objects. Modern paints are low in lead and are not usually a problem, but if a dog chews some wood with old paint on it, this can cause symptoms. Signs are either depression or excitability, blindness, abdominal pain, convulsing and vomiting. Treatment is by your vet with sodium calcium edetate.

Drugs. Reactions can occur if animal drugs are given at the inappropriate dose. Do read the label properly and keep the bottle out of the dog's reach. Do not give human drugs to dogs without asking your vet if it is appropriate. Paracetamol and aspirin are safe at recommended doses, but are very toxic at human levels. Ibuprofen is quite toxic to the kidneys and can lead to renal failure and death and should never be given to dogs. Accidental ingestion of the owner's drugs by the dog is a common occurrence in the home but it can be avoided by keeping all medicines in a cupboard. If you suspect your dog has eaten your tablets, phone the vet's surgery and describe the name, strength and approximate number of tablets which might have been consumed. Then your vet will be able to advise accordingly.

Pesticides. Many of these products can be toxic to dogs and it is as well to check that the farmer has not been spraying the fields and hedgerows before a shoot. If your dog does suffer any odd symptoms immediately following a shoot, ask the farmer if he has sprayed and what with. Occasionally there are antidotes for some products, but you do need to know exactly what has been used. Herbicides can be very nasty and care should be taken that they are used correctly and empty containers disposed of carefully. Do not allow your dog to drink from any discoloured puddles while out, in case they have formed after spraying. Most toxic herbicides cause liver damage and bloody diarrhoea, leading to death.

Insecticides tend to produce nervous signs of excitability, vomiting, inco-ordination and salivation. There is little you can do as a first aid measure except keep the dog as quiet as possible, reduce light and noise and get to your vet, who can give sedatives and antidotes if the type of insecticide is known. Examples of insecticides include organophosphates (OPS) BHC, gammexane, lindane, DDT (now banned). Metaldehyde is a slug bait and is palatable to dogs. It causes salivation, hyper-aesthesia (extreme sensitivity to touch) and convulsions. Treatment is to sedate the animal but the outcome is poor.

Rat Poison. The most common one to cause poisoning is Warfarin. It acts by interfering with normal blood clotting and affected dogs show multiple bruises on their gums and body. A single dose of Warfarin is unlikely to cause any problem and the antidote is Vitamin K. Alphachloralose is used to kill mice and pigeons by anaesthetizing them, causing the body temperature to drop resulting in

hypothermia and then death. If your dog eats such a poison, keep the dog warm until the poison wears off. Red Squill is a safe rat poison as it causes vomiting in dogs and so cannot be absorbed.

Creosote/Oil. Contamination of the coat with oil can cause skin problems but can also be toxic to the liver if the dog licks substantial amounts from the coat. To remove use a substance called "Swarfega" but, if this is not available, use cooking fat and then wash this off well with soap and water. If the dog has licked a contaminated coat, give a bulky meal e.g. mashed potatoes, bread and butter with extra vegetable oil added to it. This will reduce the amount absorbed from the intestines into the body.

The list of poisons is enormous and is ever-changing. If you ever think your dog has eaten anything toxic, phone your vet, take a sample of the poison, the box and any vomit with you if at all possible. In the house some plants are toxic. Laburnum, mistletoe and various mushrooms can cause problems in the garden. There are no specific antidotes and treatment is to minimise absorption and control any symptoms.

SNAKE BITES
Obviously countries differ in the variety and venom of their snake population. The only indigenous venomous snake in the UK is the adder. It has a characteristic "V" or "X" on the head and dark zigzag markings on the body. It is found most commonly on well-drained heathlands. It tends to bite the head and neck of dogs when they sniff and disturb the snake's sunbathing. Following a snake bite the tissue swells rapidly and often the fang marks are not visible. The swelling can cause restricted respiration if the bite is near the trachea. The dog is often depressed and should be discouraged from moving as this can move the venom around the body. In severe cases the dog can have respiratory

A dog suffering from oedemotous following an adder bite. Photo coutesy: Gillian Averis.

distress, collapse and die. First aid treatment is aimed at reducing the spread of the toxin and reducing any potentially serious swelling. Cold compresses applied to the bite can help but veterinary attention should be sought without delay, where corticosteroids, antihistamines and diuretics are used to decrease swelling.

TOADS
Toads secrete a toxic venom on their body surfaces. If a dog mouths a toad this can cause excessive salivation and occasionally nervous signs. Treatment is with atropine and steroid injections.

WASP AND BEE STINGS
These stings often occur on the face, lips and feet. They will not cause any serious problems unless the sting goes into the bloodstream or the dog is allergic to them. Wasps tend not to leave the sting but bees invariably do. If you can see the sting, remove it with a pair of tweezers, but grasp in at the base where it enters the skin and not by the sac, as that will release more poisons and make the situation worse.

The sting will cause a local swelling, irritation and pain and, if inside the mouth near the larynx, then there is a risk that the swelling could block the airway. If the dog seems to have any trouble breathing, telephone your vet immediately. Swelling elsewhere in the mouth or skin is best left alone or bathed with bicarbonate of soda (a dessertspoonful in one pint of water). Occasionally the dog can suffer a severe reaction and collapse in a state of shock after a bee or wasp sting and treatment must be sought immediately.

HAEMORRHAGE (BLEEDING)
Severe bleeding must be dealt with promptly as it can be life-threatening. Arterial haemorrhage is the most serious form of haemorrhage. The blood is bright red and spurts out from the wound with every heart beat. The amount of blood lost depends on the size of the artery. Venous bleeding is easier to control because the pressure is less, but it can still be fatal if a large vein is involved. Bleeding can be external and seen easily, or internal, where detection and control is much more difficult. Internal haemorrhage can follow road traffic accidents, gunshot wounds or trauma and can be fatal. Signs are those of shock, i.e. pale gums, rapid weak pulse, rapid respiration rate and cold limbs.

Haemorrhage can be controlled by:
(a)   Direct digital pressure. Apply pressure with finger and thumb and, if the wound is large, with your hand. If necessary, place a piece of material over the wound – gauze swabs or, if not available, a handkerchief, scarf etc. – and bandage it firmly in position. Be careful not to press too hard on the wound if it lies over a fracture. If the bleeding continues, apply another bandage. Pressure bandages should not be left on too long as tissue damage may occur, so seek veterinary advice within eight hours. If the pressure bandage is applied part way up a limb, it may stop the flow of blood from the feet back to the body, which will cause the foot to swell. This will become extremely painful, so any dressing should be applied enclosing the whole limb if possible.
(b)   If needed, a tourniquet can be applied above the wound. Tie a piece of cloth or a

APPLYING A TOURNIQUET
Photos: Keith Allison.

To stop bleeding, a tourniquet may need to be applied. Tie a lead above the site of the wound and knot it as tightly as possible (left). If necessary, insert a twig through the knot and twist it to tighten the tourniquet further (centre and right).

dog lead above the wound and pull as tight as possible. If the bleeding continues, you can put a pen or twig through the knot and twist it to tighten the tourniquet further and stop the bleeding. The tourniquet should not be left in place for longer than 15 minutes or the tissues of the leg will become starved of oxygen. Slowly slacken off the tourniquet and, if the bleeding starts again, you can reapply pressure after one minute.

CUTS AND GRAZES

Abrasions. These can be caused by a glancing blow either by a car or a solid object such as a tree. The wound is superficial and bleeding comes from capillaries. The wounds are not usually serious but are very painful and always contaminated. It is not necessary to dress them, but do prevent the dog licking them as this will exacerbate the problem. The wound will need antibiotics and, depending on its extent, painkillers.

Incisions. These are often caused by glass or a sharp object. The edge of the wound tends to gape and bleeding can be quite substantial depending on the size and depth of the wound. Damage can easily include deeper

tissues, tendons and nerves, so all should be checked out by a vet. Cut tendons need suturing quickly if there is to be no permanent damage. Usually the skin wound will heal quickly. In the field, the wound can be temporarily protected by a bandage or handkerchief dressing.

Lacerations There are caused by barbed wire, dog fights and road accidents. The edge of the wounds are irregular and there may be loss of skin. The loss of blood tends to be small because the tearing of the skin seals a lot of the blood vessels. There may be deep damage to underlying tissue and deep haemorrhage. The wound is likely to become infected due to ingrained dirt, saliva and bacterial contamination. The wound needs extensive cleaning under anaesthesia, suturing and antibiotic therapy. Painkillers are usually essential.

If the wound is gaping, a large bandage should be applied to protect the underlying tissue from further contamination. A cotton shirt can be tied around the body of a dog with a large chest wound in order to protect the wound. Try minimising the movement of the dog with a large cut, as this will reduce pain and further blood loss. With most wounds it is not advisable to try cleaning the wound while in the field. Stop any haemorrhage, protect it from further contamination, keep the wound still and seek veterinary help.

ROAD TRAFFIC ACCIDENTS (RTAs)
These accidents can happen all too frequently and often prove fatal. If your shoot has roads crossing it, do be careful to watch your dog near these areas. It might just be a country lane but the one car a day may come along just as your dog goes to retrieve that long bird. Also be careful when the shoot vehicles are arriving and/or moving to the next drive. Too many accidents happen at this time.

There are many types of injury that can happen after an RTA, from minor bruising to massive internal bleeding. Once the condition of the dog has been assessed, if possible move the dog off the road and keep the dog warm. Stem any haemorrhage, clear airways and check the pulse. Look at the gums. If they seem to be getting paler, rush to the vet as quickly as possible because there may be ongoing internal bleeding. Sometimes there is not a mark externally but the dog still dies from haemorrhage from a ruptured liver. It is quickest to go to the vet rather than call him out so, if you can move the dog, do so. If need be, place a muzzle temporarily on the dog's head to prevent helpers being bitten. If the dog has just been bumped and seems OK, you can give a paracetamol or aspirin, but do still keep a close eye on the dog and get a check-up from the vet as soon as you get home.

FRACTURES
Broken bones can be seen after road traffic accidents, or they can happen as easily as by tripping up a step. The signs of a broken bone are sudden-onset pain and usually 100 per cent lameness if the fracture involves a leg. Pain is caused by the broken ends of the bone rubbing against each other. If the

fracture is incomplete there will be little movement and hence limited pain. If the ends of the bone override and are badly displaced, again the ends will not rub against each other and so the pain is not as great as if the broken ends are close together.

The site of the fracture will soon become very swollen due to haemorrhage caused by the broken bones and damage to muscles and soft tissue surrounding it. The limb will be carried to some degree, depending on the site of the damage. One fractured toe may only cause limping, whereas an overridden fracture of the femur (thigh bone) will cause 100 per cent lameness.

It is possible to feel the grating (crepitus) as the broken ends move against each other but you should not try and feel for the fracture as this crepitus is very painful and you could cause more damage to the surrounding tissues by moving the sharp ends of the broken bone. Indeed, your responsibility, if you think your dog might have broken a bone, is to immobilise the fracture if possible. If the dog becomes distressed by your attempts to bandage/splint the broken bone, then stop. You may cause more damage and the best course of action is to get the dog to the vet as soon as possible with the minimum amount of movement of the fracture site. It is only possible to apply a splint to the leg below the elbow or below the stifle in the hind leg. If the fracture is in the toe, it is possible to bandage the whole foot, thus using the unbroken toes as a splint.

If you need to apply a splint to the leg itself, you can use anything which will support the leg – a roll of newspaper, a smooth stick etc. It should be long enough to immobilise the joints above and below the fracture. When applying the splint, support the leg on both sides of the fracture to avoid moving the broken ends. Get some assistance to do this if possible. Pad the leg with cotton wool if available, or a scarf, and then strap the splint to the leg with a bandage or, if that is not available, a scarf, sock, jumper, lead etc. Leave the foot exposed (unless it is a low fracture) so that you can check that the foot stays warm – which shows that you have not cut off the blood supply by applying the dressing too tight. If the dog starts to bite or chew at the splint, it may be on too tightly or it is causing pain and should be removed. If the dog can move and is not too distressed, it can be better to leave the leg undressed and let the vet decide if it needs support until it is repaired.

Fractured ribs are uncommon and, because the ribs are closely held by muscles and jointed to other ribs, a single fracture can often go unnoticed as there is little displacement or clinical signs, but they are painful. If several ribs are involved, the situation can be quite serious as the fractured ends can puncture the lung, allowing air to escape from the chest and collect under the skin. This is felt as a crackly sensation under the skin. If this air continues to escape, it can cause difficulty in breathing. You can reduce the loss of air by bandaging the chest (see Bandaging Techniques). Usually the damage is only to one side of the chest and the opposite lung should be able to function, so, as long as the dog is not stressed, this will be OK until you reach your vet.

FRACTURED SPINE
This is a serious injury which can leave the dog permanently paralysed. If the bones of the back are displaced, the spinal cord will be permanently damaged and it is usually necessary to put the dog to sleep as the use of the legs will not be regained. Signs of spinal injury are paralysis of the hind legs, occasionally an arched back and stiff, extended front legs. If you suspect that there is a spinal injury, only move the dog with great care. Try to slide the dog on to a rigid stretcher and do not twist the back at all. Veterinary attention must be sought immediately.

GUNSHOT WOUNDS
The reaction of the body to gunshot wounds depends on the severity of the wound and its position. Treatment is basically the same as for a road traffic accident. Make sure there is a pulse and the dog is breathing. Control haemorrhage with pressure and dressings if possible and seek veterinary help immediately. Keep the animal warm and still until you get to the vet, who will treat the dog for shock, giving intravenous fluids to replace fluid loss and restore the dog's circulation. It is not always necessary to remove all the shotgun pellets from the dog as, if they are not near vital organs or joints, they are unlikely to cause any future problems.

BURNS
Burns can occur on any part of the dog and are often caused by spills of boiling drinks. They are extremely painful but their damage can be limited by immediately flooding the area with cold water. If the burn is caused by fat, use a detergent and water to removed the fat. As a first-aid measure, cooling the area is the most important action and then the area should be dressed by a vet. This may have to be done under an anaesthetic, depending on the depth and extent of the burn. It is often better not to cover the burn initially as this is very painful and you may cause more pain to the dog than is necessary. Electrical burns can occur when dogs, usually pups, chew through electrical cable. *Do not touch the dog* until the electricity has been switched off. If the dog has not been killed, treatment is the same as for any other burn, i.e. cooling, cortico-steroids, painkillers and antibiotics.

HEAT STROKE (HYPERTHERMIA)
This happens when there is an elevation of body temperature due to excessive heat production or defective heat loss. Heat stroke is commonly found when dogs are left in cars in the sun or, for our gundogs, if they

run excessively in the sun with inadequate access to water. The dog's temperature will quickly rise and the dog can die immediately in respiratory distress or may survive only to die days later due to the damage caused to internal organs, which have been almost cooked. Treatment is aimed at reducing the dog's body temperature and this is best done by immersing the dog in water. Continue until the dog's temperature is back to normal (101.5 to 102.5). Veterinary attention must be sought immediately to prevent the dog suffering from shock and toxaemia.

Always carry plenty of water in the car, or with you if you are out in open country. At the beginning of the season the temperature can still be very hot and there is often little natural water in such areas. It might be a nuisance to have to carry your own water but it is vitally important for the dog. Black Labradors are particularly susceptible to heat stroke.

Never leave a dog in a car when the sun *may* come out.Even as early as April and as late as September, an enclosed car can soon become very hot if there are no windows open. Even a partly opened window will not keep the internal temperature of a car at bearable levels so *do not* risk it and, wherever you live, always take your dog out of the car if the sun is likely to break through the clouds. You can buy "space" blankets to cover your car and help keep the temperature down and these, combined with heavily tinted windows, can help to keep the car cool, but always keep a check on any dogs left in such a protected vehicle.

FOREIGN BODIES

Occasionally a stick or bone can be wedged across the hard palate, trapped on the upper molars. The dog will paw frantically at the mouth. Removal can be difficult and is best achieved by levering it out with a broad, flat, blunt object such as a spoon or fork handle. The hard palate may be cut and bruised, so get your vet to check it.

Foreign bodies in the eye will cause sudden-onset pain and the dog will hold the eyelids closed. If the foreign body is floating free on the surface of the eye, try washing it out with clean water or cold tea, but if it has penetrated the surface of the eye, let your vet try to remove it. If you are not careful you could cause further damage. Most foreign bodies can be removed easily with no significant damage but if your dog continues to squint, then do get the eye checked out by your vet.

Fish hooks can sometimes embed themselves into various parts of a dog. Usually you can see the incriminating tail of a fishing line and if this is followed it will lead you to the hook. Because of the barb, you cannot pull the hook back out of the skin, so you must cut off the line and the end of the hook and then push the hook on through the skin. If in doubt, let your vet do this under local anaesthetic.

Thorns can become embedded in the pad causing sudden lameness. Often the dog will nibble at the affected pad and you can see the end of the thorn. It is helpful to use tweezers to remove the thorn, but probably antibiotics will be needed to make sure no infection has been left at the bottom of the wound.

FITS
Fits fall into two main areas:
(a) Epileptic fits.
(b) Metabolic fits.

Epileptic fits usually happen immediately after the dog has been asleep, gets up, takes a few steps and then collapses into a fit. This is covered in the Chapter on Inherited Conditions.

Metabolic fits – uraemic, hepatic and hypoglycaemic – are not related to rest. The most relevant type of fits for gundogs is a hypoglycaemic fit which occurs when the blood glucose drops to a low level. These are relatively common in working gundogs. They are prevented by making sure the dog has frequent meals during a shoot. Give the dog a small breakfast before setting out in the morning and make sure that your dog has some lunch when you do. Some high-quality food, high in calories, or a handful of biscuits will often help, but I usually give my dog a Mars bar as this is packed with calories. Do not give pure chocolate as it can be poisonous to dogs. Often the dogs will not go into a full fit but will not work as well towards the end of the day because, as their blood glucose gets low, they become a little light-headed and lack concentration. They slow down, so reducing their energy needs, and manage to carry on with a lower work load. Uraemic and hepatic fits can occur when there is severe kidney or liver failure but treatment is aimed at improving the dog's health. They are most likely to occur in animals in poor condition.

If you do find a dog having a fit it is important to keep as calm and quiet as possible. Avoid the temptation to hold the dog still; this restraint is likely to stimulate the dog and prolong the fit. Ideally keep as quiet as possible. If at home, turn the radio off, dull the lights and just keep watch to make sure the dog does not harm itself. The dog is not conscious of pain or of surroundings while in a fit and so could roll on to a fire, or fall down stairs, etc. A dog starting to come round from a fit may be dazed and confused, so be a little bit cautious. Some can be aggressive for a short time until they remember where they are. Offer a small drink and food, particularly if the fit has been caused by low blood sugar – a Mars bar or other high-calorie source is ideal.

BANDAGING HINTS

One of the main considerations when applying a bandage is to make it tight enough so that it does not slip off but not so tight that it cuts off the blood supply to the area below the bandage! We are lucky in that you can use the Elastoplast to stick to the dog's hair and hold a dressing in place, but avoid direct contact of Elastoplast with the dog's skin as it often causes a skin reaction. Do not use safety pins or elastic bands. Generally, if bandaging a lower limb, include the foot in the dressing or it may swell and become very painful.

EARS Many of the gundogs, but particularly Weimaraners, Vizslas and GSPs, can cut the tips of their ears and these bleed profusely. With a little nick you can use a small Elastoplast to cover it over and leave on for 24 hours.

If the Elastoplast will not stick or the cut is a bit bigger, it is necessary to bandage the ear to the top of the head. You can stick both ears together on top of the head using zinc oxide tape but you should place some material, e.g. cotton wool or a sterile dressing, between the two ears to prevent sores. It is not necessary to apply the tape tightly and it should be done carefully so that there is no chance that the blood supply is compromised. Check the dressing daily and, if there is any pain or sores, remove it.

An alternative method is to bandage one or both ears to the head. Again, place padding (see above) between the head and ear and between the ears if both are to be included. A conforming bandage is then placed around the head in a figure of eight – making sure it is not so tight that it chokes the dog! It is necessary to use a strip of Elastoplast on the front of the bandage, just overlapping the hair, so that it sticks to it and prevents the dressing slipping backwards.

If only one ear is enclosed in the bandage the other one can help to anchor the dressing. Again, check the dressing regularly because if it is applied too tightly you can cut the blood supply off from the ear and create a serious problem. A piece of stocking or sock can be used as a temporary tubular

A HEAD BANDAGE Photos: Keith Allison.

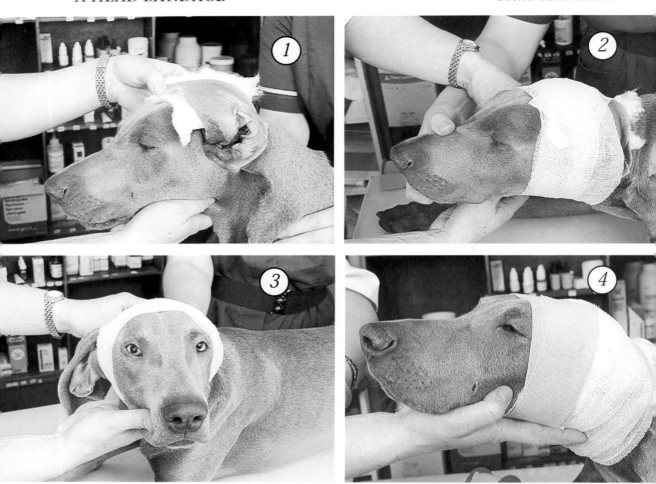

1. *Position the ears upward and cushion them with cotton-wool. 2. Use a light gauze bandage and wrap it around the head in a figure of eight. 3. The bandage should sit well clear of the eyes. 4. The bandage can be secured by adhesive tape to stop it slipping forward.*

dressing by cutting the foot off and then sliding it over the head and ears. This is not perfect but it can help on a temporary basis.

LIMBS Any wound should be covered with a non-adhesive sterile dressing. To prevent rubbing and sores, place small pieces of cotton wool between the toes, around any dewclaws and on the stopper pad. Then use a conforming bandage over the foot first, and then carefully wind it up the leg, overlapping each twist with the next. Do not pull the bandage too tight, and keep an even pressure. As you unwind the bandage, pull a 12ins length, then release the tension before applying it to the leg. This will reduce the

A FOOT BANDAGE

Photos: Keith Allison.

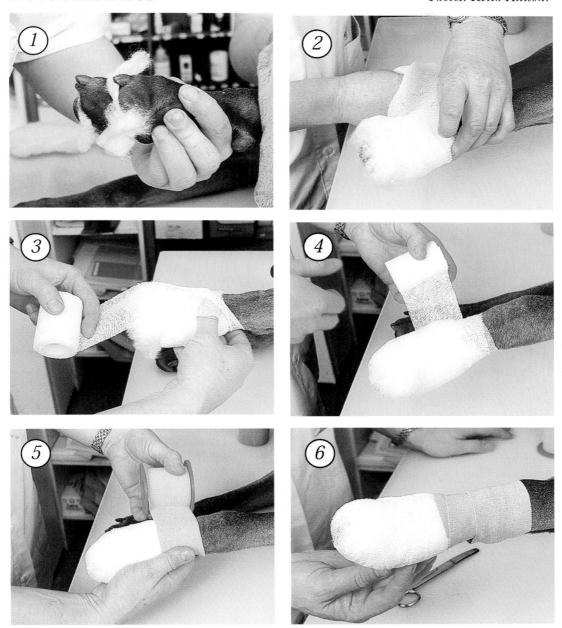

1. Place small pieces of cotton-wool between the toes, around the dewclaw (if present), and on the stopper pad. 2&3. Start by bandaging the foot and then move up the leg. 4. The bandaged foot should look like a close-fitting sock. 5&6. Adhesive tape is used to secure the bandage.

A TAIL BANDAGE

Photos: Keith Allison.

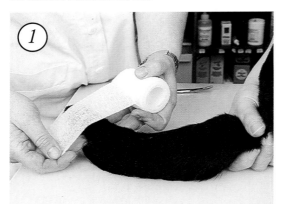 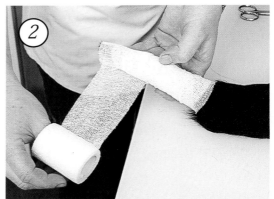

1 & 2. Use a light gauze and start at the tip of the the tail. Wrap the bandage around the tail to below the site of the injury, narrowly overlapping the bandage with each turn . Then work your way back.

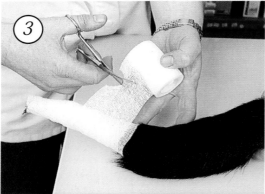 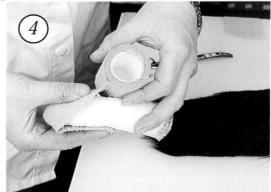

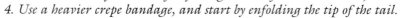

3. Continue until you are halfway along the tail for a second time, and then cut the bandage.
4. Use a heavier crepe bandage, and start by enfolding the tip of the tail.

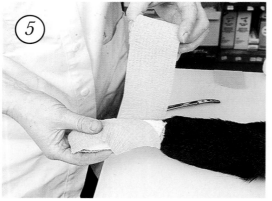 

5 & 6. Continue bandaging until the gauze bandage is fully covered, and then cut the crepe bandage.

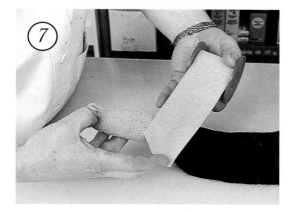

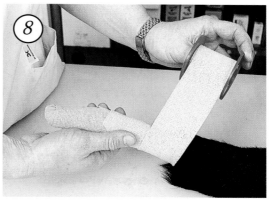

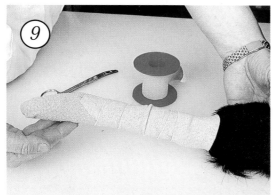

7, 8 & 9. Use zinc oxide tape to stick the bandage to a good length of hair and tail.

tape. If the tail is not too sore, just bandage the injured part using a length of bandage, up and down the tail. Carefully wrap round the tail starting at the top, and moving down the tail, then wind back up again. Then use zinc oxide tape to stick the bandage to a good length of hair and tail. And the best of luck!

CHEST BANDAGES It is unusual to need to bandage a chest, but if there is a large skin tear across the chest, or air collecting under the skin, you may need to apply some pressure and protection. A tee shirt can be put over a chest to protect a wound from further contamination. If pressure is needed, the bandage can be wrapped around the chest and then secured by passing it around the front of the chest and between the legs. The dressing tends to slip down the body with the lie of the coat, so it is necessary to use some adhesive to try holding it in place.

ABDOMINAL BANDAGES These are very unusual and not very successful and should be left to the professionals.

ROBERT JONES DRESSING This is used to give support and prevent movement. It is

chances of your applying the dressing too tightly. A final waterproofing layer of Elastoplast can be applied, using two 6ins strips applied at right angles to each other to cover the foot. A small amount of Elastoplast can overlap the bandage at the top of the dressing to stick it to the hair and hence anchor it. If you need to add support to the dressing you can place a layer of cotton or cotton wool in the dressing.

TAILS These can be very embarrassing to bandage as the dressing is likely to fall off with the first wag. I feel I have scored a victory if the bandage does not fall off before the dog leaves the surgery! Keep the dressing light. If the end of the tail is damaged you can protect it with a cylinder of plastic, then stick that to the tail with bands of zinc oxide

A CHEST BANDAGE

Photos: Keith Allison

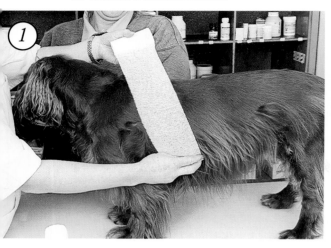

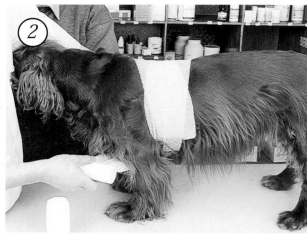

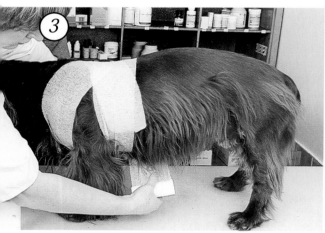

1. If you need to apply a chest bandage, use a wide roll of gauze bandage. 2. Start by wrapping the bandage around the chest. 3. Wind the bandage to the front of the chest and then back again. 4. The bandage may need to be held in place with tape.

a useful first aid dressing for a fractured limb. It involves alternative layers of cotton wool and conforming bandages. First cover any wounds with sterile gauze or non-adherent dressings, and then wrap the leg tightly with a sheet of cotton wool, more bandage etc., for about three layers. The dressing is very bulky but is comfortable for the patient; it can however slip down due to its weight, so a final strip of Elastoplast at the top, sticking to the hair, can be useful.

CARE OF BANDAGES Keep all bandages dry. A wet bandage can encourage infection,

GIVING TABLETS

Photos: Keith Allison.

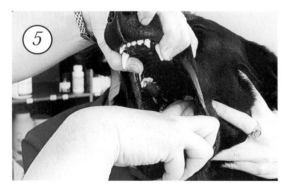

1. Hold the top jaw in one hand, hold the tablet in the other hand and apply light pressure behind the canine teeth. 2 & 3. Ease the mouth open, holding the tablet ready . 4 & 5. The tablet must be placed right at the back of the mouth so that the dog cannot spit it out.

lose its shape and cause pressure sores. If the dog goes out when it is wet, put a plastic bag on the bandaged foot. Do not leave this on all the time, as it will sweat and become damp inside. If a bandage starts to smell it should be checked by a vet or other traained person to make sure all is well and there are no sores or infection. One of the main problems with bandages is keeping the dog from removing the dressing! Often the only way is to apply an Elizabethan collar so that the dog's mouth cannot get to the dressing. These collars are a nuisance at times and cause chaos to your shins and paint-work but

95

GIVING MEDICINE

Photos: Keith Allison

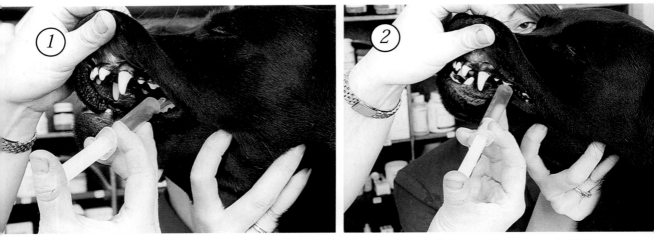

1. Use a syringe to administer medicine , and if possible, enlist the help of an assistant to hold the dog. 2. Lift the dog's upper lip, and squirt the medicine into the back of the mouth. Your assistant should hold the head, tilting it upward.

they are better than allowing the dog to remove the dressing and so prevent the wound healing. An alternative is a new, stiff neck collar which stops the dog's neck bending and so restricts the movement of the head. Children's T-shirts can be used to protect dressings on the body and chest – any colour is fine!

ADMINISTERING MEDICINES

Tablets are easily administered to dogs. Usually! I always prefer the easy option so, if the tablet can be given with food (check first with the vet), try that. Give a very palatable and tempting Trojan horse! A lump of chicken or cheese will often do the trick. If the dog is suspicious, give an undoctored morsel first and let the dog enjoy it. Then give the tablet in the same type of food, quickly followed by a third undoctored piece. Most dogs will swallow the bit with a tablet in it without realising it.

If they are clever and spit out the tablet, then you must manually put the tablet in the dog's mouth. Hold the top jaw with one

hand, hold the tablet in the other hand, and use this hand to open the mouth with slight pressure behind the canine teeth. With the index finger and thumb place the tablet right at the back of the mouth – almost causing the dog to gag. Quickly close the mouth and stroke the neck to encourage swallowing. If this fails, try spooning water into the mouth to cause the dog to swallow. The problem usually is that the tablet is not placed far enough back in the mouth.

TREATMENT TIPS

Skin. There is no point applying ointments, cream etc. to the skin of a dog who then promptly licks it off. After applying any preparation, distract the dog by offering food, exercise or play, so that the medication has a chance to work. When using medicated shampoo be careful not to allow any of it to get into the dog's eyes and ears. Plug the ears with cotton wool but do remember to remove the plug afterwards! If the shampoo needs to be applied around the head, use an eye ointment to prevent any accidental splashes into the eyes. Do follow any veterinary instructions to the letter, particularly about the frequency of washes and the disposal of the solution afterwards.

EYES Clean eyes with damp cotton wool before applying any treatment. Cold tea is an old-fashioned but useful liquid with which to bathe sore eyes. Tip the head up slightly and prise open the eyelids with gentle pressure. Apply the drops or ointment to the centre of the eyeball making sure you do not catch the surface of the eye with the bottle. Only use eye ointment for one dog, as you can get cross-contamination from one dog to the next.

EARS Hold the dog's head and raise the ear flap. If need be, it can be easier if two people do this. Apply the drops or ointment into the ear canal and then gently massage the base of the ear to encourage the drug to move down into the middle ear. After a few moments you can allow the dog to shake the ear. Do not use cotton buds to poke down the ear to clean them. Only remove matter that you can see. It can be a prudent idea to put the ointment and drops in the dog's ear while you are outdoors so that the house does not become redecorated with splattered ointment when the dogs shakes his, or her, head!

9 *LAMENESS IN GUNDOGS*

Lameness in dogs comes in many guises, ranging from the very mild to one hundred per cent lameness, and from transient to permanent, but whatever the form, it usually happens at the least convenient time – the day before a big shoot! There are numerous causes of lameness. In this chapter I am going to discuss the most common of them. Often the first problem is deciding which leg is causing the lameness! As a general rule the sore leg will be on the ground for a shorter period of time, the dog's head may appear to drop when the affected leg is weight-bearing and the length of stride will appear shorter. It is quite easy to confuse a front leg with a hind leg lameness, so study the dog's movement carefully. These problems obviously only apply to mild lameness – if the dog is holding up the lame leg this makes life a lot easier! Questions to ask yourself include the following: is the lameness present at all times? Is it worse after rest? Is it worse after exercise? Is there any swelling? What age is the dog? Has any known trauma occurred?

PADS
If a dog suddenly goes lame while outside, with no known trauma occurring, always check the pads for evidence of thorns, or cuts. Spikes from blackthorn and brambles can become embedded deep into the pad or the skin around them and cause one hundred per cent lameness. The dog may try and bite or chew the foot, so examine the pads carefully. Most dogs have ticklish feet and, if you touch their toes, they will pull their foot back. This is often confused with the dog being in pain, but if you press gently on a pad with a foreign body in it, you will get a much more marked reaction. If you do find a deeply embedded thorn, it can usually be removed with your fingers; but it would be advisable to get some antibiotics to stop any infection, because part of the thorn penetrates deep down and the small stab wound can heal over quickly at the top, leaving trapped infection at the wound's base.

Another common cause of lameness found in the pads is inflammation of the skin between the pads. This can be due to infection, allergy or irritation. All these conditions are seen as red, inflamed moist skin between the toes and between the pads. The skin can become quite swollen and wet. With both conditions the dog will be lame all the time and will try and lick the affected tissue. A common cause of irritation is nettles, and the dog will suddenly pick up its feet and try to bite them. The picture of a cat on a hot tin roof is brought to mind! Newly-cut grass is a common allergen, although the onset of lameness from this is gradual. Some disinfectants will cause irritation to the skin of the pads, so do be careful to read the instructions carefully on your kennel's disinfectant and dilute the chemical correctly. I have seen a valuable stud dog go lame, due to the use of a cheap farm disinfectant as a kennel wash that inflamed his feet, which then became infected. They were then so painful that he refused to mate any bitches. Some dogs will develop interdigital dermatitis (inflammation between the pads) if they walk on roads which have been gritted in the winter. The combination of salt and sand can cause an acute painful ID and owners of these dogs have to be careful where they exercise their dogs in the cold winter months.

Nail-bed infection can occur when the skin around the base of the nail is damaged and infection gets in. The skin around the base of the nail gets swollen, red and painful, and it may weep. The dog will be lame and will try to lick the infected nail. Contrary to popular belief, dogs do not lick things better, they usually make matters worse. Nail-bed infection needs antibiotic therapy.

A common medical condition which can cause foot pain and can look like a foreign object sinus, is an interdigital cyst. Some dogs seem prone to them and their cause is not always known. Some dogs are more likely to get them in dry weather, others in the wet, and some have trouble when there is salt on the road. They are red, painful, soft swellings between the toes which blow up over a few days, causing irritation and pain, and will eventually burst if not treated. Antibiotic treatment will normally settle them down quickly.

The ground on which your dog walks can cause problems. Anything which sticks to the hair between the pads can cause lameness. In the depths of winter, snow balls can form between the pads which will cause pain. You can try breaking the snow balls up but, if you trim the hair before the dog encounters the snow, the problem will be unlikely to occur. In contrast, in the heat of summer, melted soft tar can start a nasty dermatitis with inflammation and pain. This can be removed by clipping the hair away and using a spirit-based cleaner, but do wash this off as the treatment will cause as much irritation as the tar itself. Mud can also collect on the hair between the pads, so check carefully if you have a well-coated breed.

In late summer and early autumn your dog might pick up harvest mites from the fields. They are just visible to the naked eye and appear as a reddish deposit around the nails and sometimes on the abdomen. They can cause licking and a skin infection but are usually well-tolerated in dogs. If your dog has a problem, you can wash the feet in an insecticidal shampoo and that will kill the mites. However, it is necessary to do it daily, as the dog can pick them up every day when going out into the fields.

CUT PADS
Cut pads are an all-too-common occurrence on gundogs. Usually the cause is broken glass, but any sharp object can cause a nasty cut. Cuts can be superficial or deep. Deep cut pads will bleed profusely and it is essential that a pressure bandage be applied as soon as possible to prevent blood loss. This means putting on a bandage with plenty of padding, if available, but with the dressing on fairly tightly. Do not leave the tight dressing on for too long or you could cut the blood supply to the foot, leading to serious consequences, but it will be OK if it is only left for two to three hours before receiving the attention of the vet.

A thin slice off the pad will settle quickly and just needs cleaning and protecting. However, deep cuts may need suturing. Pads can be troublesome to heal. This is because of two main problems. The first is that there is no blood supply to the outer, hard part of the pad and so it cannot knit together again, and the other problem is that every time the dog bears weight on the damaged pad, the healing process is disrupted and this makes it more likely that the sutures will pull out. On balance, though, it is better to have a deep cut sutured, as it will heal better than if it is left with just a bandage for support. Often the cut is across the pad and then all that can be done is to remove the flap and allow the pad to heal across by itself. This obviously prolongs the healing process but it is usually all that can be done.

Occasionally a dog will go lame without any sign of injury, but is obviously conscious of its feet. It may be that the pads are bruised or sore. This can occur if the dog has run across very hard and uneven ground. Often there is very little to see, but if pressure is put on the pads the dog will show signs of discomfort. The only treatment is rest and avoiding hard rough ground in the future. An unfit dog, or a dog with thin pads and flat feet, is more likely to suffer from this condition.

As mentioned earlier, foreign bodies, often grass seeds, can penetrate the skin between the pads and cause infection and lameness. If the hair between the pads is kept short and groomed regularly, you are less likely to see this problem.

NAILS

Torn nails are extremely painful and can easily occur if the nails are not kept short. As the nail grows it has a tendency to curl and form a hook, which makes it more likely that it will catch on something and tear. Once a tear starts it will creep up the nail, so the nail needs to be cut above the crack to stop it running. Often this needs a general anaesthetic if it requires cutting above the quick, which is very painful. If the nail is torn above the line of the quick, or pulled off completely, it can bleed profusely. As with deep cut pads, a thick pressure bandage should be applied to stop the haemorrhage.

Dewclaws are the worst nails for being torn. As I have said earlier, I can see no justification for leaving dewclaws on any dog. I have listened to the arguments that they help dogs to grip when going up steep terrain, but I have seen many a dog with no dewclaws cover the ground perfectly easily, so I am not convinced. Having seen the pain that their damage can cause, I feel it is far better to have them removed when the puppies are newly born. When they are removed before the pups' eyes open – I like to do them before the puppy is four days old, preferably at a day old, which is far kinder – they can be cut off with a pair of curved scissors and any bleeding stopped with either a silver nitrate pencil or potassium permanganate. If you have never removed dewclaws or seen it done by an experienced person, please get your vet to do it. Done correctly it is a simple procedure but it should not be attempted by an untrained person. If the dewclaws need removing when the dog is older, this necessitates a general anaesthetic, removal of the now-calcified bones, control of bleeding, skin sutures, dressings and antibiotics.

If the skin around the base of the nails is damaged at all – and this can occur with such a little thing as the skin being pushed back and bruised – an infection can develop in the nail bed. This is seen as a red, painful swelling around the base of the nail, which can be cleared up quickly with antibiotics. However, if the infection spreads down the base and into the joints of the toe, this can mean a prolonged course of antibiotics and, in some cases, may lead to amputation of the toe. The lesson to be learned is to treat these infections quickly and then the outcome is usually successful. A complication of nail-bed infection is that the subsequent growth of that nail can be affected and it may grow in an abnormal fashion which has to be checked regularly to make sure it is not growing into the pad.

100

CUTS

Cuts are not just confined to the pads. Small stab-type wounds between the pads or below the wrist (carpus) can cause copious bleeding and some lameness. From the carpus downwards there are four bones which become the four toes. Each of these bones has four arteries and four veins associated with them, so, with a total of 32 vessels, it is no surprise that deep cuts to this area can lead to a lot of bleeding.

As with cut pads, the most important initial act with such a bleeding cut is to apply a pressure bandage to stop the flow of blood. There is an old adage that a little blood looks a lot – but with so many blood vessels in the lower leg there is a chance that the blood loss can be life-threatening, so do take cuts seriously. If you have not got a bandage on you – and who does carry one in their pocket! – use a handkerchief or tie a sock tightly above the leg. If all else fails, apply pressure with your thumb until a bandage can be applied.

A complication with deep cuts of the lower limb is that the tendons to the toes can also be damaged. If the tendons on the lower side of the metacarpus are cut, the dog will not be able to grip with that toe and it will stick up or appear long. Apart from looking unsightly, this toe is more likely to be damaged and will have lost its anti-concussive properties, its spring. Often the tendons can be sutured together again and, if they heal right there will be no lasting problems, but this needs to be corrected as soon after the injury as possible because, if not, the cut ends of the tendon will shrink back and then it is not possible to stitch them back together.

TRAUMA

This is another cause of acute lameness. We have all seen the dog that has run into a tree, screamed and then limped off on three legs. Hopefully the damage is just bruising and often, with a little gentle massage, a

miraculous recovery happens. Later on in the day of the accident the leg may well stiffen, but the problem will soon resolve. Sometimes the collision with the tree affects the tendon of the biceps muscle, at the point of the shoulder. This will result in a moderate degree of lameness, usually worse after rest. Occasionally the swelling on the tendon can be felt as the whole shoulder appears a little bigger, but with rest and anti-inflammatory drugs the condition will resolve, with no long-term effects.

Bruising can occur anywhere on the dog's legs and will cause a mild degree of lameness. Mild bruising is often not noticeable but with more severe bruises you will see some swelling and redness of the skin. A bruise occurs when a blood vessel is ruptured and forms a haematoma or blood clot. These can vary in size from a pin head to that of a football. If possible, apply a bandage to a large swelling to reduce the amount of bleeding from the damaged vessels under the skin. A large bruise, as well as being painful and interfering with the normal use of the leg, is also a potential food source for bacteria and hence infection, and so it is worthwhile having veterinary attention to provide antibiotics or anti-inflammatory drugs.

SPRAINED JOINTS

Sprained joints will either cause acute lameness, or the lamenesss may appear after rest, the initial twist not having been noticed. A sprain is when a joint moves beyond its normal range. The movement of a joint is restricted by the shape of the joint, the ligaments surrounding the joint, and the muscles and tendons which act on the joint. The joints of the limbs are called synovial joints. They are formed by the articulation of two or more bones, the ends of which are covered with cartilage. The joint is enclosed by a capsule which secretes a lubricating fluid called synovia.

If the joint is inflamed by an abnormal

EXAMINING THE FRONT LEG

Photos: Keith Allison.

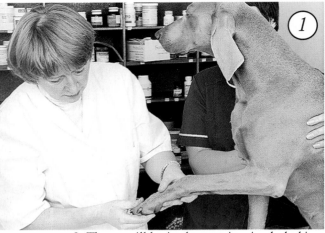

1. The vet will begin the examination by looking at the foot, the pad, the nails and the toes.

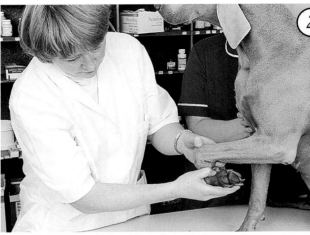

2. The wrist joint is flexed, and the dog's reaction noted.

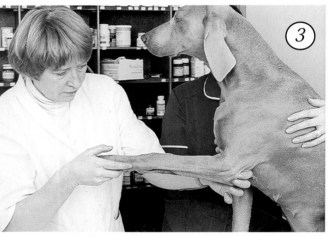

3. The front leg is then extended straight out from the elbow.

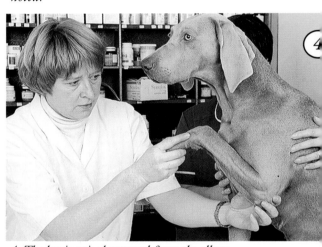

4. The leg is raised upward from the elbow.

movement, it will become swollen and painful due to the inflammation of the synovial membrane and the increased production of synovia. This will obviously cause lameness and pain. Treatment is aimed at restricting any abnormal movement with support bandages, if possible, and reducing the inflammation with anti-inflammatory drugs. Mild sprains will settle, with no long-term effects, but any inflammation to the joint is likely to lead to degenerative joint disease later in life. Prompt treatment can reduce the extent of this chronic damage.

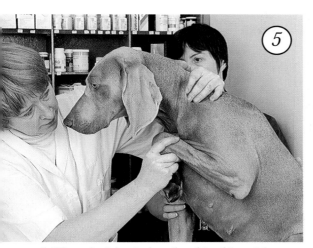

5. *The wrist joint is then flexed in this position.*

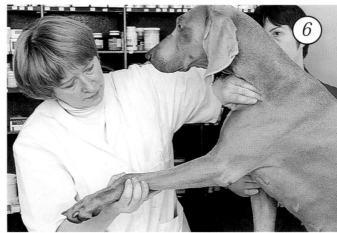

6. *Finally, the front leg is extended out from the shoulder.*

DISEASES OF THE JOINTS

The importance of proper limb conformation is not always stressed enough. If the angulation of the bones and their configuration with each other are not good, this can place abnormal stress on the bones of the joint, which leads to damage and then to degenerative joint diseases. Straight stifles, elbows turning out and cow hocks are all examples of such structural shortcomings. The cow-hocked dog can have several problems because of this poor angulation of the limb. With cow hocks you will also often find that the stifles, when viewed from the rear, turn out, giving a bandy-legged appearance. This causes the pull of the main muscle of the hind leg, the quadriceps, to be off-centre. Apart from being energy-wasting, it also puts a strain on the movement of the patella (knee cap) as it runs up and down the patella groove, causing more pressure on the medial ridge of the groove, which can lead to erosion, arthritis and, eventually, the patella slipping medially out of the groove completely. This will cause the dog to limp for a few strides until the patella slips back into position. In some cases the patella can remain permanently luxated and the dog will have very weak hindquarters. The abnormal pull of the quadriceps and the odd angle of the knee joint will also affect the way the head of the femur articulates with the pelvis at the hip joint and is likely to lead to re-shaping of this joint, for example hip dysplasia (HD) which can cause arthritis and pain.

Some abnormalities in conformation are acquired and are not congenital (present at birth). This can happen after a bone fracture, if the end of the broken bone is not aligned correctly, producing a twist or bend in the bone. A case which comes to mind is that of a Weimaraner puppy who broke his femur when about 12 weeks old. At that time the dog's legs were straight, with no sign of HD or cow hocks. Unfortunately, the fracture healed with a bow in the leg. This caused the patella to slip slightly medially, turning the stifle out, and the hock in, on the affected leg. This led to osteo-arthritis of the patella groove, and pain. At the other end of the repaired bone, the articulation of the hip

103

EXAMINING THE HINDLEG

Photos: Keith Allison

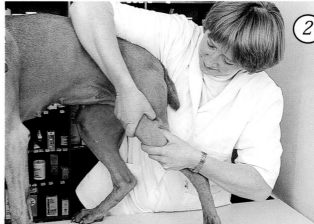

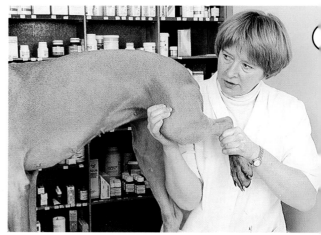

1. The vet begins the examination at the foot, checking the pad, the nails and the toes.

2. Pressure is applied to the thigh, feeling for tenderness.

3. The hindleg is lifted, bending the stifle.

4. The leg is flexed downward and backward, so that it is at full stretch.

5. Finally, the leg is lifted away from the body and outward.

joint was affected and the hip changed shape and developed HD. The poor young fellow had to undergo a major operation when he was 10 months old, when his hip joint was removed (arthroplasty) and he is now pain-free but has an odd-looking hind leg.

As I explained in the chapter on nutrition, the long bones grow in the young dog at the growth plates. Once these plates close, the bone cannot grow in length any more. Damage to the growth plates can cause them to close prematurely. Normally, this does not cause much of a problem, but the exception is if the growth plate of the radius or ulna is damaged in the front legs. These two bones run parallel to each other and, if one stops

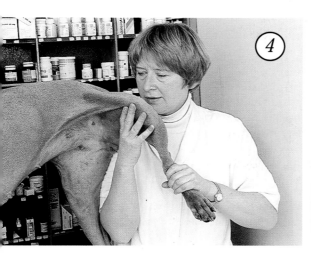

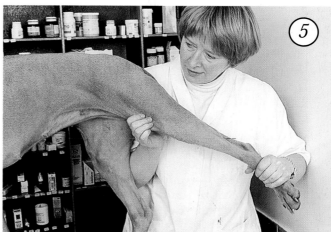

growing while the other continues, this will cause a limb deformity. If the radial proximal growth plate (near the elbow) is damaged, it will close, but the ulna will grow, pulling the elbow joint apart. Correction of this problem involves breaking the radius and realigning the elbow joint by means of bone screws.

A similar problem can occur at the other end of the bone when the ulna stops growing, the radius continues to grow and the leg becomes bowed, turning the foot out laterally.

DEGENERATIVE JOINT DISEASE (DJD)
This is a common cause of lameness in a dog and can follow damage to the joint caused by abnormal movement of the joint, or normal movement on an abnormal joint. These changes lead to arthritis. The clinical signs of DJD start with a reluctance to move, but without any obvious lameness. The next stage is stiffness and lameness after sustained activity or brief over-exertion. After a few days of rest the stiffness disappears. As the DJD progresses, stiffness can be more noticeable after rest, but the animal will "warm out" of the lameness

following a little movement. Cold and damp weather often makes the stiffness worse. In the final stages the lameness is more or less constant and the dog may be a bit irritable because of the constant pain.

DJD involves several processes but, basically, it causes production of bony growth around the joint and thickening of the synovial joint capsule which surrounds the joint. The cartilage acts as a smooth, gliding surface for the joint, absorbs concussion and protects the underlying bone. The loss of cartilage exposes that underlying bone, which then wears away and can be re-shaped. Exposure of the underlying bone causes pain. The thickening of the joint capsule causes stiffness and decreased movement of the joint.

DJD can happen on any of the joints. In its mildest form the dog is lame after periods of exercise, or after rest, but will soon be able to walk soundly. As the damage to the joint increases, the amount of lameness increases and the dog will be reluctant to move. If the DJD is in the hind leg, the dog will be reluctant to jump into a car or on to a seat. The joint can appear swollen and/or hot, but this is not always the case. The lameness from DJD is not always constant and can disappear for prolonged periods, and then have an acute flare-up following a sprain or extra exercise.

Treatment is medical and managemental. Medical treatment is with anti-inflammatory and analgesic (pain-killing) drugs. It is important to provide the anti-inflammatory drugs which will reduce the permanent damage to the joint. There are numerous types of anti-inflammatory drugs which your vet might use, and new ones are always coming onto the market. It is often a question of trying several drugs before you find one that suits your dog. Occasionally a dog might develop stomach pain and diarrhoea when on these drugs. If this happens, that particular medication should be stopped and an alternative tried. Some of the drugs used to relieve joint pain in dogs are the same as those used in humans, but there are some exceptions, so do not assume that your painkillers are suitable for your dog.

Aspirins can be given at a dose of 20 mg/kg twice daily but they can cause stomach bleeding, so should be used with care. Paracetamol can also be given, with care, and tends to produce fewer side-effects. *Do not give Nurophen, Brufen (Ibuprofen)* as it is extremely toxic to the dog and will cause damage to the kidneys, which can suffer acute renal failure and death will result. Olive oil and codliver oil can have a beneficial effect on inflamed joints and are an excellent supplement to the diet of the older dog. These oils have high concentrations of gamma-linolenic acid, an important chemical which the body uses to counteract inflammation, and hence decrease the pain in joints. They are useful in both acute and chronic pain and, sometimes, will be sufficient, and do away with any man-made painkillers.

ARTHRITIS (Inflammatory Joint Disease)
Bacterial infections can cause arthritis in the joints of dogs. The infection can be by trauma and direct penetration of the joint, or via the bloodstream. The most commonly affected joints are the shoulder, elbow, hip and stifle joints, and previous damage will make a joint more susceptible. The joints are painful and the overlying skin may be swollen and red. The synovial fluid becomes thick and cloudy and the bacteria can erode the cartilage and allow the infection to go into the bones and cause osteomyelitis. Bacterial arthritis can leave the dog with a very stiff and badly damaged joint and, if osteomyelitis occurs, the prognosis can be very bad. Treatment is with oral antibiotics, although sometimes the joint can be flushed with antibiotics as well. Treatment is usually continued for two to three weeks after all signs of infection have gone. Viruses, mycoplasma and fungi have also been found to cause arthritis, but their incidence is less common than bacterial disease.

There are several types of non-infection arthritis but they are quite rare. Canine rheumatoid arthritis is one of these conditions. It is first seen as a stiffening lameness, sometimes with signs of a fever, anorexia and swollen lymph nodes. The disease causes erosion of the joint surface and dramatic remodelling of the bone. Treatment is with corticosteroid and cytotoxic drugs but the prognosis is not good.

EXERCISE AND ARTHRITIS
Regular, consistent exercise will also help with chronic arthritis. Apart from preventing stiffening, it will keep the muscles and tendons active, and they will protect the joint from any more abnormal movement. The exercise should be geared to what your dog can do comfortably. It should be daily and be consistent. The average surgery is often full on Monday nights with hobbling, older dogs who have sat around all week and then been walked off their legs all weekend. As well as the dogs having stiff muscles, the

joints are also inflamed and painful. Several short walks a day are better than one long daily walk. Avoid any twisting and turning exercise for the dog with joint disease, as this is more likely to put abnormal pressure on the damaged joints. Swimming can be excellent exercise, as the muscles are used but no weight is put on the joints. However, not many rivers are at body temperature and, if the dog is allowed to stay cold after the swim, this will lead to joint pain. A dog who does like swimming – and so many gundogs do – must be dried off quickly and kept warm straight after the swim. In the summer this is usually not a problem and, as it can be beneficial to the muscles and tendons, it is well-worth encouraging this form of exercise.

OVERWEIGHT DOGS

Overweight dogs cause more damage to their joints and experience more pain to already damaged joints. As owners, we like to see our dogs eating and are guilty of giving in to pleading eyes and drooling jowls and so give tidbits. Too much food will lead to a fat dog. A fat dog is an unhealthy dog. As well as causing joint pain, obesity can also lead to heart disease, liver failure and bladder problems. As a vet I have heard many reasons why a client's dog is not overweight: "She has a lot of body"; "He has a big frame"; "His mother was big"; "He only eats one meal a day"; "She hardly eats anything" etc. It is selfish and cruel to allow your dog to get fat. If you are in doubt as to your dog's correct weight, ask your vet, get your dog weighed and then act on the answer. It is a good idea, as I have said before, to weigh your dog every month so that any change can be seen early and action taken.

Tidbits are the usual major cause of obesity. That last little bit of biscuit (or two), your corner of toast, the drop of tea, etc. all add up and if you put them all together, by the end of the week you would probably have at least another meal there! Milk is full of calories and is not needed by your dog. Do not feed it to an overweight animal. Buy a smaller food bowl and weigh the food daily. It is very easy to give a bigger handful if your dog gives you the "old sad eyes"!

To start with it is often sufficient just to reduce your dog's food by a third. If you are feeding meat and biscuits, reduce both by a third. Stay on this diet for one month and then re-weigh your dog. If the weight has not reduced by 2 lbs (1 kg), it is probably well worth putting your dog on one of the calorie-reduced diets which your vet can supply. They have increased levels of vitamins and minerals to compensate for the reduced calorie intake. You should aim for a weight loss of about 2lbs (1 kg) every two weeks, so it is not a quick job, but is well worth it for your dog's health's sake.

OSTEOCHONDRITIS DISSECANS (OCD)

This is a common cause of transient or chronic lameness in the larger breeds of dogs and in Brittanys. It may cause clinical signs of lameness with subtle gait abnormalities and usually first becomes apparent when the dog is six to nine months old. Clinical signs persist for weeks or months and will lead to degenerative joint disease.

OCD can happen in most joints but is most often seen in the shoulder, elbow, hock and stifle. It happens in fast-growing breeds and it appears that there is bruising under the cartilage of the joints which leads to damage to the cartilage. A flap of cartilage develops and the bone beneath is poorly calcified. The weight-bearing part of the joint is normally affected, which backs up the theory that it is trauma to the young joint which causes the damage. Dogs fed on an unbalanced diet, where the Calcium:Protein is incorrect, are more prone to developing OCD.

The treatment depends on the joint. If the damage is in the relatively simple shoulder or stifle joint, it is probably better to have the flap of cartilage removed, and the joint usually heals very well. But in the elbow and hock, which are very complicated joints, it is often better to control the pain with anti-inflammatory drugs because the surgery causes as much disruption to the joint as the flap of cartilage. In these cases, rest and drugs for one to two months, followed by a gentle return to normal movement, will usually settle the OCD down, but later in life the joint will suffer arthritis.

CRUCIATE RUPTURE
The cruciate ligaments are found in the stifle (knee) joint. Rupture of one of these is often a cause of acute leg lameness. Rupture can occur in one of two ways. The classical cruciate rupture happens in a middle-aged to older dog who puts a foot down a hole while running, and twists it awkwardly. The dog will cry in pain, hold the leg up and be one hundred per cent lame. The initial pain will settle quite quickly and the knee can be moved without any pain, but the dog will not put much weight on the leg, because the joint wobbles and so is uncomfortable. If the joint is not repaired it will lead to massive DJD and arthritis.

More recently, another group of dogs has been seen with cruciate rupture. These dogs are usually about three years old and belong to the large breeds of dogs, for example Rottweillers and Bullmastiffs, but we are seeing it in gundog breeds such as the Golden Retriever, Chesapeake Bay Retriever and the Curly Coated Retriever. The lameness comes on gradually and is transient, then it eventually becomes permanent lameness. In these dogs the ligament becomes inflamed and gradually weakens, allowing some abnormal movement of the joint. Eventually it snaps, leading to instability and DJD.

The stifle joint is a hinge joint and the cruciate ligaments, which are situated in the centre of it, prevent any sliding movement.

They cross in the middle of the joint, hence their name – cruciate. When these ligaments are damaged, replacement ligaments should be put in place as soon as possible to reduce the amount of arthritis which will occur in the future. The operation is quite a major one and needs six weeks' complete rest afterwards, but the results are always better than if the joint is left with no surgery. In a young dog, if one ligament tears, it is quite common for the one in the other leg to give way at a later date.

TENDON DAMAGE
Tendons are fibrous, strong structures which attach muscles to bones. They can become inflamed due to trauma or infection and will then cause lameness due to pain. The main causes of lameness where tendons are involved are with inflammation of the biceps tendon at the front of the shoulder, and when the tendon to the toe is damaged. A small stab wound to the foot can cut the tendons which keep the toes flexed and the foot tight. If the tendon is not repaired the toe will drop down and the nail will appear to stick up in the air. The toe is more likely to be damaged because of this, so it is often advisable to have the toe removed. For this reason it is essential to take any cuts between the toes seriously, as they may look minor but they might be hiding serious injury.

If the cut tendon is seen to promptly, it can be sewn together again and, with rest, full function can be restored. However, this sewing is a difficult procedure, because the tendon is made of many fibres lying parallel to each other and the suture will just pull through them. It is necessary to use a special type of suturing to form a cross, and this will hold it in place.

BONE CANCER
Osteosarcoma is the most common bone tumour in dogs. It is usually seen in the long bones near the carpus (wrist) and around the stifle, distal femur and proximal tibia

(around the elbow). The onset of lameness is usually rapid over a two to five day period and there may be swelling around the growth. The dog can be off food and may have a temperature. Diagnosis can usually be made on X-ray. Treatment with drugs is poor and early amputation is often advisable; but the growth may have already spread to the lungs. Amputation will relieve pain but may not prolong the dog's life: it is worth contemplating, if an early diagnosis is made, as it will alleviate discomfort, and most dogs manage very well on three legs. Survival time, post amputation, is generally no more than five months.

HIP DYSPLASIA (HD)

Hip Dysplasia is found in many breeds but is more common in the larger, heavier breeds. Its development is complex and involves not only genetic factors, but also environmental and nutritional ones. In HD the joint is abnormal in shape and function and will develop DJD and arthritis. At birth all dogs are born with normal hips but some, subsequently, undergo progressive structural changes. The hip is a ball and socket joint. The ball part of the joint, the femoral head, is held in the pelvic cup (acetabulum) by a ligament in the centre of the ball (the teres ligament) and by the shape of the acetabulum, the joint capsule and the dog's muscles.

In HD the hip can subluxate, or be loose in the socket, allowing abnormal wear of the joint because of abnormalities in one, or all, of the structures which keep the hip firm. Pain results from damage to the joint surface, osteoarthritis around the joint, and thickening of the joint capsule. On X-ray examination the degree of hip dysplasia can be assessed, but the bony changes are not

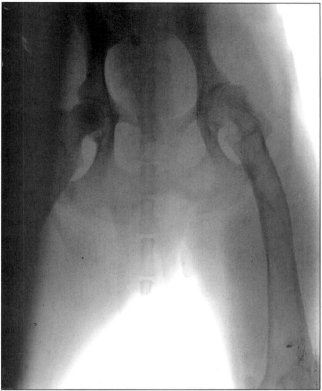

Hip dysplasia in the left hip following a fractured femur which has produced abnormal alignment of the hip joint.

always as dramatic as you would expect from the pain the dog is suffering.

There are considerable variations in the degree of clinical signs – the time of the onset of structural changes, the age of the dog when the clinical signs occur and the rate at which the dysplasia advances. Joint laxity is the earliest sign of HD and gait abnormalities, without any lameness or stiffness, will precede DJD. Many dysplastic dogs have a period of mild lameness when under one year of age, but then show no signs of clinical lameness until two to six years. Young dogs with loose joints tend to have odd periods of lameness after exercise. If the dog is overweight, or has poor muscle tone, the joint is more likely to be stressed and have more bouts of pain and a greater chance of developing DJD. In the young dog with dysplastic hips, treatment of lameness is aimed at protecting the joint with rest, painkillers and anti-inflammatory drugs. If this does not alleviate the pain, it may be necessary to consider surgery, but often this is not necessary at this stage.

Too much, or too little, exercise can make hip dysplasia worse. As mentioned earlier, the muscles help to hold the hip joint stable and prevent abnormal movement. If a dog is not fit, the muscles are slack which allows abnormal hip movement and, eventually, DJD. If the young pup is over-exercised, you may put excessive stress on the joints and cause damage and inflammation, leading to DJD. Similarly, if your dog is overweight, that will cause more wear and tear and stress on the joints, and the progression of DJD will be quicker. An unbalanced diet will also increase the chances of the joint being damaged, by not having a correct Ca:P balance, or by having too many vitamins in the diet. So, by good animal husbandry, you can reduce the chances of your dog developing HD. The disease has an inherited base, but the degree of development can be helped by moderate, regular exercise, by giving your dog an appropriate balanced diet, and by keeping weight at the correct level.

Retrievers and Setters seem more prone to showing signs of HD than other breeds. It is very unusual to find clinical HD in the Spaniels. Sussex Spaniels are particularly prone to having poor hips when seen on X-ray, but they rarely produce any lameness. This may be because, with shorter legs, less stress is put on the joints and also because the joint is held firmly by the muscles and ligaments. I am sure that the laxity of the joint is the main reason why dogs develop clinical lameness, and it is more important than the shape of the joint. I have reached this conclusion after examining numerous dogs under general anaesthetic. Often the

Golden Retriever or the Labrador Retriever has good-looking hips but, under general anaesthetic, the hip can be raised out of the socket to a marked degree. In the Spaniels and HPR breeds, this is not as apparent. Goldens and Labradors are more likely to suffer hip lameness than Spaniels. In many countries there is a scheme whereby the hips are scored – the lower the score the better. Details of the scheme are in the chapter on Inherited Diseases. In the USA a new test is now available which also assesses the laxity of the joint and I feel that this test will give a better guide as to which dogs are likely to develop HD. Because HD has a genetic basis, all dogs should be X-rayed before they are bred from.

Surgery of the hip joint is required if anti-inflammatory drugs are not working. In the young, growing dog an operation called a pectinectomy can be performed. A muscle on the inside of the leg is cut and this changes the angulation of the femoral head with the acetabulum and can relieve pain and encourage a better shape to the hip joint. If there is much evidence of DJD this technique has limited value.

A more complicated measure, but one which tends to be more successful, is changing the angle of the femoral head to the acetabulum by reshaping the pelvis. This involves cutting the pelvis in three places, re-aligning the pieces and holding them in place with bone screws and plates. This can be very effective in a young dog, but it is a major operation and would only be done in special cases.

Arthroplasty, or femoral head resection, sounds an horrific option, but many dogs do extremely well and subsequently work as normal. The operation involves removing the femoral head and then allowing a false joint to develop. The hind leg is then attached to the body by a muscular, fibrous joint in the same way as the front leg is attached to the body. The pain is removed because the inflamed bone is not rubbing against more bone. Most dogs do extremely well but, occasionally, the joint remains stiff and painful. Hip replacement is becoming more common and in this procedure a false hip joint is inserted into the dog. The results are improving and so the operation can be worth considering in a large dog. This is a very specialised operation and will only be done by a few orthopaedic surgeons in veterinary hospitals – and it is expensive.

Hip Dysplasia can develop as a result either of direct trauma, or by a trauma which alters the way that the femur articulates with the hip. This can be seen after a fracture of the femur, when the bone does not heal with good alignment. Fractures of the pelvis can also alter the relationship between the femur and pelvis; or damage to the hip itself can do the same, leading to inflammation and bone changes.

HIP DISLOCATION
Hip dislocation can occur because of a rupture of the ligament which holds the femoral head deep in the socket. The dislocation can be simple, or there can be hip fractures which will lead to complications. The dislocated leg usually moves forward and upward, and causes acute lameness. Replacement of the hip back into the socket is a very difficult procedure because of the large muscle mass around the hip, which makes manipulation very hard. Sometimes it is possible to replace the hip under general anaesthetic, but often there is damage to the joint capsule and acetabulum, leading to instability in the joint. This can mean that every time your vet manages to manipulate the hip back into the socket, it flips out again.

There are various surgical procedures that can be tried if the hip will not stay in the socket on its own, but often it is a better option for the dog to have a femoral head resection if there is any damage to the cartilage of the joint, because DJD will follow. If the femoral head is removed, the dog will not have pain in the future. If the

joint is not badly damaged, a false "teres" ligament can be put in, or the hip held in position with a metal rod. After the hip has been relocated, by whichever method, the leg is often strapped up so that the hip is rested for one to two weeks.

FRACTURES
Obviously broken bones will cause lameness. The amount of lameness will depend on which bone is broken and if there is displacement of the two ends of the bone. Fracture of the main long bones due to trauma will cause one hundred per cent lameness. The leg will become swollen and is painful. It is possible to feel crepitus, or a grating sensation, but this will cause pain to the dog. The leg should only be felt with care.

It is usually not practical or beneficial to the dog to try a splint to support the damaged leg. If the skin has been broken you should attempt to protect the wound from being contaminated by covering it with a long piece of clean cloth, if available. If there is a lot of bleeding you should apply pressure at or above the wound, as described in the First Aid chapter, but do not touch the fracture, as that would cause pain. The dog should be taken to a vet as soon as possible so that the leg can be X-rayed and the fracture repaired. If you think your dog will need an X-ray, do not feed or give water before the visit to the surgery, because a general anaesthetic will have to be administered.

Depending on the type and place of the fracture, the bone can be repaired by applying a cast, plaster of Paris, or a splint, but usually the bone will heal better by using bone pins, plates or screws. The long bones have a hard, calcified outer surface and a central medulla filled with bone marrow. The bone pin is placed in the middle of the bone, and the two broken ends are slotted together, with the pin holding them firmly together from the inside. This allows the bones to heal quickly and the dog will soon begin to use the leg again. The pin can be left in place, but may need to be removed once the bone has healed because the dog sometimes becomes lame again after the bone has healed and this is, usually, because the pin has moved a bit, causing pain.

A more complicated form of fixation is by bone plates and screws. These are used when the medullary cavity will not take a pin, or if the fracture is complicated and involves several pieces. The plate is laid across the fracture and the screws placed through the bone. Once the bone is held firm, healing can take place. If the plate needs to be removed this is often harder than putting it there in the first place, because some of the plate can be covered by bone and fibrous tissue, and it is not always easy to find it – let alone remove it!

Fractured toes are quite a common occurrence and can be the result of quite a minor trauma. The affected toe will soon become swollen and is quite painful. If only one toe is fractured it is possible just to strap the toes together, which will allow healing to take place. If all the toes are fractured it is necessary either to pin the toes, or to use a plaster cast or a splint. Most fractures take approximately three weeks to heal, but recovery can take longer because the muscles associated with the fracture will have become weaker and fitness has to be regained before the dog is back to normal.

10 RESPIRATORY PROBLEMS

The respiratory system of the dog must work efficiently if it is to deliver sufficient oxygen to the blood to allow the dog to work properly. A lap dog who has a mild respiratory disease will not suffer any great decrease in ability when walking round the block. But in our gundogs, where we expect prolonged periods of work, often over hard terrain, the slightest decrease in respiratory function will reduce the dog's capabilities. Sub-clinical disease, which does not show any obvious outward signs, is of particular signficance, in that it will not only reduce the dog's stamina but, if the dog is pushed hard, could lead to permanent damage e.g. emphysema following bronchitis.

INFECTIOUS BRONCHITIS (KENNEL COUGH)

Infectious bronchitis can be caused by several agents, but the most common is a bacterium called bordetella bronchiseptica. It causes a dry, persistent cough which usually does not cause the dog much of a problem but is more of a problem to the owner hearing it constantly, often at night! The cough is usually dry and non-productive and is readily controlled by antibiotics. Occasionally the irritation caused by the infection persists and the dog can continue to cough for weeks, despite treatment. If the dog is exercised excessively while experiencing infectious bronchitis, permanent lung damage can result.

Infectious bronchitis is also known as Kennel Cough because it is very commonly found in kennels. This is not the fault of the kennels but, because the infection is very virulent, airborne, and present before the dog coughs, it will spread rapidly through a kennel and the dogs, causing the owner nightmares! There is a nasal vaccine against bordetella which most reputable boarding kennels will require, but it only gives protection for five months, so it is usually administered in early summer to cover the months when the infection is at its greatest. The vaccine is sprayed into the nostrils which can produce problems if the dog is not co-operative. My dread is when a client comes in and says they have just come for kennel cough. If the dog co-operates the vaccine takes 30 seconds to give, but if the dog does not want me to squirt liquid up its nose, and most do not, it can take a lot longer and considerable energy is expended by all!

The incubation period for infectious bronchitis is three to five days. Occasionally other infectious agents can cause kennel cough, but normally bordetella has to be present as well. Infection with the para influenza virus can cause serious complications, with the dog becoming depressed and having a mucopurulent discharge from the nose as well as a cough. Treatment is with antibiotics to prevent secondary infection and usually the dogs will make a complete recovery, but they can be quite poorly for a week and are more prone to other complications. I have seen several dogs with Para Influenza develop swollen painful joints and osteodystrophy. Treatment of this painful condition is with Vitamin C and corticosteroids. Although it is very dramatic and painful, most dogs respond quickly to treatment.

LARYNX

The larynx is the voice box and can close to prevent food or foreign bodies from entering the trachea and lungs. Traumatic injury to the larynx and surrounding soft tissue is not uncommon. Bite wounds from other dogs are the main cause but other trauma such as gunshot wounds, or the overzealous use of the choke chain, can also cause damage. This can result in swelling of the larynx and a narrowing of the lumen, causing respiratory distress. Occasionally a tear in the larynx can allow air to escape and collect in the soft tissues under the skin. This can be felt as a crackling under the skin. Treatment is not usually required but, if the air continues to escape, a lightly applied pressure bandage can be used, making very sure that the windpipe is not compressed, which would cause severe respiratory distress. Any bandage should be checked every half hour.

Injury can cause permanent damage to a nerve in the neck, causing laryngeal paralysis. This causes a collapse of the larynx on one side and this interferes with the free flow of air. Laryngeal oedema will cause a narrowing of the lumen of the larynx and respiratory distress. The most common cause is due to a bee sting and it can be life-threatening if the swelling completely occludes the larynx. If your dog is stung by a bee and if there is any sign of respiratory distress, seek veterinary advice immediately.

TRACHEA

This is the tube which links the larynx to the lungs and it is supported by C-shaped rings of cartilage which hold it open during the changes in air pressure which occur during breathing. Tracheitis is the most common disease of the trachea and is often caused by bordetella bronchiseptica leading to kennel cough. Tracheitis usually produces a dry, non-productive cough.

Bacteria and viruses (distemper and adenovirus) can cause tracheitis but a common cause is continuous barking, which leads to inflammation of the trachea. Inhalation of smoke or noxious gases can also lead to irritation of the lining of the trachea. A parasite, filaroids osleii can cause nodules in the trachea and a persistent cough. Infection is usually seen in dogs under two years of age, and it comes from infected bedding and the larvae penetrating the skin on the feet and migrating to the lungs. Treatment with Fenbendozole is effective. Inhaled foreign bodies can lodge in the trachea and cause coughing. Pebbles, nails and grass awns are common inhaled foreign bodies. Diagnosis of the cause of tracheitis can be confirmed with X-rays, endoscopy and tracheal washes.

PULMONARY OEDEMA

This is a collection of fluid either in the tissue of the lungs (intestinal oedema) or within the air passages (alveolar oedema). It is usually a complication of another disease such as heart failure (left-sided), infection, toxic inhalants or allergy. When fluid fills the alveoli, the animal is in danger of drowning in its own fluid and it can be a real emergency if the condition is acute. The signs of pulmonary oedema can also be chronic. The signs are increased rate of breathing (tachypnoea), increased depth of breathing (dyspnoea) and fluid sounds in the lungs.

Intestinal oedema does not interfere with the flow of air in the alveoli, but increased pulmonary circulation during exercise may lead to the entry of fluid into the alveoli, leading to restlessness and coughing at night. Intestinal oedema is a common presenting sign with chronic heart failure. Acute oedema can be life-threatening and veterinary attention should be sought immediately. Treatment is with diuretics to remove the fluid, bronchodilators, antibiotics and, if need be, oxygen therapy.

LOWER RESPIRATORY DISEASE

The clinical signs of lower respiratory disease include fever, cough, dyspnoea (difficulty breathing) and exercise intolerance. Infections can cause bronchitis, both bacterial and viral. Canine distemper, adenovirus and para influenza are the most common viruses involved, but many other bacteria can also cause problems. Allergic causes of bronchitis are not as common as infection, but they have been found.

Inflammatory bronchitis due to inhalation of smoke, tobacco smoke in particular, can and often does cause chronic bronchitis in dogs. I have seen many a client's dog with chronic bronchitis nearly as bad as the owner's tobacco-induced cough! Chronic coughing can cause damage to the alveoli and a condition known as emphysema. This is permanent damage to the end alveolars; they are broken, allowing air to pass into the lung tissue itself. This causes extra effort to be needed to breathe properly. Treatment of bronchitis is with antibiotics and drugs to dilate the airways to facilitate breathing. Care should be taken not to over-exert the dog, which could lead to emphysema and permanent damage.

PNEUMONIA

Pneumonia is inflammation of the lung tissue itself. It is usually caused by infection. The signs of pneumonia are fever, lethargy,

depression, weight loss, moist, productive cough, and dyspnoea. Due to the infiltration into the lungs, they are less easily inflated and so breathing is shallower and more rapid than normal. Viral, bacterial and occasionally fungal agents can be implicated in pneumonia. Inhalation of food, or small foreign bodies, can cause inhalation pneumonia. This is often caused by puppies being fed too much milk too quickly, and some milk is inhaled. This results in a marked reaction in the lungs and is often fatal. Aspiration pneumonia can also happen following anaesthesia if the dog vomits and has decreased laryngeal reflexes due to the anaesthetic. Treatment of pneumonia is much the same as for bronchitis – antibiotics, anti-inflammatory drugs, bronchodilators and oxygen therapy if the dog is distressed. Pneumonia is a more serious disease than bronchitis but both can have a poor prognosis.

NEOPLASIA

Cancer of the lungs can be primary or secondary. Because of the large blood supply to the lungs it is very common to find secondary tumours in the lungs from tumours elsewhere in the body. Primary cancers can occur but they are not as common as secondary tumours. Signs depend on the position of the tumour, but usually the dog is bright, but coughs or breathes rapidly, has weight loss and often has decreased appetite. Diagnosis is based on X-ray examination and blood analysis. Treatment has to be medical, as surgery is not a realistic option. Drug therapy can give the dog a feel-good factor, prolonging a satisfactory life, but a dog who starts to suffer should be put to sleep immediately.

PLEURAL DISORDERS

The lungs and the chest wall are covered by a thin membrane called the pleura. Normally there is very little gap between the pleural surfaces covering the lungs and the chest wall. Occasionally various fluids or air can collect in the pleural space and this prevents the lungs from expanding properly. Because of the great reserve capacity of the respiratory system, the dog may not appear to be ill for some considerable time, and then the symptoms may appear to be acute. Clinical signs can include a dry cough, increased rate of breathing, shallow breaths and, if infection is present (Pyothorax), fever, anorexia and lethargy.

Hydrothorax, when a thin clear liquid collects in the pleural cavity, can occur with right-sided heart failure or diseases where protein is lost from the body. Pyothorax is when the fluid is thick and often contains a lot of pus. Common causes of Pyothorax can include penetrating wounds to the chest, complications from pneumonia and blood-borne infections. Treatment of any fluid in the chest depends on the cause, but may necessitate draining the chest to improve the dog's breathing. Pyothorax may need several months of antibiotics therapy to prevent recurrence.

Blood can collect in the pleural space (Haemothorax) following trauma or clotting defects caused by eating rat poison. If a major blood vessel is damaged, death follows rapidly. Signs are weakness, rapid poor pulse, pale lips and gums and respiratory distress. If the blood vessel is a minor one within the lungs, the blood loss is usually not severe and the condition will correct itself. Occasionally air can escape from a damaged lung into the pleural cavity. This prevents the lung from expanding because the dog cannot form a vacuum and mechanically expand the lung. Usually the damage is only to one side of the chest, so the other lung can cope and provide enough oxygen for the dog while at rest, but the dog would soon become breathless with any exertion. If the damage is small it will heal over and the escaped air can be reabsorbed or, more often, it is drained mechanically from the chest to allow the collapsed lung to reinflate.

BROKEN RIBS
Broken ribs can follow crushing injuries or gunshot wounds. If the broken ends of the rib damage the lungs, this can allow air to escape out of the chest and collect under the skin. With each breath the dog can suck more air under the skin, and blow up like a balloon. Treatment is to produce increased pressure over the damaged area with a bandage and this stops the air escaping. If air is escaping under the skin, you can feel it like a crackling under the skin. Unless the damage is massive, it will usually heal very well. Broken ribs can be painful: drugs should be given to alleviate this, together with antibiotics to prevent infection in the lungs.

HEART DISEASE
Heart disease is a major cause of respiratory distress. Congenital abnormalities can cause heart disease in young puppies. The most common abnormality is when the duct which allows blood to by-pass the lungs in the unborn puppy fails to close at birth and so the efficiency of the heart at pumping blood through the lungs is decreased. The puppy tends not to grow well and a heart murmur can be detected by stethoscope. Correction is a specialised procedure but can be successful. Other congenital abnormalities which are, as yet, inoperable, include narrowing of the main arteries exiting from the heart, gaps in the muscle wall separating the two halves of the heart and lack of valves within the heart. All these conditions will result in a stunted, weak puppy.

MITRAL VALVE FAILURE
Mitral valve insufficiency is the most common cause of congestive heart failure (CHF) in the dog. The mitral valves should close when the ventricle of the heart beats, preventing blood flowing backwards in the left auricle, or the collecting area for blood from the lungs. When the deficiency on the

valves is only minor, no clinical signs will be seen because the heart has a large reserve capacity and can afford to be a little inefficient. A murmur can be heard with a stethoscope.

Clinical signs are usually seen on middle-aged to older dogs, although the disease can start much earlier, but the heart compensates satisfactorily for several years. As the disease progresses, the lungs start to become slightly waterlogged due to back pressure, and intestinal oedema occurs. This can lead to some exercise intolerance and nocturnal coughing. As fluid backs up in the lungs, it also interferes with the working of the right side of the heart, causing heart enlargement and ascites (fluid build up in the abdomen). The duration and frequency of coughing increases and respiratory distress is soon evident with moderate exercise.

Treatment is aimed at reducing the load on the heart and increasing the output of the heart. By reducing the load, the fluid in the lungs is reduced and so oxygenation of the blood is improved. Vasodilators, diuretics and a low-salt diet are used to reach this goal. There are

A heart examination to detect if this Sussex Spaniel has an abnormal heart beat.   *Photo: Keith Allison.*

commercially available low salt diets but they tend not to be very palatable. Be careful not to give your dog any savoury snacks. One crisp or chip contains a significant amount of salt and can cause more water retention and a deterioration in the condition. With treatment the heart can compensate and cope for considerable periods of time and many dogs lead normal lives for many years. It is worth treating dogs before they become

seriously ill, as this reduces permanent damage to the heart and liver.

TRICUSPID VALVULE INSUFFICIENCY
The tricuspid valve prevents the back flow of blood from the right ventricle into the right auricle which collects blood from the body. Insufficiency of the tricuspid valve causes congestion of the liver, ascites and engorgement of the superficial veins of the

117

body. The dog has a pot belly, exercise intolerance and puffy limbs. Treatment is to reduce the venous engorgement with diuretics, reduce the load and increase the efficiency of the heart. Often mitral and tricuspid valvular insufficiency are found together.

MYOCARDIAL DISEASE

The most common form of disease of the heart muscle is dilated cardiomyopathy. This is usually seen in the large breeds of dogs, from three to eight years of age. Clinical signs are related to right and left sided heart failures, i.e. general debility, weakness, abdominal enlargement, coughing, dyspnoea and fainting. The heart rate is rapid and the heart can be heard over a large area of the chest. On X-ray examination the heart is massively enlarged and on ECG irregular heart beats can be found.

The heart muscle wall is thin and the heart itself is much bigger than normal. The stretched flabby heart cannot contract efficiently, so its output is reduced. Treatment can improve the condition of the circulation but the heart muscle will remain thin and treatment must be continued for life. Dilated Cardiomyopathy is a common cause of sudden death in dogs. Myocardial disease can also take the form of abnormally thickened muscle, and restrictive disease, where the heart cannot fill properly with blood and so heart output and circulation are compromised.

11 INHERITED CONDITIONS

Inherited conditions are passed on from one generation to the next. Their appearance is governed by pairs of genes which are passed on to the offspring by their parents. Gundogs are no more, or less, vulnerable than other breeds. Sometimes the inherited gene is not expressed because it is controlled by a recessive gene and, if the other half of the pair is a dominant gene, the recessive gene will not express itself. If the dog has two recessive genes, the recessive trait will be expressed. With the introduction of DNA testing for genetic defects, it may soon be possible to blood-test parents to find out what hereditary conditions they may pass on to their pups. However, the dog has 39 pairs of chromosomes, compared to 23 pairs in humans, so the mapping of the genes will be much more time-consuming in the dog.

HIP DYSPLASIA

Hip Dysplasia (HD) is a disease found in most breeds of dogs, but is more common in the larger, heavier, fast-growing breeds. It is controlled by complex genetic factors but environmental and nutritional factors are involved as well. Both sexes can be equally affected. Dogs with this problem are born with normal hip joints that subsequently undergo various degrees of change which can lead to lameness or abnormal gait. In severely affected dogs lameness can be seen in the young dog, often with bouts of pain. This will sometimes settle, and then the dog will develop osteo-arthritis in middle to old age. Changes in the hip joint include joint-loosening, flattening of the femoral head, a shallow acetabulum and damage to the cartilage – all leading to secondary arthritis.

If the growing dog is over-exercised or fed an inappropriate diet, HD is more likely to occur. As HD is more often found to be a clinical problem in the heavier, fast-growing gundogs, it is very important that these animals are exercised and fed properly. Too little exercise can lead to the development of HD because the muscles and ligaments surrounding the hip joint will not develop adequately, so the joint will not be held firmly together. At the other extreme, too much exercise will cause excess pressure on the growing joint and is more likely to lead to abnormal development of the hip joint. You must hit a happy medium.

Correct feeding is important. If the dog is allowed to be too heavy and fat, the extra weight carried by the hip joint can allow HD to develop. If the bones are weak because the calcium balance is wrong, this will also allow the development of HD. Dogs which are kept lean and fit are less likely to develop

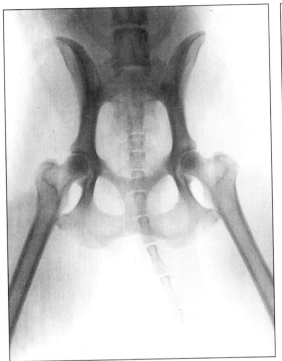

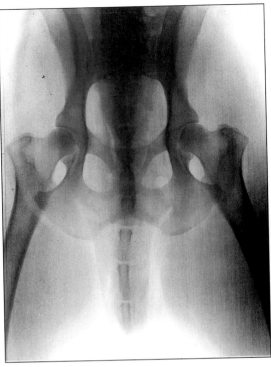

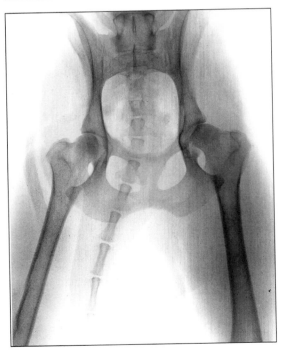

Above left: The centre of the femoral head on the right hip is only just inside the hip joint (score of 2 sublaxation), whereas the left hip is deeper (score of 1). The cranial acetabular edge is not closely fitting to the femoral head (score of 2 on each hip). The overall score of 7 is excellent.

Above: The centre of the femoral head is only just inside the hip joint, and so scores 2 on both sides.

Left: The centre of the femoral head is well outside the hip joint. This will give a high score for sublaxation and norberg angle.

HD than an overweight dog. This does not mean that you should starve your growing pup, but you should monitor the dog's weight and keep it at an acceptable level. Labradors and Golden Retrievers are particularly prone to lameness due to HD. Often their hips on X-ray do not look too bad, but under general anaesthetic it is possible to test the laxity (looseness) of the hip joint and sometimes the femur and femoral head can be pulled one to two centimetres (up to an inch) out of the hip joint. This laxity can cause erosion of the joint surfaces and the development of osteo-arthritis and pain. I feel that joint laxity is as important, if not more important, in the development of lameness due to HD than the shape of the hip joint.

Because the development of HD is partially controlled by genetic factors, the hip status of any breeding dog should be assessed. In the UK the Kennel Club and the British Veterinary Association run a joint scheme in which the hips of dogs over one year of age are scored for HD. The lower the score, the fewer signs of HD are found. When dogs are scored under this scheme they are X-rayed, usually under general anaesthetic, and the registration number of the dog is put on the X-rays which are then assessed by a special panel. The depth, shape and confluence of the femoral head and acetabulum are noted for both hips, and a score given. The maximum possible score is 106, each hip giving a possible total of 53. There are various other schemes to assess hip status in different countries. In the USA there is a new test called the Penn Hip, which assesses the laxity of the joint as well as its shape, which I feel is an improvement on the plain X-ray schemes. In some countries the hips are not scored but graded.

Any dog with a total score of less than 20 is unlikely to have any hip problems. Each breed has an average score and, ideally, you should aim to lower that score, but it is important to remember that hips are not the whole dog, and so the choices of stud dog should not be made solely on the HD score of the dog. This is particularly important when you remember that probably only twenty-five per cent of HD is controlled by the dog's genes. I would happily mate any bitch with a score under 20. I would mate a bitch with a score up to 30, with a little bit more emphasis put on using a partner with producing low scoring hips. If I had a bitch with a higher score, I would still consider breeding, but only if she was otherwise an excellent example of the breed, with good temperament, hunting ability, conformation and no sign of lameness. The choice of a stud dog for such a bitch would be made not only on his own conformation and breed type, but also very much on his hip status, his parents' hip status and that of his offspring.

Hip dysplasia is found in all gundogs but usually will not cause any lameness in the smaller breeds. As I have said, Labradors and Golden Retrievers are possibly the gundog breeds most often seen with hip problems but Sussex Spaniels can have horrendous hip scores and rarely suffer any lameness. This may be due to their shorter legs and charateristically slower pace.

PROGRESSIVE RETINAL ATROPHY
This is a group of conditions which can be split into two forms, generalised and central (CPRA). Both conditions occur due to the degeneration of the light-sensitive retina. They are usually progressive and lead to total blindness. They are not painful or accompanied by any other sign in the dog, but there is no treatment.

Generalised PRA is controlled by an autosomal recessive gene. That is, it has to be carried by both parents to produce the disease in the offspring. Night blindness is the first sign of trouble. The dog can often see straight in front but may have poor peripheral vision e.g. a dummy thrown straight in front of the dog is seen, but not one thrown across the dog. The disease gradually progresses until total blindness occurs. The age at which it can be diagnosed by the use of an ophthalmoscope varies according to the breeds. The Irish Setter can be affected within a few weeks of age and can be totally blind by the age of one year. An Irish Setter who is clear at three years of age is likely to remain so. The Cocker and the English Springer Spaniel are usually only first diagnosed after one year old but the condition can occur up to five years.

In the UK control of the disease has been encouraged by a joint BVA/KC scheme of certification, with temporary certificates used up to the age beyond which PRA is unlikely to develop and then a final certificate is gained. The condition is seen in English Cocker Spaniels, American Cocker Spaniels, English Springer Spaniels, Gordon Setters, and Irish Setters.

In central PRA the central area of the retina is destroyed and so sight is poor in bright light when the pupil is small, so light only falls on the central diseased part of the retina. In dull light the pupil dilates, light can fall on the unaffected edges of the retina and hence sight is improved. Dogs may walk into large, stationary objects directly in front of them but can see a pheasant flying across the sky. The disease tends not to progress to total blindness, as it does with Generalised PRA, unless both conditions occur – as can happen, particularly with English Springer Spaniels. It is believed to be inherited, possibly by a dominant gene, but its mode of inheritance has not been completely discovered. Breeds affected can be Labrador Retrievers, Golden Retrievers, English Springer Spaniels, Pointers and Chesapeake Bay Retrievers.

CATARACTS

Cataracts are opaque lesions in the lens of the eye. They can be partial or complete, unilateral or bilateral, congenital, traumatic or hereditary. Most forms of primary hereditary cataracts are inherited by a simple recessive gene, i.e. both parents must carry the gene for the offspring to show signs. Most are not present at birth but can be seen after the first year of life. Congenital cataracts often have other signs of eye abnormalities e.g. persistent hyaloid arteries, but hereditary cataracts are not accompanied by other lesions.

In most breeds, the age at which a cataract appears and its appearance are characteristic of that breed, and can be used to decide whether or not the cataract is likely to be hereditary. American Cocker Spaniels and Golden Retrievers tend to show the first signs in middle age, that is up to six years of age, and the cataracts are not always symmetrical. The Welsh Springer Spaniel can develop cataracts from two months to three years of age and they are usually bilateral and symmetrical.

The BVA/KC have a scheme in the UK to certify dogs with temporary or final certifiable cataracts as seen in English Cocker Spaniels, American Cocker Spaniels, Large Munsterlanders, Golden Retrievers, Labrador Retrievers, Chesapeake Bay Retrievers, Irish Setters, Pointers and Welsh Springer Spaniels. There is no treament, and control is through breeding from unaffected stock. This can be difficult in the breeds which develop this condition later in life as often they have already been used for reproduction before sgns of the disease appear. The cataract can be removed surgically by a specialist if it is felt that there are no other lesions in the eye.

GLAUCOMA

Glaucoma is an increase in the fluid pressure inside the eyeball. This reduces the health of the retina or sclera, damages the iris and will eventually lead to blindness. The blood vessels on the white part of the eye are often enlarged, red and prominent. The condition is often seen as an acute problem, with pain, but there may be several smaller episodes

Glaucoma in the right eye.
Photo courtesy: Dick Lane.

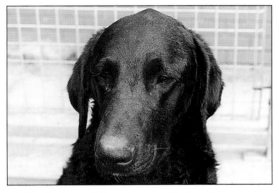

A Curly Coated Retriever suffering from entropion.   *Photo courtesy: Dick Lane.*

A Sussex Spaniel suffering from ectropion.
Photo courtesy: Gillian Averis.

which go unnoticed. Treatment is aimed at reducing the pressure within the eye. This can be surgical or, initially, often with drugs to increase the drainage from the eye or reduce the formation of fluid. Surgical treatment is specialised and would only be undertaken if the case did not respond to drugs. Glaucoma is seen in Welsh Springer Spaniels, American Cocker Spaniels and English Cocker Spaniels. The precise mode of inheritance is not known.

ENTROPION

Entropion is a condition where the eyelids rotate inwards and cause irritation to the eye and excess tear production and pain. The eyelid can be rolled out, showing the edge of the eyelid reappearing from where it was rubbing against the eyeball. Treatment is by surgery and involves removing a wedge of skin to keep the eyelid turned out, and then the dog should have no further problems. Entropion is not a simple hereditary disease. Many genes influence the shape of the eye and can cause entropion. Usually it is the lower lid which is involved, but it can affect the upper lid as well. It is seen in Chesapeake Bay Retrievers, American Cocker Spaniels, English Cocker Spaniels, English Springer Spaniels, German Short-haired Pointers, Golden Retrievers, Irish Setters, Labrador Retrievers, Pointers, Weimaraners and Italian Spinones. Surgical correction should be left as long as possible to allow the head to grow and attain its adult shape. Sometimes the condition will correct itself as the head develops and changes shape. However, if the condition is causing distress to the dog then it should be corrected immediately.

ECTROPION

This is the opposite of entropion i.e. when the eyelids roll outwards. In themselves they do not cause any irritation or pain, but they act as a pocket and collect dirt and debris which will cause irritation to the eye, conjunctivitis and pain. Treatment is surgical and is more complicated than entropion, in that the shape of the eye has to be changed. Often just regular cleaning of the eye is sufficient to relieve any clinical problems. It is seen in Clumber Spaniels, American Cocker Spaniels, English Springer Spaniels, English Cocker Spaniels and Gordon Setters.

DISTICHIASIS

This is a condition where there is a double row of eyelashes. The abnormal row can rub against the surface of the eye, causing irritation, epiphora and pain. It is not known whether this is hereditary or not. If the eyelashes cause a problem they should be removed either by electrolysis, or by cutting out the hair follicles. Surgery should not cause any problem to the dog in the future. Many dogs have some degree of distichiasis without it causing any problem.

EPILEPSY

Epilepsy can be an inherited condition and usually starts to show signs between one to four years of age. Fits can be triggered by many causes, so you should not assume that it is an inherited problem. They can occur through metabolic disturbances (e.g. low blood glucose), trauma, toxins, drugs, tumours, or they have no known cause and are termed idiopathic. A fit is an abnormal electrical discharge in the brain which can cause a variety of signs, depending on its severity. The most mild form is "petit mal" which lasts only for a few seconds and often the dog will just "switch off" and stare into space for a few seconds.

From petit mal you can go to the other extreme where the dog has a classic epileptic fit and will fall over, salivate, paddle the legs, defecate, urinate and lie stiffly. Usually this will last for only a few seconds, but it can feel a long time if you are watching it. On recovery the dog may be disorientated and may be aggressive, so be cautious. The dog will usually get up, be a bit staggery for a short while and will often be hungry and thirsty. During a fit the dog doesn't know what is happening and is not in pain. Try to resist the urge to hold the dog during a fit, because this may further stimulate the dog and can prolong the episode. If your dog has a fit, watch carefully to make sure the dog does not come to any harm, turn down any music and switch off lights, as they can stimulate the dog and maintain the fit. If the dog continues to fit for more than five minutes, call your vet, who may need to anaesthetise your dog to stop the seizures.

If your dog comes round from the fit and appears OK, it is sensible to go to the vet as soon as possible and have the dog checked. With epileptic fits there are usually no clinical abnormalities or any changes seen in any blood samples. It is possible to have scans to try to identify the cause of the fit, but this is expensive and only available at a few specialised research institutions. Treatment is usually successful, but various drugs may have to be tried until a suitable one is found. If your dog is only having an occasional fit, it is best not to give anti-convulsive drugs, as there is no point in keeping your dog sedated permanently, if treatment is only needed every three months. If the interval between the fits decreases, and often it will, then when the fits are occurring at least monthly, treatment should be started.

Most epileptic fits happen after rest. Classically, the dog will have been resting, then stands up, takes two steps and then falls over and goes into a fit. It is unusual for them to happen outside during exercise. Anti-convulsive drugs can cause liver damage, and so bi-annual blood samples are often taken to monitor the effect on the liver. Treatment is usually successful, although sometimes it is not possible to stop a prolonged fit (Status Epilepticus) and euthanasia is the only course of action.

Breeds which have hereditary epilepsy are Brittanys, American Cocker Spaniels, Flat-Coated Retrievers, Irish Setters, Golden

Retrievers, Labrador Retrievers, Pointers, Long-Haired Weimaraners (recessive gene) and Welsh Springer Spaniels.

INGUINAL HERNIA

An inguinal hernia is a soft swelling in the groin. It can be unilateral or bilateral but should be repaired, because loops of bowel, bladder or uterus can become trapped in the hernia and become strangulated, requiring immediate surgery. No dog which has an inguinal hernia should be bred from.

UMBILICAL HERNIA

This is a soft swelling on the middle of the dog's abdomen where the navel should be. I do not feel these are hereditary. I have seen them in purebred and mongrel dogs. The first bitch I had produced many puppies with umbilical hernias in her first litter. In the second litter there were none, because I cut the umbilical cords myself and did not allow the bitch to drag the pups around by their cords. If the hernia is small it is best left alone and, as the abdominal muscles strengthen, they will close the hernia and, occasionally, a small bobble of fat will be caught in the hernia and this will seal it. If the hernia is large, the size of your thumb, it will need surgical correction.

MEGAOESOPHAGUS

This is a condition where the muscles of the oesophagus do not work properly and food is not passed down the oesophagus into the stomach. The oesophageal muscles stretch and the oesophagus becomes a flaccid tube, not a muscular propulsive vessel. Food collects in the oesophagus and causes periodic vomiting. The pup does not thrive because the majority of the food is not passing into the stomach and so is not digested. Most affected puppies appear normal while feeding from the bitch, but start vomiting once they begin to eat solid food. Often the oesophagus billows at the neck, giving an appearance similar to that of a frog. There is no corrective treatment, but some dogs will improve if they are fed a liquid diet and have their front legs raised while eating, to encourage the food to pass through the oesophagus by gravity. If it is possible to tube-feed the pup, then there can often be an improvement and the condition will appear to resolve at four to six months of age. But, as the conditon is hereditary, possibly an autosomal recessive with incomplete penetration, other pups in the same litter may be affected or be carriers and should not be bred from. Diagnosis is made by X-ray examinations using barium to show the size of the oesophagus. A complication often seen is inhalation penumonia and is caused by inhaling vomited food into the lungs. This can be fatal if not treated promptly. This condition is seen in Irish Setters, Weimaraners, English Springer Spaniels, Flat-Coated Retrievers and Labrador Retrievers.

12 THE REPRODUCTIVE MALE

Dogs, like bitches, reach puberty from six months of age but usually they cannot mate a bitch until they are eight to nine months old. Full sexual maturity is reached at 15 to 18 months and a dog can remain fertile throughout his life; there is no canine menopause. However, although a dog can often mate a bitch and produce a litter from nine months of age, it would be unwise to use a young dog on too many occasions because it may affect his future fertility. Once he is a year old he can be used on a regular basis without any detriment.

THE TESTICLES
The testes are oval to round in shape. They sit side by side, with one slightly in front of the other. They are enclosed in the scrotum and, due to their external position, are kept at a temperature just below that of the dog's body. In cold weather the cremaster muscle pulls the testes closer to the body and, conversely, lowers them in warmer weather to help cool them. If the temperature of the testes rises, it can damage the production of sperm and lead to infertility. The testes descend into the scrotum early in life, normally by the sixth week. With some dogs this may not happen until they are six months old, but this is very unusual. The epididymis is the bundle of ducts which exit from the testes carrying the sperm. They form a knot at the caudal end of each testicle. They are quite pronounced in the dog.

PENIS AND PREPUCE
The penis has a long narrow bone (os penis) that reaches from the glans at the tip of the penis to about half-way down. This gives the penis rigidity during penetration of the bitch, as the engorgement of the tissues around the penis, the corpus cavernosum, will occur after the penis enters the bitch's vagina. During the engorgement the diameter and length of the penis increases, and behind the os penis a bulbular swelling grows – the bulbus cavernosus. During copulation the muscles of the bitch's vagina tighten behind the bulbus carvernosus and form a tie so that the male cannot withdraw his penis until the bitch releases her grip. When the dog is finally released, the penis is still engorged with blood and will look large and vascular. This is normal.

THE PROSTATE
The prostate gland is the only accessory sex gland in the dog. It is situated within the abdomen at the front of the pelvis. The urethra, which carries urine and the

ejaculate, passes through the middle of the prostate. After ejaculation the prostate produces a fluid which helps wash the semen into the bitch and up to the cervix and uterus.

PROBLEMS WITH THE MALE

TESTICLES Undescended testicles is an inherited defect and affected dogs should not be bred from. It is known as Cryptorchidism. The problem can be unilateral or bilateral, the testicles can be in the abdomen or in the inguinal (groin) region. If an eight-week old puppy has not got both testicles descended into the scrotum, there is a real risk that they will never drop and this would render the dog unsuitable for show or stud, so do check your pup if he is intended for show and/or for breeding.

Because of the raised temperature in the environment of the retained testicle, the production of sperm is disrupted and that testicle will be infertile. If one testicle is in the scrotum it can still produce normal sperm and can be fertile, but the dog should not be bred from because he is likely to pass on this fault to his offspring. In some breeds e.g. Welsh Springer Spaniels, the testicles can drop as late as six months but this is rare. Castration is the best treatment for these dogs. As well as the hereditary point, from middle age the retained testicle is more likely than a testicle in the scrotum to develop a sertoli cell cancer which, although not life-threatening, will cause alopecia and feminising symptoms.

The testicles can sometimes be encouraged to drop in a young pup by the use of chorionic gonadotrophic hormone injections, but this treatment must only be used if the owner is aware that, if it is successful and the dog is used at stud, he is likely to pass on this fault to future generations and so should not be used at stud.

ORCHITIS This is an infection of one or both testicles. In acute infection the testicle is hot, swollen and painful, and if not treated it can lead to fibrosis of the testicular tissue and ducts, leaving blocked ducts and a smaller nodular testicle. Acute infection will cause infertility due to a rise in the temperature of the testicle. If treated successfully, fertility will return within three to six months, but if the main collecting ducts are blocked by fibrosis the testicle will remain useless. Brucella canis is a common cause of orchitis in America, although it is very rare in the UK. If the infection is in one testicle, and the infection is severe, it may be necessary to remove the infected testicle to reduce the chance of the infection spreading to the other one, and also to reduce the damage done to the normal testicle by the increased heat of the adjacent, infertile testicle.

TUMOURS The most common testicular tumour is the sertoli cell tumour which is fairly common in dogs over seven years of age. Cryptorchid dogs are 14 times more likely to develop sertoli cell tumours, which is why castration of these dogs is advisable. Sertoli cell tumours usually cause feminisation of the dog, with loss of libido, shrinkage of the unaffected testicle and sometimes hair loss. They are usually benign and do not spread to the rest of the body, but they should be removed to stop the feminisation, to ensure they cannot turn cancerous and also because they can grow to such a size as to cause physical problems.

EPIDIDYMITIS Infection or inflammation of the epididymis is not uncommon in the dog. It is often seen with orchitis but can be caused by trauma as well. Epididymitis will produce a low sperm count due to the reduction of the passage of sperm, but also the motility of the sperm will be affected because it is in the epididymis that the sperm acquire their "motors" to allow them to swim up the bitch's reproductive tract.

PENIS AND PREPUCE

TRAUMA OF THE PENIS This is usually caused by bruising or laceration, the latter being accompanied by profuse bleeding. Treatment is with antibiotics, painkillers and tranquilisers as necessary. If the urethra, the duct in the centre of the penis which carries both the urine and the ejaculate, is damaged, it is necessary to place a catheter inside it to keep the orifice open and maintain the flow of urine. If urine cannot be passed due to damage or pain, the pressure in the bladder can increase and cause back pressure into the kidneys, with resulting damage. Most lesions will heal completely with treatment. Fracture of the os penis is possible but rare. Usually it is necessary to operate on any fractures if the broken bones are displaced.

PHIMOSIS, PREPUTIAL ADHESION OR PERSISTENT FRENULAM PHIMOSIS Phimosis is when the preputial opening is too small to allow exposure of the penis. It can be congenital or due to trauma. Surgical correction is usually completely successful and mating can then take place.

PARAPHIMOSIS This is when the penis cannot be retracted. It can be due to phimosis, strangulation (e.g. with a rubber band), infection of the sheath (blanoposthitis), trauma of the penis, masturbation or fracture of the os penis. Treatment depends on the cause. Lubrication with vaseline or a solution such as 'Pevedine' can often be useful, but if the penis is very swollen and oedematous it can be worth applying sugar to the surface, as this draws fluid from the penis by osmosis and this may then allow retraction. Veterinary help should be sought if the penis cannot be retracted one hour after mating. If left exposed, the penis is prone to damage and infection.

After mating the penis will be exposed for a short time. The dog will usually lick the penis to encourage retraction, which usually takes place within five minutes of separation. Make sure the prepuce is completely everted, and no hairs are caught in the preputial orifice, because this can cause severe irritation, for example in English Setters and Flat Coated Retrievers.

Blanoposthitis is usually of no clinical problem to the dog. A yellowy-green discharge is seen at the preputial orifice and, if not profuse, it is best ignored. If the dog is conscious of the discharge, or leaving marks on the carpet, and licking himself profusely, the infection should be treated. Treatment is not always totally successful but should reduce the discharge to an insignificant amount.

PROSTATE

PROSTATIC HYPERTROPHY This occurs frequently in older uncastrated males. It is a symmetrical increase in the size of the gland. Often it does not cause any problems but the increased size of the prostate can cause difficulty in defaecation as it presses against the rectum in the pelvic canal. This can lead to excessive straining to pass faeces which, in its turn, can lead to perineal hernias – a soft swelling at one or both sides of the anus.

A perineal hernia should be surgically repaired because, if left untreated, the bladder or loop of bowel can be pushed into the hernia, causing a potential crisis if the blood supply is interrupted. Correction of perineal hernias should also be accompanied by castration, as this will lead to a decrease in the size of the prostate and hence less straining, and so less chance of the hernia recurring.

Treatment of uncomplicated prostatic hyperplasia is either by castration or, if the animal is not a good candidate for surgery, by administration of female hormones (diethylstilboestrol or medroxyprogesterone acetate) or anti-male hormones (Tardak) which will cause a reduction in the size of the prostate. Treatment must be continued or the hypertrophy will reoccur. Castration is a permanent cure.

PROSTATITIS This can occur at any age but is more common in the mature dog. It can be acute or chronic. In acute disease the prostate is swollen and painful and the dog may well walk with an arched back, have stiff hind legs, pass blood or pus from the penis, is often pyrexic (has a raised temperature) and can be extremely ill.

Abscesses from within the prostate can cause interference with defaecation and urination due to adhesions between the prostate and the rectum. Diagnosis is made by palpation of the swollen irregular painful gland, X-ray examination and bacterial culture of the post-ejaculate which contains prostatic fluid. Treatment is aimed at removing the infection with antibiotics which can penetrate into the prostate (i.e. lipid binding antibiotics) such as Erythromycin, Tribrissein, Chloramphenicol and Enrofloxacin (Baytril). The drugs must be given for a minimum of four weeks and it is advisable to reculture the prostatic fluid before treatment is stopped, but treatment may have to be continued for months. If the dog is not to be used at stud, castration will also improve the condition, but obviously it is not good if you want the dog to sire puppies. Fertility will be reduced with prostatitis but can return after six to twelve months with successful treatment. Only one third of dogs will be cured, so the prognosis is not good.

Chronic prostatitis can follow from a partially-treated acute phase, or if the initial infection was not very large. The dog may not show any signs but may have reduced fertility and sometimes will drip blood when sexually active, e.g. after mating a bitch, or when a bitch is on heat. Often an affected dog will start to mate a bitch but, when penetration occurs, will withdraw, as it becomes painful.

This can happen both with prostatic hypertrophy and chronic prostatitis but, in the latter, bacteria can be cultured from the post-ejaculate. Antibiotic treatment can be beneficial but, if it is not a valuable stud dog involved, it is kinder to have the dog castrated and a course of antibiotics given.

INFERTILITY
Any process which interferes with the production and/or carriage of sperm will render a male infertile. It can be congenital, i.e. the dog was never fertile, or acquired. If a dog mates four bitches and only one – or none – becomes pregnant, his semen should be examined. This involves a collection of the ejaculate. This is best done with an in-heat teaser bitch, and the semen is collected via an artificial vagina. Ideally a bitch of the same breed should be used, as it has been shown that you will get a better collection than if a bitch of a different breed to the dog is used. Also, apparently, the dog can control his sperm quantity if he doesn't think he is really mating the bitch! A vet who is experienced in collection should be used, in order to get a good sample. The ejaculate will be separated into three portions:
1. Pre-ejaculate (clear and watery)
2. sperm-rich fragment (thick and creamy)
3. post-ejaculate (clear and watery).

The semen must be examined immediately to assess motility, concentration and any abnormalities. The colour of the collection is assessed to look for urine, pus or blood. Culture of these fluids can help to pinpoint the source of infection.

A normal ejaculate contains 350 to 450 million sperm per ml, and the volume of sperm depends on the size of the testicles and will range from 0.5 ml up to 4 ml in giant breeds. Most of the gundogs will normally produce 2 ml. The sperm takes 62 days from the start of production to becoming motile and fertile and they pass through the collecting ducts and are stored in the epididymis, the knobbly part on the end of the testicle. If sperm production is interrupted, the dog can still produce fertile sperm for up to two weeks afterwards, due to the sperm stored in the tubules of the testes.

Sperm production can be interrupted by various causes: Heat – a rise in temperature caused by something as simple as kennel cough can cause temporary infertility; Drugs – steroids are a common cause of sperm production failure; Trauma – damage to the testes will cause increased blood supply and hence an increase in temperature and infertility; Toxins: systemic disease, e.g. hypothyroidism, Cushing's disease etc. and malnutrition.

After a temporary interruption to sperm production, it can take three to six months for fertility to return to normal. Giving male hormones will not increase the production of sperm; it can actually hinder production as

excess testosterone shuts down the mechanism that causes spermatogenesis (production of sperm).

It is often a good idea to have a routine blood sample taken from an infertile dog to make sure there is no underlying disease, such as hypothyroidism which may be causing the infertility. Hypothyroidism can be treated with thyroid supplements but, as there is a chance that it is an inherited disease, the future potential problems should be thought through thoroughly before using such a dog at stud.

Vitamin E is now very much in favour in human male infertility and its use in dogs has helped increase fertility in some cases, so it is well worth giving this as a supplement to a dog with low fertility. Sperm production will decrease if the dog's nutrition is not adequate, so, again, make sure the dog is on a top-quality diet.

13 THE WORKING BITCH

The claim that it is "good" for a bitch to have a litter is a fallacy. It will not fulfil her, calm her down or prevent future false pregnancies or uterine infections (pyometra). Bitches will start to have seasons, and hence become capable of having puppies, from six months onwards, but should not be bred from until they are physically mature; around 20 to 24 months is usually recommended for a first litter. At this age the body has just about stopped growing, but there is still some flexibility in the bones of the pelvis, and this makes whelping easier. If you mate your bitch too young, she will still be trying to grow and mature herself at the same time as rearing a litter and it is difficult to do two jobs at once!

If you wait and mate your bitch for the first time when she is over five years, you are more likely to run into problems because it is a little bit like a 40 year-old woman giving birth for the first time – the risks to mother and child are greater, and the same holds for dogs. If the bitch has had a litter when younger, the pelvis will be wide enough to enable her to give birth, and the uterus should be in good condition. You will not have the same problems as if it was her first litter.

UNDERSTANDING SPAYING

If you decide not to mate your bitch, it is a sensible idea to get her spayed at the earliest possible time. Just before her first season is best. Spaying is a major but routine operation and, if done on a young, fit bitch, will hardly be noticed by her. When she is spayed, your vet will remove her ovaries and uterus so she will not come on heat. This is an obvious advantage for both you and her, because the three weeks of her season can be guaranteed to fall in the middle of the shooting season and so she is out of action for this time. You also have to make sure you do not get any unwanted puppies. If you live in a built-up area, walking her from home for exercise, you may soon have a few devoted suitors on 24-hour duty outside your home. The other problem is that if she is in the house, there is always the possibility that someone will let her out without thinking – and nine weeks later you have the cross-bred litter.

Also, for the few weeks before their season, bitches often suffer a form of PMT (pre-menstrual tension) where they are a bit grumpy towards other dogs, moody and distracted from work. Following a season, most bitches have a degree of false pregnancy. Some just develop mammary glands, whereas others become lethargic because they must protect their imaginary unborn puppies, or will produce gallons of milk, or stop eating, or start digging up the garden or the carpet. Some will hide behind the settee, carry squeaky toys around, and be totally miserable. After about two weeks of these severe nesting signs they usually snap out of it and carry on as usual – until the next season!

The hormonal changes involved with each season have an effect on the mammary glands and can cause cancer. Mammary cancer is the biggest cancer killer in dogs. If a bitch never has a season, it is almost impossible for her to develop breast cancer later in life. By stopping her seasons you are reducing the chance that she will develop this potentially fatal condition.

Another serious consequence that can follow several seasons is a condition known as pyometra. With pyometra, the uterus becomes full of pus and toxins, making the bitch very ill. It usually happens during the nine weeks after a season. She will be depressed, thirsty and may have a smelly, cloudy pink discharge. If this condition is not resolved by either spaying or the use of strong drugs, she will die. Surgery in the older bitch is more complicated than if she had been spayed as a puppy, but the drugs used to empty the uterus of the pus cause dramatic side-effects and are only used if surgery is contra-indicated. When I was at university we were told that if a bitch had a litter it would stop her from developing a pyometra, but this is not true. I have seen numerous bitches who have had litters and then developed pyometra when they were older. A litter does not prevent this condition.

There are disadvantages to spaying. As I said earlier, it is a major operation requiring general anaesthetics, but most anaesthetics are pretty safe and it is a routine operation. A small number of bitches can develop urinary incontinence after the operation, but this can normally be treated with tablets and

medicine. The third disadvantage is that a spayed bitch is more likely to put on weight, but that is only because she is eating too much and so her food should be reduced and her weight monitored. Spaying is not a reason for obesity.

I know quite a few people feel that a spayed bitch does not work as well as an entire one. I do not see how this can be the case. An unspayed bitch goes through various stages of her cycle; anoestrus when the female hormones are dormant, pro-oestrus, oestrus and dioestrus when she is preparing for mating and then thinks she is pregnant. During this stage, as I have said, she can have PMT, mood changes and be lethargic. How can this make her a better working bitch? When spayed she is in a permanent anoestrus state and has a more stable and predictable temperament and does not have her mind diverted by hormones!

Weighing up the pros and cons of spaying, it is much more sensible to stop the seasons of a young bitch if you decide not to breed from her. Spaying is preferable to injection or tablets, because with the latter you still have a uterus in situ which can develop pyometra and you have to remember to go back for repeat treatments or she will come on heat.

While talking about heat control by means of drugs, not surgery, I would never advise anyone who desperately wants to breed from a bitch to interrupt her season with any drugs. They can cause infertility and, if you are really wanting to breed from a bitch you can guarantee that she will be the one to become infertile after heat control. Having said that I do not like drugs to interfere with seasons, if I have to use them I would use proligestone (delvosteron, conivan) as I have found this drug produces the least chance of side-effects. If it is not the end of the world if you do not have a litter, and your bitch's seasons fall at the wrong time, it may be worth using some drugs for heat control for a short time. However, if you do not want a litter, get her spayed.

FREQUENCY OF LITTERS

It is unwise to mate a bitch more than once a year. If she has reared a normal-sized litter, she will benefit from a rest to allow her body to recover. If she had a very small litter and was in excellent condition at her next season, and was an excellent mother, and you had people waiting for her puppies, it could be argued that it would be all right to mate her at the next season, but I would then make sure she had a long break before another litter.

The number of litters a bitch should have depends on the condition of the bitch, the quality of the puppies she produces and her mothering ability. Some bitches blossom when pregnant, are easy whelpers and rear good strong puppies. If her puppies then grow on to be a credit to the breed, she should be bred from again. If she is a poor mother, or produces poor puppies, I would strongly advise you to think seriously before allowing her to have another litter, and it would probably be better to have her spayed.

The total number of litters a bitch has must be assessed with each case. If she is in good condition, producing quality puppies with ease, then I can see no reason not to breed from a bitch up to seven years old – but she would have to be producing exceptional puppies to have more than three litters. In the UK the Kennel Club will not register more than six litters from a bitch, or when she is eight years of age.

THE BITCH'S CYCLE

Puberty in bitches occurs from 6 to 24 months; usually sooner in smaller breeds, but this is not always the case. Not every dog has read the book and knows what is expected of her! The cycle can be split into four parts: pro-oestrus, oestrus, dioestrus and anoestrus.

Pro-oestrus is the first stage where the vulva swells over a few days and a bloody discharge is produced. In some bitches the discharge is not always obvious if the bitch is very clean, or if she has a lot of coat e.g. Black Cocker Spaniels. At this stage oestrogen, one of the female hormones, starts to rise in the blood and the cells lining the vagina change from small round cells to square 'cornified' cells. She will be attractive to dogs but will not stand to be mated – or at least, she should not! During pro-oestrus the ovaries, which produce the eggs, come to life and eggs begin to develop and get ready to be released into the fallopian tubes. Pro-oestrus can last for a variable time, but it is usually about ten days.

Oestrus follows on from the pro-oestrus when the body produces a sudden wave of a hormone called luteinizing hormone (LH). At the same time the hormone progesterone starts to rise and, over the next few days, reaches a plateau, which is maintained until whelping, when progesterone suddenly falls, or it gradually tails off in a non-pregnant bitch from about seven to nine weeks. Ovulation of the eggs occurs two days after

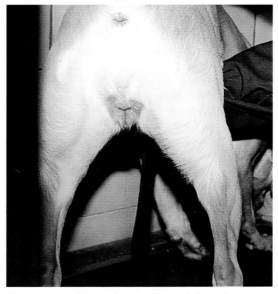

Pro-oestrus: The vulva swells and there is a bloody discharge.   Photo courtesy: Dick Lane.

the start of the rise of progesterone, but uniquely in the dog, the eggs are not fertile for another two days. They then remain viable for three to four days.

The bitch will stand for the dog during oestrus – well, she should! Due to the rise in progesterones, if tickled around the vulva, she will curve her tail to one side, in an arched fashion, and some bitches will push their vulva upwards and stand for the dog to mount. Some bitches are not as obvious when oestrus begins and are often quite aggressive to the attentions of a strange male. Patience can result in the bitch accepting the male, but sometimes her behavioural signs will not coincide with her hormone changes. Her hormones are more important with regard to her fertility than her behavioural signs.

Most text books state that in oestrus the bloody vaginal discharge will change to a straw-coloured discharge, but I would say that at least fifty percent of bitches bleed throughout their cycle, and so the change in the colour of the vaginal discharge is not an accurate indication about when the bitch is ready to be mated. Behavioural oestrus can occur four days before, or up to six days after, the rise in progesterone, but the fertile period will still be four to seven days later than the rise in progesterone.

Eight days after the surge in LH hormone, the square, cornified vaginal cells suddenly change back to the small, round cells and this can be a useful count-back mechanism to see when ovulation actually occurred, if the exact time was not known. The change in the cells marks the start of dioestrus. During this time the hormones are virtually the same whether the bitch is pregnant or not, so hormone levels cannot used to find out if a bitch is pregnant. During dioestrus the bitch will often behave in a matronly manner, her mammary glands will swell slightly and she is likely to put on weight and be a little lethargic. Her appetite will usually increase. If the bitch is not pregnant, she

may progress through dioestrus and into anoestrus without any great change, but a lot of bitches go through some form of false pregnancy. The average length of time of dioestrus (Metoestrus) is 75 days. Some or all of the following signs can be seen during a false pregnancy: abdominal enlargement; uterine engorgement; mammary development plus milk production; nesting behaviour; aggression and anorexia.

Most will have some mammary development, but the degree of behavioural changes can vary. Quite a lot of bitches will hide in suitable nesting areas, behind chairs, under beds and in dark areas. They may dig up the carpet or the garden, take squeaky or cuddly toys and guard them jealously. Some will completely go off their food and have a distracted look – go out for a walk quite happily and run normally but, on returning home, suddenly remember their imaginary pups, dive behind the chair, dig furiously and cuddle up to their toy.

These behavioural signs are due to falling progesterone levels and rising prolactin (a hormone responsible for milk production) and often are best left untreated, because the hormonal drugs used to stop a false pregnancy will only postpone this natural change in hormone levels and the symptoms will often reoccur. Most false pregnancies will last for 14 days. If the bitch has masses of milk it can be worth treating but certainly you should watch that the milk in the glands does not become infected. If this happens, one or more of the glands will become hard, red and painful and veterinary attention should be sought immediately.

Anoestrus is the period of relative hormonal inactivity, when the ovaries of the bitch are 'switched off'. It can vary in length from as little as 15 days up to 265 days, but the average length is 125 days. The interval between one oestrus cycle and the next can range from 4 to 13 months but once the bitch has established a pattern she will always tend to have the same inter-oestrus interval.

The most common is twice a year, with the bitch having her first 'season' at about nine months, but some will not start until well over a year old, with no decrease in fertility.

DELAYED PUBERTY

Officially the first oestrus (season or heat) is related to reaching a specific body weight. Roughly the oestrus will occur two months after reaching 70 per cent of the mature body weight. For example, a Cocker Spaniel's seventy per cent of body weight equals 5 kg and this is reached at 4 months, therefore the first heat occurs at 6 months of age. A Labrador's 70 per cent of body weight equals 25 kg which is reached at 8 months, so the first season occurs two months later, at 10 months. The formula sounds feasible, but it does not always happen exactly to the strict rule, in my experience. I would never be worried about a delayed first season until the bitch is two years old. Some bitches can be as late as this and be quite normal, but once you start to manipulate the cycle with hormones you are likely to cause more harm than good.

A delay in reaching puberty can be caused by several factors: it has been unobserved; delayed maturity; drugs; intersex, or developmental. Kennel management can be at fault if a season is missed. Some bitches are meticulously clean and will not leave any tell-tale drips of blood on their coat, bedding or run, as tends to happen with Gordon Setters. If they have a full coat and are not inspected regularly the season could pass unnoticed in a breed such as the Flatcoated Retriever, especially if the bitch lives on her own and there is no experienced stud dog in the vicinity. If you are suspicious that you may have missed the season, it is possible to do a blood test to see if the bitch has high progesterone levels. If she has, she has been on heat in the last eight weeks.

Some lines within a breed mature slowly physically and so tend to come on heat later, like Chesapeakes. If the bitch has been ill, or on poor nutrition, she will not reach the necessary body weight to stimulate her hormones. A blood test can be done to check that she has no underlying illness which is the cause of the delay.

Several drugs can stop a bitch's reproductive cycle and development. Obviously heat-controlling drugs and male hormones will have a deleterious effect. Corticosteroids given in large or prolonged doses will also suppress oestrus.

Occasionally an apparently normal female with normal female external genitalia has male internal organs, i.e. testicles instead of ovaries and an enlarged clitoris. Obviously if the dog has testicles there will be no oestrus cycle. An enlarged clitoris, like a small penis, can sometimes be seen just inside the lips of the vulva. Occasionally it protrudes outside the vulva and can be damaged, which leads to the bitch licking herself excessively. DNA testing can be carried out to see if the bitch really is an intersex, although often it is obvious and does not need further clarification. Why intersex develops in dogs is not known. It may be hereditary but I would think it is more likely to be due to hormonal influences of a litter mate on the developing foetus. Usually the dog shows no clinical problems and the condition is self-limiting as the dog is sterile.

Other developmental abnormalities of the female reproductive tract in normal females can lead to no signs of the bleeding associated with her being on heat. An imperforate hymen, or no uterus or cervix will not stop a season but will interrupt the flow of blood and so there will be no external bleeding.

A long inter-oestrus interval can be due to genetic reasons but any gap up to one year can be normal – although frustrating if a mating is desired. Stress will increase the time between seasons and sometimes one cycle seems to be missed completely, although it might have been a silent heat, with no real bleeding and hence a missed season (usually not missed by the stud dog!). Stress in the bitch can be caused by a change of environment, bullying in a pack, or trauma. Systemic or debilitating disease will delay a bitch's season, e.g. hypothyroid, disease of the adrenal glands, malnutrition due to diarrhoea, heavy worm infestation and cancer.

Treatment of an abnormally long inter-oestrus period is not very successful but is aimed at stimulating the ovaries. Regimes of treatment with hormones are with FSH (follicle-stimulating hormones), PMSG (pregnant mare serum gonadostrophin) and LH (luteinizing hormone and oestrogens). A full, detailed history should also be taken into account to rule out earlier disease, stress, or other possibilities, and a blood sample taken to check blood levels, cells, biochemistry and hormones. Increasing day length can act as a stimulus for oestrus, as can running with other bitches who are in season.

If the interval between seasons is less than 120 days, i.e. less than 4 months, it can be very difficult for the bitch to become pregnant. The hormonal changes following on so rapidly from one season to the next don't enable the uterus to be in a suitable state to maintain a pregnancy, and infertility often results. If the bitch is a particularly good dog, it may be worth considering preventing the next season with proligestone (covinan, delvosteron) and then mating her at her next season. It should be remembered that there may be a genetic reason for her short cycle and so you could be perpetuating a breeding fault.

PERSISTENT BLEEDING

Persistent vaginal bleeding can be due to failure of ovulation. The most common cause of failure of ovulation is cystic ovaries. Treatment with a progesterone, proligestone, or ovarid can resolve the situation, but there is an increased chance of endometritis (inflammation of the lining of the uterus) and so treatment should not be initiated unless the season has lasted for at least four weeks. Sometimes hypothyroidism can be the cause of lack of ovulation and hence prolonged bleeding. This can be corrected with thyroid replacement but, as hypothyroidism may be hereditary, breeding from affected bitches should be considered carefully.

PREGNANCY DIAGNOSIS

Once you have managed to get your bitch mated you will probably get anxious about whether she is pregnant or not. Because the hormones of the bitch are virtually the same whether she is pregnant or not, blood tests and urine tests are of no use. There is a blood test which you can have done at 28 to 35 days but it can give false positive results and because of this I would not recommend it. The earliest reliable method of PD is to have an ultrasound examination. This can be done from 21 days but – a word of warning – do not rely on the number of foetuses seen on the ultrasound being accurate. I have heard, all too often, the sad tale of owners who had expected a certain number of puppies, so when that number had been born, they then assumed the bitch had finished and so she was left to look after them on her own. Then they found, next morning, that she had produced some more puppies, who were often dead due to lack of supervision or a prolonged labour. However, ultrasound is a very reliable pregnancy diagnosis and causes no harm to the bitch and unborn puppies.

It is possible in slim bitches to feel the foetal sacs from 21 to 28 days when they should feel like a row of golf balls. After 28 days they lose their firm round shape and cannot be felt. It is often difficult to explain to people that you can feel a pregnancy at three and a half weeks but not at six weeks, but this is because of that loss of turgidity of the foetal sac and not due to the lack of skill of your vet. Having said that, I find it very difficult to feel foetal sacs at three to four weeks unless the bitch is very thin, so I do not find that abdominal palpation is a good form of pregnancy diagnosis.

Doppler examination can pick up the heart-beat of the puppies from four and a half weeks up to birth. This is a useful test, as the viability of the pups can be checked. The number of puppies cannot be given by this method of PD but it will not give false positive results. The foetal skeleton can be seen on X-ray from seven weeks onwards and there is no need to worry about X-raying the puppies at this age. At this time all the body organs are present and are unlikely to be damaged by X-ray. I would be reluctant to X-ray a bitch up to five weeks into pregnancy, as this is when the eggs are differentiating into all the many parts which form a puppy, and there is an outside chance that the X-rays could cause an abnormality.

My favourite method of pregnancy diagnosis is to wait until six weeks, when you will get abdominal enlargement and the teats will be prominent and bright pink. If the bitch is just getting fat, her teats will not be bright pink, but also she will be fat all over her body. If she has a little bulge behind her sternum (breast bone) and you can feel her back bone, the chances are she is pregnant.

I often wonder why people need to know if a bitch is pregnant any earlier than six to eight weeks, because she should be treated just as though she was not pregnant up to this time. If you are wondering whether you should enter this show or that trial, I would say do enter, because then you can guarantee she will be pregnant and you will not be able to compete! OK, so you have lost your entry fee, but I feel that is a small price to pay to ensure "Sod's (Murphy's) law" is enforced and she is pregnant! If you don't enter, she won't be pregnant. There is also the danger that if you find she is pregnant at four weeks and you do not enter anything, she will then abort or re-absorb the pups.

Do not treat your bitch any differently after she has been mated until she is six weeks in whelp. Keep working her, feeding her and grooming her as normal. The only precaution you should take is not to give any unnecessary drugs during the first three weeks of pregnancy as *some* may cause defects in the pups.

THE PREGNANT BITCH

The body weight of your bitch should increase by twenty to fifty-five per cent during pregnancy, the majority of the change occurring after six weeks. At six weeks in whelp worm her with fenbendazole (Panacur). This is the only wormer at present which can kill the larvae as they migrate from the bitch to the foetuses. I find that worming the bitch over a period of three days at six weeks in whelp with a full dose of fenbendazole each day is effective. Six weeks is when most of the worm larvae move across from the bitch to the puppies. Worming the bitch prior to mating has no effect on the number of worms affecting the puppies.

If your bitch is on a good quality complete diet there is no need to alter that. If she is not on a suitable diet, gradually change her to one of the premium ranges and the one suitable for pregnancy, usually thirty-three per cent protein and twenty per cent fat. Do not give any supplements. For the first six weeks continue to feed the normal amount of food and exercise her as normal. Pregnancy is a condition, not an illness.

After six weeks start to increase the amount of food so that at whelping she is eating two thirds as much food as before mating. Also watch her weight and adjust accordingly. If her backbone is very prominent, try to increase the amount of food. If you cannot see it, then go steady with any increase. You want her to be fit, not fat, at whelping. As the puppies take up more room in the abdomen, your bitch will not be able to eat the increased volume of food in one or two meals. Start to feed her smaller, more frequent meals so that she can remain comfortable.

Continue to allow her as much exercise as she wants until she whelps. She is likely to adjust her pace to her ability. Many bitches become quite sedentary once mated and will only trot quietly at heel, whereas others exercise as usual right up to the whelping. If your bitch is fat and has poor muscle tone due to lack of exercise, she is going to have a much harder labour than if she were in good condition.

PREGNANCY PROBLEMS

Most bitches have no problems while pregnant but, occasionally, the puppies can be aborted or re-absorbed. If the bitch is unwell with an infection or with toxaemia, she may lose the puppies. Often nothing is seen, because she will lick and clean up any discharge, but the owner may notice that the bitch did look pregnant and then did not continue to bloom. I used to think people had been a bit optimistic in thinking the bitch was pregnant when she was not, but ultrasound has shown that a pregnancy was there, but no pups were born, indicating that they had been re-absorbed or aborted. Infection within the uterus is a common cause of re-absorption. Beta haemolytic streptococcus is a common bacterium responsible for foetal loss which can be isolated by testing a vaginal swab. Other bacteria can also be involved. They need not be in the uterus, but if they cause the bitch to become ill, this may lead to abortion. Severe trauma, or shock can lead to abortion or a re-absorption of all or part of the litter.

Sometimes a litter will be born along with a mummified foetus which may have died due to infection, or due to congenital abnormalities incompatible with life. If you think logically about what happens between the time when the sperm fertilises the egg and a viable normal puppy being born, I find it amazing that any are born "normal", and yet most people are horrified at the thought of even one puppy being born not perfect. It may be that many foetuses do not complete the normal division and specialisation necessary to sustain life and, hence, they die. In a multiparous animal (that is one that has many young in one pregnancy) the loss of the odd abnormal foetus will often not be noticed. Nature is a wonderful organiser and magician – because so many puppies are born quite normally!

INFERTILITY

One of the biggest problems during pregnancy is that the bitch was never pregnant in the first place. Due to the normal change in hormones, whether the bitch is pregnant or not, her body will take on the demeanour of pregnancy, false or not. So why was she not pregnant?

The most common cause is being mated at the wrong time. The most accurate way to determine when to mate a bitch is by having blood samples taken on alternate days from about seven days into the season. The blood test will tell you when there is a surge in progesterone and this is a good guide that ovulation will occur two days later. As the egg is not fertile for another two days, it is best to mate your bitch three to five days after a positive test. Most of the tests tell you to mate her within 48 hours of a positive test which is normally all right because most healthy semen will remain alive for five to seven days inside the bitch. But if the semen is not strong and dies early, you will not obtain a pregnancy.

The next cause of infertility can be that the male is not producing motile sperm. The fact that a dog has sired puppies in the past does not make him permanently fertile. A short period of fever, or trauma to the testicles, can lead to infertility for up to six months. If he has sired puppies immediately before your bitch and afterwards, then he is likely to be innocent, but his fertility should be checked if there is any doubt.

If there are any changes in the lining of the

uterus which will not allow the embryos to implant, this will lead to infertility, endometritis or early pyometra, and is unlikely to support a pregnancy. Inadequate production of progesterone by the ovaries throughout the pregnancy will lead to the loss of the litter. Treatment of a bitch which on previous cycles lost litters with no evidence of infection, can be worth considering, but there is a risk of foetal abnormalities and treatment must be terminated in time to allow birth. Treatment is with progesterone (25 to 50 mg injection 1 to 3 times weekly) or Medroxyprogestorerone acetate 2.5 to 10 mg orally daily. Treatment for lack of luteal function should only be done when all other examinations prove fruitless.

There may be an obstruction to the flow of semen to the eggs – in the cervix, uterus or oviducts. Previous infections can lead to blockage of the oviducts and there is no treatment for this.

14 PRINCIPLES OF BREEDING

Never embark upon breeding from your dog unless you have asked yourself some very serious questions – and answered them correctly. Is it because you want another puppy? Are the dog and the bitch good specimens of the breed, free from hereditary faults and of good temperament? Have they been screened for Hip Dysplasia and eye disease? It would be foolish to breed from a dog if these tests had not been done. Have you the time and facilities to rear a litter properly and find suitable homes for the puppies? What would you do if suitable homes cannot be found at eight weeks of age? Would you be able to run on a litter up to 12 weeks or even six months of age until good homes were found? Can you afford to rear the litter properly? What about the stud fee, which can be nominal or very high, depending on the quality of the dog? There is the feeding of the bitch and the pups to consider. In addition, you must provide extra heat for the puppies, who will also need a suitable whelping box and bedding. Remember also that once the puppies are five weeks old they will be better off in an outside kennel and run – with heating. Then there is always the possibility of vet's fees. There will certainly be wormer needed for the bitch and pups – but suppose she needs a caesarean section if there are problems at whelping? And she might need treatment afterwards for metritis, or mastitis or any other post-whelping problems.

You may lose the litter – so do not bank on the money from the pups paying for your new kitchen or car. Rearing pups correctly will not, and never should be, an easy way to make money. Some bitches make wonderful mothers, whereas others hate it and you may have to hand-rear the pups. Having weighed up the pros and cons, it may be a lot easier to buy in another pup rather than to try to breed your own!

GENETIC CONTROL

A common misconception with breeding purebred dogs is that if you mate a big dog to a small bitch you will get medium-sized dogs. This is not true, you will get some big and some small. Every physical characteristic in a dog is controlled by two genes. These genes are situated in a pair of chromosomes which contain thousands of genes. Basically genes can be usually either dominant (D) or recessive (r) for a particular feature. You can then have three combinations of genes for each feature. DD, Dr and rr. If a dominant gene is present it will mask the recessive gene. If the genes are both recessive, the recessive feature will be expressed. Recessive genes are not inferior to dominant ones but cannot be expressed in the presence of a dominant gene. In the formation of the foetus, the genes of both parents mix together and one half of a pair of genes from each parent join together to form a new pair. Depending on whether they are dominant, or are two recessive genes, a certain character will develop.

CHOOSING A STUD DOG

However, if you have decided that you would like to breed a litter and your bitch fulfils the criteria I have mentioned – her hips are good, her eyes are clear – how do you choose a dog? Do not use the dog down the road because he is of the same breed and it will save any travelling. I will talk here about a bitch owner looking for a suitable stud, because it is highly unlikely that the owner of a proven stud dog would search out a bitch for his dog. The bitch has the pups so the bitch owner chooses the dog. If you got your bitch from reputable breeders, ask them for their advice. If you have a litter, the aim should be to produce stock which is typical of the breed, good workers, good temperament and better than your bitch. You should always be looking to improve the line. There are several methods of breeding to help you achieve this.

OUT-CROSSING

This is when two dogs are mated together and they have no common relations in the pedigree. An advantage of this method is that a characteristic missing from one line can be introduced; but one of the big disadvantages is that, along with the good new characteristic, you are as likely to get

There are many important considerations to weigh up before breeding a litter. Photo: Carol Ann Johnson.

bad ones. From a breeding point of view, the genetic make-up of puppies produced from an outcross is not predictable; and these litters can be very variable in type. Out-crossing is a useful method for breeders if both lines are closely bred and then the gene pools of these two dogs will be restricted, so you will not get quite as much variation in the resulting litter as if the parents are themselves the result of an outcross. Quite a number of successful breeders will do an outcross in every third generation when the rest of the matings involve more closely related animals.

LINE BREEDING

This is when two related animals are mated together e.g. grandparent to grandchild, aunt to nephew, cousins. This system is commonly used by many kennels to concentrate the influence of a particular dog, and it increases the number of genes shared with the dog's relatives and hence similar characteristics. If line breeding is continued for many generations it will produce ever-increasing homozygosity (same genes) and the pups will become more uniform in appearance and behaviour. This is how breeders develop their type. Their type must still fit in to the Breed Standard but it makes a particular kennel's stock easily recognisable. It is paramount to line breed only to an outstanding individual. There is no point concentrating on the qualities of a mediocre dog.

When line breeding, it is important to know the dogs in your pedigree. If your bitch is a wonderful hunter but lacks speed, you would want to line breed to a dog in her pedigree which was a good hunter but also excelled in speed. If you did not know the attributes of the various dogs, you could be line breeding to a dog which was also a bit slow, and then you would be reinforcing this slowness, not improving it.

It is important that you are honest with yourself regarding your bitch. It is no good pretending she is something that she is not, because her genetic make-up will not be deceived and all you will do is not produce the dog you require. This is where it can be useful to ask the advice of the experienced people in the breed. Do not be offended if they point out your bitch's bad points as well as the good; it will allow you try to improve on them. Kennel blindness (not being able to see the faults in your own dogs) is the best way to keep breeding mediocre dogs.

INBREEDING

This is a further development of line breeding, but here the matings are much closer, brother to sister, mother to son, etc. It is used to develop and fix a strong type in a breed, but it can also bring out bad characteristics lurking, previously unseen, in the genes. It will not create monsters if

monsters were not present in the genes originally. The general public are quick to blame inbreeding for all the ailments of purebred dogs, but they are misinformed, because inbreeding cannot produce abnormalities. It only allows them to appear if the genetic make-up of the dogs carries them, but it also allows superior dogs to be produced. It has some advantages and some disadvantages over line breeding.

It is vitally important that inbreeding is only used on good specimens and that their attributes are thoroughly and honestly assessed before a mating takes place. If two dogs are inbred and they both have an undesirable characteristic, it will be even more concentrated in the next generation and will be very hard to eliminate later. Conversely, two exceptional dogs can concentrate their qualities and produce an outstanding litter.

If you inbreed two dogs which carry a recessive undesirable characteristic, but do not physically show it themselves because they have a dominant gene to mask the recessive gene, the resultant litter is likely to produce some puppies with the undesirable characteristic.

B = Beautiful and is dominant over u= Ugly

Bu mated to Bu can produce
  BB – beautiful
  Bu – beautiful
  uB – beautiful
  uu – ugly

It must be appreciated that with inbreeding you may produce a pup which has the undesirable characteristic and is not suitable for show, work or even as a pet, and therefore should be put down.

As a breeder you are responsible for producing sound, healthy dogs, and failures should not be passed on to the public if the dog cannot lead a normal life. These occasional inferior puppies can occur in any type of breeding system, but are more likely to come to the surface with an inbreeding programme, but only if the genes were already present. However, if you are breeding from superior stock, you are more likely to produce superior stock. Most of the inferior puppies are produced when a bitch is bred with little thought about the quality of the stud dog and the pedigree, and a handy dog is used.

The big temptation when mating a bitch is to use the latest Champion and, often, the results are disappointing because, unless the pedigrees tie in and there is some degree of line breeding, you could well be diluting the desired characteristics of both your bitch and the Champion stud. If the Champion is an outcross, he will not tend to reproduce his own characteristic well, because his genes are not concentrated. If the Champion is line bred, he is likely to pass on a concentrated pool of genes and reproduce himself well. Such a sire is called prepotent.

Having decided on the right dog and the approximate time you would like to mate your bitch, you must tell the stud dog owner that you would like to mate your bitch to one of their dogs. The owner might say No! Do not wait until the day before you want to mate your bitch, as the owner of the stud dog might not be available. Either phone at the beginning of the season or, preferably, as soon as you have made your mind up.

MATING AND ITS PROBLEMS
Mating a dog to a bitch should be an easy operation – think of how many unwanted mongrel litters there are. But when you really want a mating to take place you can guarantee you are in for trouble. In theory, when the bitch is ready to be mated she will allow the male to lick her vagina, and she will arch her tail to one side. In practice she will often sit very firmly on her bottom and, if the dog persists, try to bite his head off! It is usual for the bitch to travel to the dog. He is then on home territory and will not be put

off by the smell of other males. The dog will often lick the bitch's ears and nudge her neck and body in a "water-testing" manner to check her reaction. You will often see the stud's jaw chattering when he licks her vulva.

He will then mount her and grip her body with his front legs in front of her thighs and pull himself towards her. Slow thrusting movements continue until the penis penetrates the vulva and then the pelvic thrusting becomes much strong and faster until ejaculation occurs. Now the dog will try and turn, by slipping his front legs to one side of the bitch and then lifting his hind leg on the opposite side across the bitch's back, and will then usually stand back to back with the bitch. This is what is known as the "tie". It can last from one to sixty minutes, but twenty minutes is the average time. You should hold the two dogs around their thighs to prevent any damage to the dogs when they are tied. Do not try and separate them during the tie, because you could damage the dog if you attempt to pull them apart.

Ejaculation happens during the first minute or two after the period of rapid thrusting, and can be confirmed by the rhythmic contraction of the muscles under the tail which will continue throughout the tie as the prostatic fluid is pumped into the bitch to aid the forward journey of the semen. A tie is not necessary for a successful pregnancy. The sperm are released in the ejaculate during the first minutes after the rapid thrusting, but everyone will feel happier if the tie lasts for 15 to 20 minutes.

When the bitch releases the dog he will still have a partial erection, the blood vessels will be very prominent and his penis still quite large. He will often lick himself to encourage the penis to return into the prepuce. Do check that the prepuce is completely everted and no hairs are caught in the sheath, as this would cause severe irritation, particularly in coated breeds such as the Brittany and the Large Munsterlander.

It is not necessary to wash the dog down unless the bitch is known to have a vaginal infection, but I would not recommend that you allow your dog to mate such a bitch because she is unlikely to become pregnant, due to the infection, and your own dog may catch it, with potential infertility for him.

With a young dog it is important to reassure him and protect him from a reluctant bitch. If your dog is going to be used at stud at some time, you must be careful never to tell him off for mounting a bitch when she is not willing. Just ease him off, praise him and restrict him so that he does not keep pestering her. If you drag a young dog off a bitch, and then scold him, he is unlikely to be keen to mate a bitch later on when you want him to.

Some stud owners are happy to allow the dogs to play for a while, which sometimes can give the bitch time to relax, but it is not a good idea to allow them to mate on their own. Encourage the dog to mate the bitch with the close attention of several helpers so that, if help is needed with an unco-operative bitch, you can give assistance without the dog turning into a shrinking violet.

If the dog is still reluctant, put the bitch on a lead and run her around the area in which you are trying to mate them. This will often encourage the male. The best place to mate the bitch depends on your circumstances. It is as well always to mate your dogs in one area and then they will know that when they go into that area they will be mating. A covered quiet area away from other dogs is ideal – a stable or a garage for example.

When the dog is beginning to get aroused, ask the owner to hold the bitch's head, or preferably get a helper. Bitches are often less co-operative with their owner in close proximity. If need be, ask the bitch's owner to leave until the dogs are tied. Do have one person holding the bitch's head firmly, as some will turn round on the dog and try to bite him when he mounts her – so be

prepared. A muzzle is an essential piece of equipment to prevent damage to dog and handlers. Often it is not needed but it should be used if in any doubt. If the bitch is very reluctant to be mated, and shows no sign of tail-arching, check that she is ready by taking a blood test, or by observing her reaction to a bit of tickling around the vulva. Many maiden bitches are overawed by what is happening and will not stand. However, when the dog penetrates the vulva they often stand quietly and do not move, thus showing that they really were ready.

If the bitch tries to sit down you can support her hindquarters but do make sure you are not overpowering the dog. Crouch down at the side of the bitch and give him some breathing room. I can remember trying to mate a particularly difficult bitch with three people holding her, and the poor dog stood back, looking at us and asking for a bit of room for himself.

If the dog is thrusting but not hitting the target, you can try to push the vulva towards the dog. If you try to guide the dog's penis, you are likely to put him off. Try standing a tall bitch downhill for a small dog, and vice versa if the opposite applies. If the bitch is uncomfortable when the dog tries to penetrate her vulva, an experienced handler will try feeling the vagina for any obstruction by putting some vaseline on a finger and gently inserting it into the vagina. The vagina goes upwards a little at first, and then forwards, so one must be very careful. This digital examination should only done by someone with experience – preferably a vet. Once the tie has been achieved the bitch will sometimes be quite excited for a short time, so be ready to hold her firmly to prevent any damage being done to either of them.

Sometimes the dog will not tie with the bitch and falls out immediately after thrusting. If the dog has had the rhythmic pulsation under the tail, he will have ejaculated and the bitch may be pregnant, but I would advise that you put the dogs away, go for a coffee, and then try again. This time, though, hold the two together for as long as possible. Five minutes is enough to ensure that the semen has been deposited in the vagina.

A similar situation happens when the dog seems to be making progress, penetrates the bitch – and then stops and dismounts. This can be for various reasons: pain due to a disc problem, hip dysplasia or prostatitis can be the cause, and these should be checked out. Often there is no particular reason. When the dog penetrates the bitch, try holding him in place with your arm behind him and, if you keep the penis in the vagina, he will soon start thrusting again as the bitch's vaginal muscles clamp around the penis. Thrusting can be encouraged by manually holding the penis behind the "bulb" if the dog is inside the bitch.

After the bitch has released the dog many people will not allow her to urinate immediately. This is misguided. If the dogs have been tied for 20 minutes the semen will be through the cervix and into the uterus, so it cannot fall out. The exit of the bladder is well below where the semen is deposited, so the urine cannot wash out the sperm. However, if you have not had a tie, then I would recommend that you do elevate the bitch's hindquarters and, if need be, gently insert a clean finger into the vagina to mimic the plug-like effect of the penis. As the bitch clamps round your finger you will have more sympathy with the dog in the future!

If the dog tries to mate the bitch and cannot achieve penetration, have the bitch checked for any obstruction. Often bands of tissue can be present in the vagina, probably part of the hymen, and they can be manually broken down; but they do not often cause any problem. Occasionally there may be a tumour inside the vagina which would prevent penetration.

15 THE GUNDOG LITTER

Once you know that your bitch is pregnant with what I hope is that carefully planned litter, you should prepare for the whelping. The first thing you need to acquire is a whelping box and you must decide where she will whelp. I like to have my bitches whelping in the house. I can keep a close eye on them there and notice any problems with the puppies more easily if I am sitting with them drinking coffee and looking at television, whereas in a kennel I might not be so tempted to spend as many hours watching them.

PREPARING FOR THE WHELPING

I like to have a whelping box which allows the bitch to lie stretched out across the short side, with the other side about two foot longer. For my Weimaraners the whelping box is 5ft by 3ft and 12 ins deep. Inside the box you must put a "pig rail". This is either a shelf or a pole placed four inches inside the box and four inches off the ground. This prevents the bitch from squashing any puppies against the side of the box.

Then you need to decide what bedding to use. Newspaper is a cheap form of bedding but it is cold and offers no grip to the puppies. It also can stain the puppies with newsprint, so I would not use it on its own. Some people use hay or straw but I feel that,

with modern bedding material, this is not suitable for your pups and can cause damage to their eyes. Recently I had to have a post-mortem examination done on a two-day old pup that died suddenly. A piece of straw was found in the stomach and it had caused a tear in the oesophagus. What the pup was doing swallowing straw I do not know. I assume it had some milk on it and the pup sucked on it, swallowed it and died. I have always used a synthetic bedding commonly known as vetbed. I find it excellent for the bitch and pups, because it is warm, it offers grip to the pups, and it allows all moisture to drain under the blanket or on to newspaper, but remains dry on top. It is also very easy to wash and dry and will last for a long time. If you buy two pieces, both the size of your whelping box, you can wash one while the other is in use. I find them ideal.

The next thing you need to organise is the source of heat for the puppies. It is *vitally* important that the temperature around the pups should be maintained at 80 F at all times. I use a pig heatlamp suspended about 30 inches above the box and positioned at one end of it. I feel happy if the pups are all sitting at the other end of the box, and then I know they are warm enough. If they feel cold they will move under the lamp. The heat lamp will often make the bitch pant to

One week to go before whelping.   *Photo courtesy: Gillian Averis.*

lose some heat, but I would rather she had to do that than have the puppies becoming chilled and subsequently dying. The Rolls Royce way of heating your puppies is by using electric heating pads in your whelping box, but you must make sure that the pups and mother are protected from the electric cable.

Your bitch will whelp 64 to 66 days after the surge in progesterone or a positive pre-mate test, and not nine weeks after mating. It is the time of ovulation which controls the length of the pregnancy. Having said that, because the bitch will normally only accept the mate when she is fertile, most bitches will whelp nine weeks plus or minus three days after mating. A few days before whelping the puppies seem to drop lower in the abdomen of the bitch and she becomes

more pear-shaped. Her temperature, which is normally 101.5, will drop and fluctuate from 99.5 to 101.5 F for a while before whelping, but this is not an accurate guide about when she will go into labour. Labour can be split into three stages.

FIRST STAGE OF LABOUR
This is when the cervix relaxes and dilates. It can last from one to thirty-six hours. In theory the bitch will not eat and will appear anxious. But do not rely on the idea that if she eats she cannot be in labour. Many bitches will eat despite what their bodies should be telling them. The first sign I often see occurs on the previous day which, in retrospect, is quite clear. The bitch will often sleep for most of that day, as though she is making the most of her chance to sleep while

147

Above: The first stage of labour: the bitch will become more restless as the birth approaches. Photos courtesy: Gillian Averis.

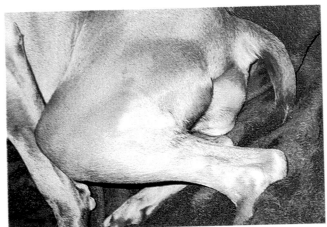

Right: The birth is imminent. Notice the bulge under the tail.

she can. The first sign of the labour proper is often that she will look at her flanks and shiver, she may pant and dig up her bed, your bed or the garden – or all three. Nest digging can occur at any stage in late pregnancy – as the enormous holes in my garden will testify!

Once she has started on the first stage of labour do not leave her on her own at any time, or allow her to go outside unsupervised. Many a pup has been born out in the garden. During this first stage she may

148

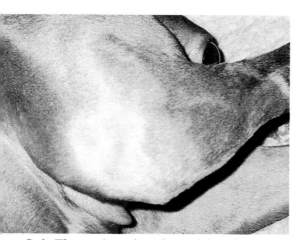 

Left: The pup is at the vulva. Right: The puppy, still encased in the sac, slides out.

Photos courtesy: Gillian Averis.

want to keep relieving herself. I had one bitch who must have walked a marathon in the first stage of labour. She kept asking to go out, walked round the garden, and then dashed back into the house to settle down in her bed – only to want suddenly to go out again. After eight hours of this I decided I would never have a litter again!

If your bitch is not happy about where she is to whelp she can interrupt labour. Do not issue tickets for the show: that is the best way to stop labour – if all the neighbours and friends have come to watch. I keep everyone out of the way until she has started in the second stage of labour, and then I only allow one person she knows well to stand by to help if need be. If your bitch is obviously in the first stage of labour and is not progressing, it is worth taking her on a short bumpy car ride, as this can often get things started.

SECOND STAGE OF LABOUR

This is usually greeted with great relief if your bitch has been making the most of her first stage. It is signalled by abdominal strains, usually an audible grunt. It is the best sound on earth when you have been waiting for positive action for 24 hours.

Once abdominal straining starts you should note the time. A puppy should be produced within two hours. If this doesn't happen, call your vet.

The bitch may stand, sit or walk around during this stage; often she feels the need to defaecate or urinate, so go outside with her – but do take a torch at night, to make sure she does not produce a pup unobserved in the garden! At this stage I try to encourage the bitch to whelp in the whelping box but, if she wants to go elsewhere, I will let her have the first pup where she wants to. One of my bitches was determined to whelp on my bed, so in the end I gave in and allowed her on to it, whereupon she rapidly produced her first pup. After a few minutes I then picked the pup up, and the bitch followed us down to the whelping box. Once she was happily installed, I quickly nipped upstairs, stripped the bed and left the sheets to soak. Once a bitch has started whelping properly she will usually continue quite happily in the box.

At a variable time after abdominal straining begins, one of the membranes surrounding a puppy, the allantochorion, will tear, releasing some "water". The bitch will lick this and clean herself quite obsessively. As the puppy in its own sac starts to pass through the cervix, abdominal contractions will increase, the bitch will arch her back, and her tail will be raised away from the vulva. Soon a large swelling will be seen under the anus and, shortly after this, a bluey-grey sac will push through the vulva opening. This is the amnion. A few more strains will push the pup's head out of the vulva and allow the puppy to be born. Most bitches will cry with the delivery of the first puppy. Be careful that she does not bite this thing that is causing her so much pain. I will help her deliver the first puppy if she is struggling, by gripping the pup behind the head and pulling it gently downwards and between the bitch's hind legs. It is advisable to have someone around to hold the bitch's head to prevent anyone from being bitten. Once she has had her first pup, the rest are usually passed without any more "Oscar" nomination performances, but there are always exceptions.

If the puppy is still covered by the amnion, the sac, I always break it with my fingers and squeeze any fluid away from the puppy's nose. Squeeze the head between your fingers from the eye towards the nose, which will make the puppy cry and breathe. I usually tear the umbilical cord unless the bitch looks as though she knows what she is doing. Usually the bitch is too busy licking up the fluid to remember to clean the pup and chew the cord through. *Never* use scissors. Hold the cord firmly with one hand nearest the puppy and, with the thumb and fore finger of the other hand, fray and tear the cord about two inches away from the pup. Encourage the bitch to eat the placenta as this will encourage further uterine contractions.

STIMULATING BREATHING
A puppy who is not breathing well should be picked up and rubbed firmly with a towel. If this does not stimulate breathing, hold the puppy in the palm of your hand with your finger over the neck and, holding firmly, move your arm down sharply between your legs. This will force fluid out of the lungs, and also the pup's diaphragm will massage the heart and encourage respiration and cardiac output. Do hold the pup firmly. On one occasion when I was doing a caesarean section on a Weimaraner, the owner was present and watched the nurses reviving a pup in this way. He was keen to help and so I said he could hold a pup. I meant him to take one that was breathing okay, but no, he grabbed the next one that was delivered and, having watched the nurse in action, shook the puppy between his legs. Unfortunately it slipped from his hand, flew between his legs and hit the radiator behind him. It certainly made the pup cry! Subsequently that puppy did very well – but I was glad it was the owner that had let go and not the nurse!

You can rub the puppy quite vigorously with a towel to encourage breathing. Most people are too gentle and ineffective when doing this. Puppies are tough little characters and if they are not breathing well, they can be rubbed quite energetically, particularly around the anus, to encourage respiration. When the puppy is born the bitch will often ignore the pup and be far more interested in cleaning the bed and herself and eating the afterbirth. This is when you need to be vigilant and give the pup a good rub if breathing appears slow to start.

BIRTH POSITIONS AND MALPRESENTATIONS
Normally fifty per cent of puppies are born head first (anterior presentation) and fifty per cent hind legs first (posterior presentation). It is best for the bitch if the first puppy comes head first, as the size of the head provides more stimulus for contraction than the rear quarters, and hence a speedier birth. In anterior presentation, the head and two front legs are presented into the birth canal, with the pup in a diving position.

Breech presentation is abnormal and often prevents delivery. Breech is when only the tail is presented and the hind legs are pulled forward. This increases the diameter of the pup, causing great problems for the bitch. Similarly, if the pup is presented with a front leg back, it is extremely difficult for that pup to be born. If the head is bent to one side or the other and only the front legs are in the pelvis, that pup cannot be delivered.

If the bitch has not produced a puppy two hours after the start of straining, call the vet. A quick walk in the garden can sometimes help either to wake up a tired bitch, or help reposition a puppy, but if the two hours is up it is time for the vet. Do not be scared to telephone your vet in the middle of the night. The call will not be welcomed with delight and jubilation, but I would rather be disturbed then and deliver a live puppy than be saved from a night call, only to do a caesarean the next morning and produce dead puppies. As I climb out of bed I want to resign from being a veterinary surgeon, but when I deliver that live little pup, I know I'm doing what I really want to do.

As stated earlier, the pup is normally born in a diving position or posteriorly, with both hind legs and the tail coming first. If your bitch is straining and nothing appears, you can gently have a feel and see what is happening. If you can feel a head and two feet, or a tail and two feet, just give the bitch a little more time, but if you are unsure, telephone your vet. The two-hour rule should be observed. If she is straining for two hours and nothing appears, telephone your vet.

Once you see the bulge under your bitch's tail, a puppy should be produced quite quickly. If your bitch is having trouble, try to help her by getting your fingers behind the pup's head or in front of the hips. You may need to ease the lips of the vulva up and over the pup's head. A little washing-up liquid can help the head slip out. If you can see the puppy, but the bitch cannot pass it, do try to assist once the pup can be seen at the vulva. The umbilical cord is likely to be compressed, so preventing oxygen and blood from getting to the puppy, so you must get the pup out as quickly as possible. Hold the pup as high up as possible and pull downward and between the bitch's legs, in time with the contractions. If you are not sure what to do, phone your vet immediately who will talk you through it, or see you immediately at the surgery.

Correction of malpresentation is extremely difficult because most obstructions occur at the brim of the pelvis and this is outside the reach of a finger. There are whelping aids, forceps, but it is all too easy to rip the uterus wall as well as the puppy, with severe risk of damage, so I would never allow them to be used on a bitch under my care.

If you are unlucky the bitch will rest for up to two hours between straining for each pup which can make whelping a very protracted event. Usually a bitch will rest for 20 minutes between pups but, if you are lucky, it might only be ten minutes. Try to encourage the newborn pups to feed from the bitch, as this will encourage the production of oxytocin, which increases milk production but, more important, it causes uterine contraction.

When the bitch has finished whelping she will often sleep and look more relaxed. Well, this is what the books say, but I have seen bitches who will feed or sleep between puppies. If I think the bitch has finished, I will leave her for two hours after the birth of the last puppy and then I will take her outside to relieve herself. I will then do a gentle examination to see if I can feel any puppies in the abdomen, but this is not easy to do. The bitch will often pass urine while outside and this movement will often start any remaining puppies moving down the uterus, engaging in the cervix and starting the bitch contracting again. If you are not sure whether she has finished, phone your vet.

If your bitch needs veterinary attention it is likely your vet will ask you to go to the surgery. Many people would prefer the vet to come to the house to see the bitch, but there are several reasons why your bitch will receive better treatment at the surgery. The most obvious is that all the equipment your vet might need is there. If a puppy is stuck, it will be quicker to perform a caesarean if you are already at the surgery than if you all have to pile into cars and then travel there. Your vet will be able to examine the bitch more easily at the surgery, and she will be less distressed because the last thing she wants is for a stranger to come into her whelping area at home. Finally, the car journey will often get things going, and many a puppy is born in the back of the car travelling to the surgery!

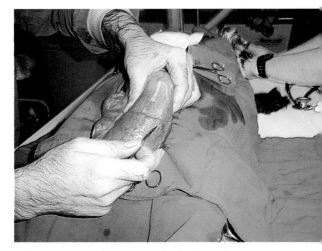

The uterus is pulled out of the body and is about to be incised.

CAESAREAN SECTIONS

If the puppy cannot be manipulated digitally, the only other option is to do a caesarean section. This is a major operation but is now much safer for the bitch and the puppies with modern anaesthetics and techniques. The problem with a caesarean is that the bitch needs to be under anaesthetic, but not the puppies! Modern anaesthetics allow vets to use a short-acting injected anaesthetic and then maintain the anaesthesia with a gas. This means that by the time the pups are delivered, the injectable anaesthetic has worn off, and the gaseous anaesthetic will soon be breathed out by the pups and so they will wake up and breath normally, but the bitch will stay under the gaseous anaesthesia.

As soon as the operation is finished, the gas is turned off and the bitch will wake up. She may be a little groggy for a while, but will soon be on her feet and nursing the pups. Be careful when you introduce the bitch to the puppies, because she may not recognise them as hers and may be aggressive towards them. Once she has cleaned them and fed them she will be fine.

If your bitch has not gone into labour, and

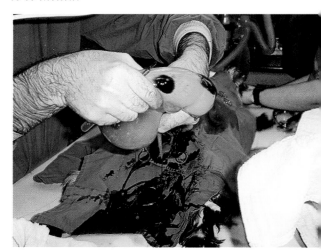

The puppy is still in the foetal sac, but has been removed from the uterus.
Photos courtesy: Gillian Averis.

has to have a caesarean, she will not have any instinctive mothering behaviour. You may have to make her lie down and feed her pups. Once her milk starts to pass through the pups she is likely to realise that they are hers and mother them. If the pups are weak and cannot suck, try to keep her milk flowing by manually expressing the milk so that when the pups pick up, the bitch will still have some milk.

Most veterinary surgeons perform a caesarean through the midline. This will not cause any problems with the milk supply, but it is important to keep the wound clean and dry. As the mammary glands hang down, the wound can become warm and moist, but an advantage is that the bitch tends not to lick it.

DYSTOCIA (Interruption in birth)
Primary dystocia is when the bitch never starts in labour. It commonly occurs if the bitch is carrying only one puppy. The stimulus to initiate whelping comes from the puppies, but a single pup will often not produce enough hormones to cause the bitch to start whelping. If the whelping date comes and goes with no action and your bitch is not very large, your vet will suggest an X-ray to see how many pups are present. If there is only one puppy it would be advisable to have a caesarean section performed, otherwise you will run the risk of the puppy dying. Another cause of primary inertia is when the uterus is extremely full and the muscle fibres are stretched so much that they cannot contract, so there will be no abdominal contractions and the only treatment is to perform a caesarean.

Secondary inertia can be caused by having too many viewers present, as some bitches do not want the world and its auntie watching her private affair. When your bitch is whelping I recommend you sit quietly in the corner, watching the television or reading a book, and keeping a sneaky eye on your bitch. You are then there to help if needed, without being overpowering.

An obstruction in the birth canal will obviously prevent delivery of the pups. An abnormally small pelvis, or one that has been narrowed due to pelvic fracture, will need a caesarean section. If the bitch was born with a small pelvis you should think very carefully before mating her, because you are going to perpetuate this inability to whelp naturally. It is unusual for there to be any obstruction in the vagina and vulva because, if the dog was able to mate the bitch and his penis could enter the vagina, there should be room for the puppies to be born. The uterus can twist, which will prevent birth and, if the bitch has an inguinal hernia, a uterine loop can fall into it and prevent expulsion of the foetus. Both these conditions are very rare but they are potentially fatal.

THIRD STAGE OF LABOUR
This stage is when the placenta or afterbirth is passed. In theory one is produced after each puppy but sometimes a puppy will be delivered from the opposite horn of the uterus before the first placenta is passed. Frequently the passage of the placenta is not noticed, as it is often cleaned up by the bitch before you have a chance to see it. I defy anyone to know exactly how many placentas have been passed! The placenta is an oval greeny-black tissue, a cross between liver and a sponge. If one is retained, it will usually be passed during the following 24 hours without any ill effects. The discharge during whelping can be dark green. This is because the blood pigments in the placenta are green and will discolour the uterine discharge.

Many people like a "cleaning out" injection once whelping has finished. I do not routinely do this as it is painful when given, and because it causes uterine contraction and abdominal pain and I feel that the bitch has gone through quite enough without inflicting unnecessary discomfort on her. However, if there is any doubt that she has finished whelping, I would give an injection of oxytocin as a precaution.

The discharge from the bitch, post-whelping, can stay greeny black for several days, but some bitches will pass blood during this period. As long as the bitch is eating and drinking and the discharge is not smelly, there is no need to have antibiotics.

153

Some bitches will continue to have a black-coloured discharge for up to six weeks after whelping. This can be normal. If the discharge is like rhubarb and custard, veterinary attention should be sought as your bitch might have metritis, a potentially fatal condition. She will be unwell, with a raised temperature, and there is a strong risk that she will lose her milk and you will have to hand-rear the puppies. Prompt attention, treatment with antibiotics and fluid therapy if needed will usually lead to a quick recovery.

Occasionally a bitch will continue to haemorrhage after whelping. This can be because the uterus does not start to shrink and the placental areas in the uterus remain vascular and bleed. If this persists over several days the bitch can become anaemic. Treatment is given to encourage the uterus to contract and, if needed, blood transfusions can be administered. It is not known why this can happen, but usually there is no problem at subsequent whelpings.

POST WHELPING

Most bitches are devoted to their puppies and spend the first few days post whelping lying with their pups, cleaning and feeding them. Newborn puppies cannot defaecate and urinate on their own and need stimulation from the bitch to perform these vital functions. If the bitch does not clean her puppies, manually stimulate them by wiping some damp cotton wool, or cotton, across the vagina or penis and rectum to stimulate the passing of urine or faeces. The first faeces that the puppy passes is the meconium. It is often dark and shiny and, from the expression on the bitch's face, does not taste all that good. Once the bitch's milk starts passing through the puppy, the faeces turn yellow and are seed-like in appearance.

The puppies will normally feed every two hours. To start with you may need to show them where the teats are, and I find it

beneficial to express some milk from the gland onto the teat, which can encourage the puppy to suck. If your puppies are having trouble suckling, check that they do not have cleft palates. A cleft palate is a gap in the centre of the hard palate, or roof of the mouth. The gap prevents the puppy from producing a good suck and milk will come down the nose. A puppy who has a cleft palate is best put to sleep immediately. Cleft palates are seen in several gundog breeds including Cocker Spaniels.

Occasionally the bitch is reluctant to feed her puppies. If this happens it may be necessary to be firm and encourage her to lie down and feed her litter. If need be, physically hold her down and allow the puppies to suckle. Once the milk from the pup comes through, and the bitch cleans them up, she will normally feed them without any help from you. Be careful that she cannot bite them if she is very reluctant to mother them. Normally once the puppies are feeding she will accept them, but this is not always the case, so watch her carefully. Some bitches like to pick their puppies up and carry them around. Although this is normal mothering behaviour, it is not to be encouraged because if she holds on too firmly, she can damage the puppy. Also, if she takes the pups out of the whelping box they can become chilled and more susceptible to infection.

Often a bitch is not concerned about eating and drinking right after whelping, but is more conerned about her puppies, cleaning, counting and feeding them. It is advisable to put food into the whelping box with her or, if need be, hand-feed her until she is eating well. Similarly, put a bowl of water into the box with her, but do not leave it in with her in case a puppy climbs into it and drowns. Immediately after whelping, your bitch does not need vast quantities of food. She is not producing much milk in the first few days and she can manage on a small amount of food. If she is reluctant to feed,

A contented litter, with all the puppies feeding.   *Photo courtesy: Gillian Averis.*

try some fresh chicken or fish. Give her some diluted milk and water if she is not eating well. It will give her energy, and liquid is important to her in the first few days.

Most bitches are quite relaxed and will lie quietly with their puppies. It may be necessary to put her on the lead to get her to relieve herself. While she is out of the way it is a good time to change the bedding in the whelping box – but be quick, because she will not stay out for long. I usually change the vet bed two days after whelping and then not again for one week. If you change the bedding too frequently you will possibly upset the bitch, because you will keep changing the smell of the whelping box from that of puppies to that of detergent. Also, if you keep the box too clean and sterile, the puppies' immune system is never challenged and can become lazy, leading to infections later in puppyhood. By this I am not saying it is OK to let the puppies be dirty, but you must hit the happy balance. Once the puppies are urinating on their own, it is

necessary to change the bedding daily, or they will start to smell. The bitch will clear up the faeces of the pups for the first three weeks, and often until they go to their new homes.

Two to three days after the pups are born you may find that the tranquillity and peace of the whelping box is disturbed. Your bitch may suddenly decide to dig the bedding up, bite the edge of the whelping box and generally look unhappy. She may pick up her pups and move them around the room. This is usually due to abdominal pain caused by the contraction and involution of the uterus. It usually lasts a couple of days and then she will become settled again. Occasionally, if she is very restless, anxious and panting, it is worth having a calcium injection as, if she is getting low in calcium, this can affect her nervous system and produce anxiety.

The puppies will lose an ounce or two after birth but will then grow rapidly, usually doubling their birth weight by the end of the first week. When the puppies are born,

If a litter is orphaned, try to find a foster mother. This Hungarian Vizsla is rearing her two puppies along with 10 Weimaraner puppies. Photo courtesy: Gillina Averis.

their eyes and ears are closed. Over the next few days the ear canal starts to develop and becomes functional by ten days. At around this time the eyes will start to open. Do not force them apart as this could cause permanent damage. Occasionally some pus collects behind the eyelids causing a swelling over the eye. Normally this will not cause a problem and bathing the eyes with cold tea will encourage the pus to discharge. If the puppy seem distressed, or the eye is red, get some antibiotic treatment from your vet. When the eyes are open the puppy still cannot see properly – the eyesight does not become developed until the puppy is about three weeks old.

ECLAMPSIA (MILK FEVER)

This is caused by a decrease in the calcium circulating in the blood. Symptoms can occur at whelping but are more usual during lactation. It is more common in the smaller, excitable breeds – Cockers, Brittanys and Welsh Springers. The symptoms start as restlessness, panting and nervousness,

progressing to ataxia, trembling, muscular spasms and seizures. If treatment is not given, the bitch will die. The progression of the condition is rapid and death can occur within eight hours of the first signs. Treatment is with intravenous injections of calcium which produce a rapid resolution of the symptoms. If the bitch is lactating it may be necessary to hand-rear the puppies to prevent a recurrence.

The calcium in the blood is maintained by taking calcium from the food or from the bones. In the lactating bitch, calcium is lost mainly in the production of milk. However, if you give your bitch extra calcium before whelping you are increasing the chances that she will develop milk fever. This is because as long as you are giving calcium, the body's mechanism which frees calcium from the bones is not needed, and so it becomes lazy. When she whelps, often she does not eat and so does not have your calcium supplement, but the body is not geared up to release calcium from the bones and so there can be a fall in blood calcium, leading to symptoms and possibly death. The maximum demand for calcium is at the time of peak lactation – two to three weeks after whelping, and this can be a common time for milk fever. If a bitch has had milk fever previously, it is worth giving her calcium supplement after whelping, but never give it before.

AGALACTIA

This is a lack of milk, which can occur occasionally. Usually as the puppies suck, as long as there is some mammary development, the milk will start to flow. Often at whelping the bitch's mammary glands are not well developed, but they soon enlarge with the stimulus of the puppies. Ingestion of the placenta will encourage milk production and because of this should be encouraged. Injections of oxytocin can cause a temporary flow of milk if the mammary glands are developed and usually this will get the pups sucking which will maintain the milk flow. If the bitch has no milk and the pups are restless, they should be supplemented.

FEEDING THE BITCH

During lactation the nutritional requirements of a bitch demand that she is fed a top-quality balanced diet. The extra energy needed depends on the number of pups in the litter and their age. The maximum demand put on the bitch is at around two to three weeks. If a bitch has six puppies aged three weeks, she will need to produce approximately four pints of milk a day. In order to do this and maintain her own weight, she will need to eat four times her normal intake of calories. To reduce the chance of milk fever, a complete food with the correct rates of calcium:phosphorus should be fed. Small frequent meals are more likely to provide the amount of energy that your bitch needs. I tend to leave a bowl of food at the side of the whelping box to allow the nursing mother to "graze" and take her energy as she needs it. If your bitch is supporting a large litter, or is not eating well, you can start to wean the pups at two weeks to try and lessen the drain on the bitch.

ARTIFICIAL FEEDING OF THE PUPS

If the bitch has no milk, or an insufficient supply, you must supplement the puppies. You can make up your own recipe by using milk (many experts are against the use of cow's milk), cream, eggs and bonemeal, but a much better way is to use one of the excellent commercially prepared replacement milks. You can get special feeders with a teat on them, but I find the best method is to let the puppy suck your finger and then gently dribble milk down the side of the mouth with a syringe. Do be careful to take your time when feeding puppies, because it is all too easy to give too much milk and the pup then inhales some of it into the lungs. This can lead to inhalation pneumonia and death. Because of this real danger, you should only

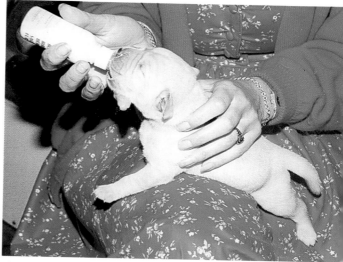

Supplementary feeds can be given with a bottle or using a syringe.

Photo: Carol Ann Johnson.

supplement the puppies if the bitch really is not producing enough milk. With a large litter, it is often better just to keep putting the smallest puppies on a teat to give them a helping hand rather than risk an upset stomach or pneumonia. To start with, a new-born puppy will take 5 to 10 ml every two hours. This can be increased up to 100 ml by two weeks of age. Hand-reared puppies tend not to gain weight at the same rate as naturally suckled pups, but they will catch up once they are on solid foods.

WEANING THE PUPPIES

I use a complete premium puppy food. I put it in hot water and allow it to soak until it forms a porridge. It is then fed warm. The first feed is usually devoured with great enthusiasm, but then the pups lie around shivering with obvious tummy ache. The next meal is usually left without much interest, but over the next few days the pups tend to get the idea. I start on two meals a day, taking the bitch out for ten minutes to give the pups a chance to have all they want, and then allow the bitch to clean up.

Weaning can be a messy business, but there is no lack of enthusiasm once the puppies get the idea.
Photo: Amanda Bulbeck.

By the time the puppies are four to five weeks old, feeding from the dam should be restricted to two to three times a day.
Photo: Amanda Bulbeck.

Gradually over the first week of feeding I increase the number of feeds to four. It is not necessary to give milk if you use a complete puppy food. While the bitch is feeding the pups I do not put any water in with them. By the time they are four to five weeks I will give them water and start to discourage the bitch from feeding them, only allowing her in with them two to three times a day.

As the pups grow I decrease the sloppiness of the food until by the time the puppies are seven weeks old, they are eating the food dry. When the pups go to their new homes, I give the owner a bag of food to continue the same diet for a few days. The pup goes through enough changes when going to a new home, so if the food stays the same there is less likelihood of an upset stomach.

WORMING

You should worm your pups and their mother at three weeks post partum. I use Fenbendazole as a liquid for the pups as it is very effective but gentle on the stomach. The bitch can have the granules. It is probably advisable to worm them for three consecutive days as this gives better results than a single dose. Worming should then be repeated at three-weekly intervals until the puppies go to their new homes.

PROBLEMS WITH NEWBORN PUPPIES

One of the major causes of death in young puppies is so-called "fading puppy syndrome". The puppies are born apparently normal but lose their bloom and die within the first few days. One pup, or the whole litter can die, and it is a heart-breaking experience for both bitch and owner. Once they start to fade, it is virtually impossible to save them. A single cause of FPS has not been found. I am sure there are many reasons for it, but a major initiating factor is the pups becoming chilled. Newborn pups cannot shiver to maintain the body temperature, so it is important that their surroundings are kept at 20C to 30C for the first two weeks. Several viruses and bacteria have been found in puppies which have died from FPS. Canine herpes virus, adeno and parvo virus have been found, and a common

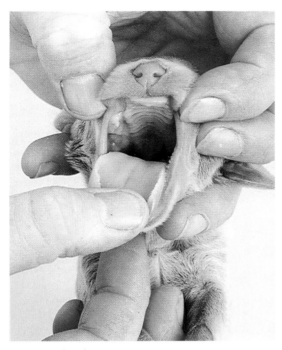

A normal palate.

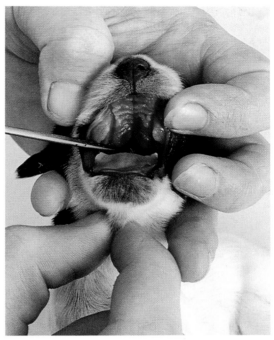

A cleft palate. A puppy with this condition cannot feed properly and will not thrive.
Photos: Keith Allison.

bacterial pathogen is beta-haemolytic streptococci. The pups should have bright pink feet (unless pigmented) and gums; they should be warm to touch and the skin should be loose. If one pup is away from the others, pick it up and put it next to the teats. If you feel one is a bit slow, smear some honey inside the mouth, and if this does not produce a rapid improvement, take the pup to the vet. Quick action can save a puppy. Congenital abnormalities can cause death if the defect is life-threatening. When you consider all the development that has to occur in the embryo it is, as I have said, amazing that so many puppies are born with no defect.

Infection can enter the pup from the umbilicus. If you have to break the cord for the bitch, I repeat, do not use sharp scissors, as these will leave the umbilical vessel open and allow infection to tract up into the pups. If you use your fingers to tear the cord, this will seal the ends and reduce the chances of infection getting to the pup. Infection from the umbilicus can lead to septicaemia, with possible fatal consequences.

Toxic milk syndrome can be caused by toxins in the bitch's milk and this causes abdominal distension, straining, and discomfort in the pups. If this happens, the pup should be taken off the bitch and artificially fed until the bitch's milk is clear. The toxins can come from infections in the uterus or mammary glands.

A problem which can happen in Spaniels is that, if the number of puppies in the litter is small and the bitch has lots of milk, the pups become so fat that they do not get onto their legs. They just feed and sleep and get fatter and fatter. For some reason the whole puppy becomes flat, looking like a plate with four legs and a head and a tail. If the pups are looking flat, gently pull their legs down underneath them in the normal position and eventually the pup will begin to develop properly. Several pups have been put to sleep because people did not realise that the puppy will eventually be all right. I had a litter of Sussex Spaniels, three of which were flat up to six weeks of age and I nicknamed them 'Cowpat', 'Flying Saucer' and 'Frisbee', but they all eventually stood up and are now completely normal.

PUPPY HEAD GLAND DISEASE
This is a bacterial skin infection which usually affects the head but can cause abscesses anywhere else on the body. The head becomes swollen, scabs develop and the skin oozes serum. The glands under the chin are inflamed and the puppy is usually very depressed. It is believed that the bacteria get into the skin through small scratches caused by the littermates' nails scratching the face. Treatment is with antibiotics and corticosteroids. The steroids are extremely important and should be continued for several weeks to prevent recurrence. If the lesions are severe this can cause permanent scarring on the face, but if treated promptly they should resolve completely.